THIS BOOK IS NO LONGER THE PROPERTY OF
THE UNIVERSITY OF CHICAGO LIBRARY

Left J 31

this music
is psychedelic

the comparative study of religions
joachim wach

Edited with an Introduction by Joseph M. Kitagawa

THE COMPARATIVE STUDY OF RELIGIONS

Lectures on the History of Religions
SPONSORED BY THE
AMERICAN COUNCIL OF LEARNED SOCIETIES
New Series Number Four

Lectures on the history of religions, sponsored by the American Council of Learned Societies.

THE COMPARATIVE STUDY OF RELIGIONS

By JOACHIM WACH

Edited with an Introduction by
JOSEPH M. KITAGAWA

THIS BOOK IS NO LONGER THE PROPERTY OF
THE UNIVERSITY OF CHICAGO LIBRARY

NEW YORK AND LONDON
COLUMBIA UNIVERSITY PRESS

COPYRIGHT © 1958 COLUMBIA UNIVERSITY PRESS

ISBN 0–231–02252–2 CLOTH
ISBN 0–231–08528–1 PAPERBACK

PRINTED IN THE UNITED STATES OF AMERICA

9 8 7

To SUSI, HUGO, and ELIZABETH

FOREWORD

This volume is the fourth to be published in the series of Lectures on the History of Religions for which the American Council of Learned Societies, through its Committee on the History of Religions, assumed responsibility in 1936.

Under this program the Committee from time to time enlists the services of scholars to lecture in colleges, universities, and seminaries on topics in need of expert elucidation. Subsequently, when possible and appropriate, the Committee arranges for the publication of the lectures. Other volumes in the series are Martin P. Nilsson, *Greek Popular Religion* (1940), Henri Frankfort, *Ancient Egyptian Religion* (1948), and Wing-tsit Chan, *Religious Trends in Modern China* (1953).

The Committee is grateful to the Columbia University Press for long, continued cooperation and to Dr. Joseph M. Kitagawa, editor of the present text. Dr. Kitagawa, after the death of Mr. Wach, not only prepared the work for publication, a lengthy task, but also added valuable contributions of his own.

ERWIN R. GOODENOUGH
For the Committee

Yale University
April, 1958

PREFACE

It was exactly fifty years ago (1905) that a professor of comparative religion at the University of Chicago, Louis Henry Jordan, reviewed the genesis and growth of this discipline (*Comparative Religion: Its Genesis and Growth*). The following lectures survey the field again, but with a somewhat different aim and goal in mind. Our study begins with a very brief summary of the development of this discipline; a discussion of its methodology follows and leads into a presentation of a theory of religious experience and its expression. The author has briefly indicated the outlines of the latter in previous publications.

Thirty years ago (1924) the author sketched a program of the study of religions in *Religionswissenschaft*. The problem of understanding religions different from our own led him to an investigation of hermeneutics (theory of interpretation) in the nineteenth century (*Das Verstehen*, 1926–33). How can the multiplicity of religious manifestations be understood? In teaching the history of religions the author felt the need for a theory of religious experience and the forms of its expression in thought, worship, and fellowship. He tackled the formidable task by first attempting to fill out the third part of the triptych in examining the sociological expression of religious experience (*Sociology of Religion*, 1944). In his *Types of Religious Experience* (1951) a chapter on "Universals in Religion" was devoted to an outline of theory of religious experience and its theoretical, practical, and sociological expression. Three decades of teaching the subject have given the author an opportunity to gather his materials and to feel ever more keenly the need for a "framework." His opportunity to formulate his methodological and theoretical views anew came with the invitation to deliver the Barrows Lectures in India (1952), and with the invitation by the Committee on the History of Religions of the American Council of Learned Societies to present lectures under its auspices during the academic year 1954–55. These lectures were given at various academic institutions in the United States.

JOACHIM WACH

CONTENTS

Introduction: THE LIFE AND THOUGHT OF
JOACHIM WACH, *by Joseph M. Kitagawa*   xiii

I. DEVELOPMENT, MEANING, AND METHOD IN THE COMPARATIVE STUDY OF RELIGIONS   3

II. THE NATURE OF RELIGIOUS EXPERIENCE   27

III. THE EXPRESSION OF RELIGIOUS EXPERIENCE IN THOUGHT   59

IV. THE EXPRESSION OF RELIGIOUS EXPERIENCE IN ACTION   97

V. THE EXPRESSION OF RELIGIOUS EXPERIENCE IN FELLOWSHIP   121

List of Abbreviations   146
Notes   147
Bibliography   195
Index   223

Introduction

THE LIFE AND THOUGHT OF JOACHIM WACH

by Joseph M. Kitagawa

When Joachim Wach died on August 27, 1955, at Orselina, Switzerland, he was in the midst of completing the manuscript for this book. His sister, Frau Susi Heigl-Wach, and the editor decided to retain his style and content as much as possible, although we were aware that Wach had intended to develop further some parts of the manuscript.

"The Comparative Study of Religions" was the title which Wach chose originally for his Barrows Lectures in India in the autumn of 1952. He felt that such terms as "Science of Religions" or "History of Religions" would be misleading to Indian audiences, while he disliked the implications of the popular expression, "Comparative Religions." Thus, he chose the more descriptive and nontechnical term, "The Comparative Study of Religions."

In many ways, Wach considered his visit to India as one of the significant events in his life. He was never more serious when he said in his introduction to the Barrows Lectures:

It has been an old and ever present wish of mine to some time visit India, the home of a great civilization and of so much that would fascinate and attract a student of the history of religions. . . . I want you to understand very definitely that *I have come as one who wants to learn* . . . . there is a very great need, I find, everywhere for true, genuine information. Certain preconceived notions, favorite prejudices, and clichés interfere with true understanding on the basis of mutual respect.

He was well aware, at that time, that he was recuperating from the heart ailment which he had had in 1950, but his anxieties were overcome by his enthusiasm for India and what it offers to a historian of religions. He said, in the Barrows Lectures:

I was educated at the University of Leipzig, a center of Indian studies. My major interest was the history of religions with philosophy and Oriental studies as auxiliaries. When I was a high school student, I met Professor Deussen, who was well known as a scholar of Indian thought. Later I had the opportunity to study under Professors Leumann and Mertel aspects of Hinduism, under Fisher, Sachan, and C. M. Becker aspects of Islam. It was Dr. Friedrich Heiler who introduced me to the study of the history of religions.

In the Barrows Lectures, Wach assigned himself a threefold task: first, to survey recent developments and contributions in the field of *Religionswissenschaft* ("the science of religion"); second, to outline a theory of religion which attempts to do justice to the universal, or general, features in the expressions of religious experience the world over and through the ages, without prejudice to any particular faith; third, to indicate the lines along which the relations between religions should be directed. One of the difficulties of his task was that his Indian audience did not share Wach's own religious and academic background and orientation. Therefore, Wach tried to avoid expounding new theories and technical aspects of *Religionswissenschaft*. Rather, he made every effort to "interpret" Western *Religions-*

wissenschaft for the Indian intelligentsia who were reared in a different religious and cultural setting. Wach was reminded that traditional Western scholarship in the study of religions, significant in so many ways, was neverthless too "Western" in basic orientation and framework. Even those who dealt with the sacred scriptures and doctrines of Eastern religions asked "Western" questions and expected Easterners to structure their experiences in a way which was meaningful to Westerners. In this situation the basic question, as Wach recorded it in the notes to his lectures in India, was

the problem of *understanding,* or more technically, of interpreting. What it means to understand other people, people different from ourselves, other civilizations, other religions. What is the nature of this process which we call understanding? Are there grades? What are the presuppositions for the interpreter? Are there kinds of understanding? And how about the limitations?

Motivated by the necessity of understanding, or more precisely of mutual understanding, Wach attempted to communicate as plainly as possible to his Indian audiences his conception of the nature and task of *Religionswissenschaft.* In response to his presentation, Wach received a number of questions and critical comments which he noted carefully. While in India, he also sought a number of noted Hindu and Moslem scholars for their views on many questions of mutual interest. Wach appreciated genuinely the comments and criticisms made by his Indian friends as correctives to his own orientation. Indeed, this was his way of attempting to broaden the religious and philosophical roots of *Religionswissenschaft,* so that it could be truly a universal discipline in the study of religions. Upon his return from India, he busied himself with a reexamination and reevaluation of his own methodology, incorporating more adequately the insights of Eastern religions. To him, this was the most urgent task for

Religionswissenschaft, if it was to be a *Wissenschaft* at all.

When the Committee on the History of Religions of the American Council of Learned Societies invited Wach to give a series of lectures in 1954, he was most eager to discuss the new perspectives which he was developing in the study of religions. In his view, the European centers of learning continue to devote great efforts to the study of the world religions. Wach, having taught in two continents, considered himself a vital link between European and American scholarship. He had high hopes that American scholars would play a significant role in the future of *Religionswissenschaft,* because he felt that Americans were less bound by the rigidity of academic traditions and were more open-minded than Europeans to an encounter with Eastern religions and peoples.

On the other hand, Wach recognized the many difficulties involved in establishing *Religionswissenschaft* in America. The strong pietistic thread of American spiritual culture and the equally strong rationalistic reaction to pietism, coupled with nature mysticism and pragmatism, tend to distort *Religionswissenschaft* into *Missionswissenschaft,* the philosophy of religion, or a positivist "scientific" study of various aspects of religions. In this connection he appreciated the constructive aspects of the recent theological renaissance in America, but he was cognizant of the inherent danger of *Religionswissenschaft* becoming subservient to systematic or constructive theology. These considerations led Wach to the task of reformulating the aim, scope, and method of *Religionswissenschaft* in the light of the contemporary situation.

At any rate, he worked on the problems which are discussed in the present volume and delivered part of the fruits of his labor in the lectures he gave at various colleges and universities in the South and East during the autumn of 1954 and the winter of 1955. In the spring of 1955 he participated in the Seventh

Congress of the International Association of the History of Religions in Rome, where he compared notes with a number of old friends and new acquaintances. Following the Congress, he planned to spend the remaining part of the spring and summer with his mother and sister in Orselina. Wach hoped to complete the manuscript for the book during the summer and then return to America. Unfortunately, he was taken ill in July and died in August without realizing his objective.

Under the circumstances, readers of this book have no way of knowing how Wach might have revised some of his ideas, and no one else can speak for him. However, a brief account of Wach's life and thought may be of some help to those who never had the opportunity to know him personally.

HIS LIFE

Joachim Wach, the oldest child of Felix and Katherine Wach, was born on January 25, 1898, at Chemnitz, Saxony. His father was the son of Adolf Wach and of Lily Mendelssohn Bartholdy Wach. She was the youngest daughter of the composer, Felix Mendelssohn Bartholdy. Adolf Wach taught law at Rostock and later in Leipzig:

[Adolf Wach's] publications and commentaries on civil and criminal law soon made him the most prominent jurisconsult in Germany. The King of Saxony chose him as his private counsellor and bestowed on him the title of Excellency. [He] died in Leipzig on the 4th of April, 1926, leaving six children. . . .[1]

Joachim Wach was descended from the Mendelssohn-Bartholdy family on both the maternal and paternal sides. His mother, Katherine, who died in the summer of 1956, was the granddaughter of Paul Mendelssohn-Bartholdy, the brother of Felix. The Mendelssohns of his paternal side (the line of the composer) use the name without a hyphen, while his mother's side (the line of Paul) uses the name with a hyphen between the two names.[2] Both lines go back to the great Jewish philosopher, Moses Mendelssohn (1729–86).[3]

Wach received affectionate attention not only from his parents but from his paternal and maternal grandparents as well. They were all highly cultured people whose homes were frequented by noted scholars, artists, diplomats, and statesmen. From his earliest years Wach was exposed to music, literature and poetry, classical languages and modern foreign languages. His sister and brother remember him as an unusually alert child. Throughout his childhood Wach rose as early as five o'clock in the morning, because for him the day was too short to do and learn the many things which interested him. His lively imagination created a land of fantasy which he named "Pelagypten," a word imbued with all the color and splendor of political and ecclesiastical offices. Every day he told his sister and brother "what happened in Pelagypten" with amazing realism.

His interest in religion started as a young boy. His governess, a devout Roman Catholic, once took him with her when she had an *Audienz* with the Bishop of Würzburg, and the Bishop gave him some religious pictures. The child decided to "celebrate Mass" with the assistance of his sister and brother, and he managed to memorize the entire Mass in Latin.

Joachim's intellectual curiosity and capacity for learning developed early in his life. When he was about fourteen years old he papered the walls of his room with the history of the world. The major historical events of each country were summarized and pasted horizontally around the walls, while the history of each century was arranged in a vertical column. He received his secondary education at the Vitzthumsche Gymnasium at Dresden, where he passed the *Abitur* examination in 1916.

In the same year, at the age of eighteen, Wach joined the

German army and was sent to the Russian front. The young officer was never separated from his two boxes of books, and he spent his leisure reading philosophy and languages. Later Wach used to say jokingly that his knowledge of Russian and Arabic was the by-product of his army experience. When he was assigned to duty near the famous Beresina River, which Napoleon's fleeing armies had crossed in 1812, he completed a summary of the history of Greek philosophy for the benefit of his sister. One memorable experience with death occurred while Wach was stationed on the Baltic Sea. In this icy, windy outpost, a young soldier lost his nerve and committed suicide. Wach was the soldier's officer and felt his own inadequacy in not being able to cope with the difficult human situation which estranged man from his Maker and from his fellow men. The problem of death absorbed him as both an existential and philosophical question throughout his life.[4]

After World War I he enrolled for a brief period in the University of Leipzig and then spent the year of 1919 at Munich. After one academic quarter in Berlin during 1920, he returned to Leipzig for two more years, where he received the degree of Doctor of Philosophy in 1922. His doctoral thesis, entitled "Grundzüge einer Phaenomenologie des Erlösungsgedankens," was later revised and published under the title, *Der Erlösungsgedanke und seine Deutung*.[5] During these years he attended lectures of Professors Husserl at Freiburg and Gundolf at Heidelberg. Gundolf, a noted scholar of the history of literature, exerted a lasting influence on Wach. In the same way, he was impressed with, and influenced by, Ernst Troeltsch, Adolf von Harnack, Johannes Immanuel Volkelt, Hans Freyer, Eduard Spranger, Hans Haas, Nathan Söderblom, Max Weber, and Rudolf Otto.

Wach majored in the history of religions and minored in the

philosophy of religion and Oriental studies, but his intellectual curiosity led him to attend lectures in medicine, psychiatry, and the arts as well. At the university, he counted among his friends young poets, dancers, physicians, scientists, and musicians. Manfred Hausmann, the poet, read his first play in the home of Wach's parents. Kurt Thomas, conductor of the St. Thomas Choir School in Leipzig, often played his compositions in Wach's house. Werner Heisenberg, now a famous nuclear physicist, was one of Wach's close friends. Wach and his talented friends once played Hofmannsthal's *Der Tor und der Tod* on the terrace of his parents' Dresden home. On another occasion, when they read Goethe's *Tasso,* Wach's sister, Frau Susi Heigl-Wach, recalls that she took the role of Leonore d'Este and Wach that of the Herzog of Farrara. With his companions Joachim also liked to travel to foreign countries—to Spain, North Africa, Sweden, Austria, Greece, and Italy. His careful preparation for these trips is exemplified by his study of the Hamitic language of the Tuareg tribe before visiting North Africa. Later, he took Hindi lessons before his trip to India.

In 1924 Wach was appointed *Privatdozent* at Leipzig in the Faculty of Philosophy. His grandfather was at that time still teaching in the University. Wach became Assistant Professor in 1929 and gave his inaugural lecture on "Die Geschichtsphilosophie des 19. Jahrhunderts und die Theologie der Geschichte." In 1930, he was conferred the Th.D. degree from Heidelberg. His European academic career, which had thus shown a high degree of promise and achievement, ended five years later.

On April 10, 1935, the government of Saxony, under Nazi pressure, terminated Wach's appointment at Leipzig. Providentially, his old friend Robert P. Casey of Brown University had invited Wach to America only a few days before. Brokenhearted yet hopeful, the German scholar came to Brown University at Providence, Rhode Island, where he taught from 1935 to 1945.

Those who were close to Wach were amazed at the personal adjustment he made in the United States, although American life was far different from his European background. He made friends in all walks of American society and was a constant interpreter of America to visitors and students from Europe.

The Second World War inflicted great hardship upon Wach. The fact that he alone was safe in America while his immediate family—his mother, brother, and sister—and friends were suffering under Nazi tyranny was almost unbearable to him. The loss of his personal library and the family fortune made his situation difficult, but his deepest concern was with the destiny of European culture and civilization.

In 1945 Wach received a call from the University of Chicago. There he became professor and chairman of the History of Religions Field of the Federated Theological Faculty. With his encyclopedic learning and inquisitive mind, he became a natural link between the theological faculty and humanistic and social scientific disciplines. His competence, modesty, and personal charm made him a unique teacher, counselor, and friend to those who came in contact with him.

Toward the end of his life, Wach received an invitation from the government of Hesse to accept the chair of systematic theology at Marburg, a position once occupied by Rudolf Otto. To him, this was a significant turn of events. Friedrich Heiler of Marburg, Wach's former teacher, has stated that this was an act which was meant to repair "that great injustice which the Nazi government had done to this outstanding representative of German science and to many others who had to leave their native country." [6] Wach admitted that it was one of the hardest decisions he had ever been forced to make—to choose between two positions which were both important to him, one in America and the other in Europe. It was only a few days before his death that Wach refused the Marburg offer with an expression of gratitude toward the country which once expelled him. His homeland again recognized his achievement in December, 1955, when the Board of the Klopstock Foundation in Hamburg (Klopstock-Stiftung, Gemeinnützige Stiftung zur Förderung der Geistes- und Religions-Wissenschaft) presented a posthumous award to Dr. Wach for his important contribution to the history of religions and theology.

Wach the scholar left behind him numerous essays, articles, and books. Chief among his books are:

Der Erlösungsgedanke und seine Deutung (Leipzig, 1922)
Religionswissenschaft: Prolegomena zu ihrer Grundlegung (Leipzig, 1924)
Mahayana, besonders im Hinblick auf das Saddharma-Pundarika-Sutra (Neubiberg, 1925)
Meister und Jünger: 2 religionssoziologische Betrachtungen (Tübingen, 1925)
Die Typenlehre Trendelenburgs und ihr Einfluss auf Dilthey (Tübingen, 1926)
Das Verstehen: Grundzüge einer Geschichte der hermeneutischen Theorie im 19. Jahrhundert. 3 vols. (Tübingen, 1926–33)
Einführung in die Religionssoziologie (Tübingen, 1931)
Typen religiöser Anthropologie (Tübingen, 1932)
Das Problem des Todes in der Philosophie unserer Zeit (Tübingen, 1934)
Sociology of Religion (Chicago, 1944)
Types of Religious Experience—Christian and Non-Christian (Chicago, 1951)

Wach taught the history of religions throughout his academic career of thirty years, but the only book he wrote in this specific field was a small volume on Mahayana Buddhism. Those who knew him, however, were constantly impressed by Wach's keen interest in and profound knowledge of many aspects of the history of religions. He insisted that the starting point of the history of religions was the empirical study of religions. And yet by temperament and by training Wach was too deeply grounded in *Religionswissenschaft,* especially in its methodological and theoretical aspects, to be satisfied by sheer historical analysis and explication of various religions.

It is interesting that Wach taught for the first ten years of his career in the Faculty of Philosophy in a German university, the next ten years in a New England liberal arts college, and the last ten years in the Theological Faculty of the University of Chicago. In each situation, he entered into the life of the school with great enthusiasm. He made a valuable contribution to each academic institution and, conversely, he must have received much from each experience. His particular environment, however, did not change his basic intellectual orientation. To be sure, he was interested in philosophy, theology, and the social sciences, but his first and last love was *Religionswissenschaft,* a field of study which embraces three main divisions: hermeneutics (or the theory of interpretation), the study of religious experience, and the sociology of religion.[7] More basically, perhaps, Wach's *Religionswissenschaft* may be characterized as a sort of "Religious Encyclopedia," which is not a collection of information but a well-organized survey of the nature, characteristics, and functions of religions. His intellectual attitude was "syntonic," to use his own favorite expression, attempting to avoid either the acceptance of one "correct" approach or an attitude of laissez-faire.

Questions have often been raised as to the nature of *Religionswissenschaft.* Is it a theological, philosophical, historical, or even social scientific discipline? On this question, Wach had an unshakable conviction that it was truly and properly a *Geisteswissenschaft.*[8] Wach's starting point was the assumption that subjective religiousness is objectified in various expressions, and that these expressions appropriate definite structures which can be comprehended. The study of such structures of religious expression is one of the primary objectives of *Religionswissenschaft*. In this sense, it is a descriptive science, following Dilthey's notion that a descriptive science "is one whose units and laws are found by empirical analysis, or close examination of what is actually given in experience."[9]

HIS CONCEPT OF MAN

Wach's descriptive science and his empirical analysis were based on a definite philosophical tradition, with man as its central focus. He said:

It appears obvious to us that philosophy should begin with a study of man—of his existence, his nature, his origin, and his destiny. Especially we moderns, brought up in the philosophical tradition of the West . . . can hardly envisage a more natural subject for philosophical inquiry than "What is man?"[10]

Wach was fully aware of the inseparableness of the three basic quests of mankind, in its striving to determine (1) the nature of ultimate reality, and its relation to the visible universe and to man (theology), (2) the nature of the universe, the origin of destiny of the world (cosmology), and (3) the nature and destiny of man (anthropology).[11] Among the three, Wach was most intrigued by anthropology, not as the study of man as a product of nature, but as the inquiry concerning man's idea about himself.[12] In the study of man Wach followed Dilthey's principle that "Human life is not only a reality, it is the reality directly accessible to us, and it is fit and proper that our best effort should go into the task of understanding it."[13] Thus, on one occasion Wach observed:

One of the most unfortunate aspects of modern scholarship has been the departmentalization of the study of man. Granted, that man is, at his best, an integral organism of which the physical, mental, and spiritual are aspects, we must deplore the fact that the inquiry into these different aspects of his nature is carried on in widely separated fields of study. But what is much more disturbing is the tendency in some quarters to deny that each of these domains of human existence, notwithstanding their interrelationship and interaction, possesses its own laws. This important fact is neglected or outrightly denied by determinists in different branches of the study of man.[14]

Wach's anthropology cannot be understood without reference to his two presuppositions: the fact of the "eternally human" (*Ewig-Menschliche*), and the fact of human corporateness (*Zusammenleben*), or man-in-society-and-culture. The eternally human does not mean a monolithic uniformity; it has within it infinite possibilities which can be actualized in various historic forms of societies and cultures. In viewing it as such, however, Wach cautions us not to accept any "breach in the development from the small, isolated, non-literate, homogeneous society which is characterized by a strong sense of group solidarity, to the larger, expansive, complex type."[15] Rather, Wach was persuaded that different cultures should be understood typologically as different ways of ordering the various human possibilities and different human responses to ultimate reality. He emphasized the importance of the study of civilizations as related to religious attitudes, and vice versa. In each civilization Wach depicted key concepts which denote the specific apprehension of spiritual reality by the people within their environment, integrated by a common historical destiny and tradition and by modes of thought and language of their own.

It was Wach's conviction that the concepts of man, his nature and destiny, are usually explained not as separate subject matter but in connection with mythical concepts which include cosmologies, histories, genealogies, and soteriologies.[16] Even in Greece, where human values were emphasized more than in any other ancient culture, the unity of life was understood in religious terms.[17] Nevertheless, Wach recognized the uniqueness of Greek anthropology in the thought of Plato and Aristotle. He argued that even the doctrine of Confucius, the "Socrates" of Asia, was grounded in ancient Chinese cosmology and possessed nothing like the notion of Socrates recognizing the sovereignty of man in man.[18]

Yet the trend of pre-Socratic philosophy was to have a profound effect upon the intellectual orientation of the West. Plato and Aristotle were, in part, acceptable to the East. *Socrates . . . was not. . . .* The free play of human reason in which we see Socrates engaged with his interrogators is not conceivable without the task of emancipation carried through by the Sophists; this play of the free spirit was to exercise considerable fascination on later ages in the West. The East has never openly welcomed it.[19]

The Occidental concept of man, in Wach's view, was decisively conditioned by Plato's doctrine of the human soul and by Aristotle's notion of "experience," which gave an empirical basis for anthropology and psychology.[20] However, while Plato was interested in salvation, Aristotle was preoccupied by perfection of life with the guidance of reason.[21] Later, Jewish and Arabic philosophers studied Plato. Under the influence of Neo-Platonism, Western philosophy resumed its interest in philosophy of religion or theology, and Western anthropology renewed its interest in soteriology grounded in cosmology.[22]

It was Wach's contention that "through the three religions of revelation, Christianity, Judaism and Islam, a philosophical renaissance occurred in the early Middle Ages in the West and East, and, with it, a renewal of interest in the discussion of the doctrine of man." [23] The Christian, Jewish, and Islamic views of man were based on the Bible, Torah, and Koran, respectively. That is to say, in all three religions anthropology as well as cosmology and eschatology was meaningless without the premise of revelation. Thus, mere speculation on the creation or the origin of the world, on the nature of man—especially the problem of his freedom—and on the nature of the historical destiny of the world was alien to the temperament of the three monotheistic religions. It was under the influence of Greek thought that the three religions developed an articulate anthropology, which involved the "emancipation of the *logos* from the *mythos*." [24] Wach was careful, however, to state that the Greek contribution to the three religions was the thought-form, and that the Greek attitude toward life was not accepted by them. While a few Hellenistic thinkers developed within the Christian, Jewish, and Islamic folds, they had to defend themselves constantly against fideists.[25] Nevertheless, in the West not only Greek thought but also "the doctrine of the three religions of revelation, with its insistence upon the creatureliness of man and his dependence upon God, his sinful nature and his responsibility, provided the framework for the anthropological quest of the thinkers." [26] In short, the Western view of man is characterized by a conviction of the intrinsic value of man.

Wach recognized a universal pattern of emancipation of philosophical reflection from its religious matrix. He not only traced this process in the histories of the three religions of revelation, but also observed that "even the most philosophical of the great world religions, Buddhism, appears at first restricted to purely soteriological knowledge," yet "the necessity for apologetics and the logic of thought tend to turn theological into philosophical reflection." [27] What distinguishes Eastern religions from the Western religions of revelation is not primarily soteriology, cosmology, or even theology; the most decisive difference is found, in Wach's analysis, in the doctrine of man. Thus, in the mystical metaphysics of Brahmanism, the ego is nothing more than a phantom not unlike a single wave in the ocean of the infinity. Wach found an essentially similar notion of man in all Indian systems, including Sankhya, Vishnuism, and Saiva Siddhanta, as well as in the great thinkers of the Indian Middle Ages.[28] The most logical, and also the most paradoxical, of all Indian systems is Buddhism, which views man as nothing more than the meeting point of different elements. In the course of time, the Mahayana thinkers, who were not satisfied with the classical Buddhist doctrine of man based on the formula of causality, developed the theory of universal illusion (Sunyata) which embraced the phenomenological nature of the Ego. Nevertheless, both in early Buddhism and in the Mahayana tradition, Buddhism ultimately recognizes only the activity— good and evil deeds—but not a personal entity as the actor.[29] Typologically similar to the Buddhist notion of man is the concept found in Taoism, one of the two main Chinese systems. According to Taoist quietist mysticism, man as an independent mind has no place in the realm of being. Only in the second major system in China, Confucianism, did Wach find a similarity to Greek thought in its emphasis on the realization of man as an ideal. Wach rightly pointed out, however, that the various Confucian thinkers found more general agreement in ethics than in their interpretation of the nature of man. At any rate, Confucian as well as Taoist anthropologies are deeply rooted in ancient Chinese cosmology.[30] The following statement may be regarded as Wach's general perspective on anthropology:

In the mythological stage thought is primarily directed to theology and cosmology, as in most preliterate cultures and in the ancient cultures of the East. A comprehensive world-view is centered in a concept of a *cosmic moral and ritual law,* on which the course of nature, of human life and society depend and towards which they are oriented. . . . The founded religions naturally bring a greater emphasis to the anthropological theme and, preoccupied as they are with the salvation of man, yet in practically all of them is safeguarded the cosmic aspect, according to which man is assigned his place in the chain or hierarchy of being. Anthropocentrism is practically unknown in the East. That is certainly true of the *Weltanschauung* manifest in the Near Eastern religions of revelation, but it is also true in India of Samkhya and even Yoga, and in Confucianism and Taoism. Greece seems to be the great exception.[31]

HIS CONCEPT OF GEMEINSCHAFT

Wach's philosophical focus on man found its counterpart in the phenomenological concept of *Gemeinschaft,* whose approximate English translation is "mutual participation." To him, the development of religious anthropologies was closely related to the development of religious communities. As stated earlier, Wach was philosophically concerned with the relation between *logos* and *mythos;* phenomenologically, he attempted to investigate the relation between the religious community and *Gesellschaft* (society). Basically, Wach shared Gerardus van der Leeuw's view that *Gemeinschaft*

is something not manufactured, but given; it depends not upon sentiment or feeling, but on the Unconscious. It need be founded upon no conviction, since it is self-evident; we do not become members of it, but "belong to it."

. . . .

Primitive man knows only one community: to him the distinction between secular and spiritual communion is entirely foreign.[32]

Wach was sensitive to two dimensions of *Gemeinschaft:* communication and the community. These two aspects were the subject matter of his lifelong research in hermeneutics and the sociology of religion, which together with the study of religious experience constituted the methodological framework of his *Religionswissenschaft*.³³

By (religious) "communication" Wach meant the art of expressing religious feeling throughout the religious community. His hypothesis was that the art of religious communication varies in inverse ratio to the degree of individual religious initiative. For example, there is a high degree of communication in a religious community which does not emphasize individual worship, as seen in the Totemic group in Australia, while there is a lesser degree of such communication in a religious group which encourages individual worship or piety. In the history of the West, Wach found that the highest degree of religious communication was in ancient Greece where the *polis* was simultaneously the religious community and the city-state, whereas later, with the disintegration of the *polis*, religious communication decreased.³⁴

Wach recognized that the problem of religious communication was inseparably related to the structural development of the religious community. For instance, in ancient India the tribe was the basis of the religious community. When this foundation became unsatisfactory and there was a concomitant decrease in religious communication, Indian religion developed along two lines. First, the orthodox Vedic and Brahmanic traditions maintained the old tribal distinction in the caste system; second, the heterodox Jain and Buddhist communities developed, disregarding the old tribal basis and placing greater emphasis on individual religious initiative.³⁵

What unites the diverse members of a religious community which is emancipated from the tribe or state? In this situation, Wach observed the development of sacred language, symbolism, and ritualism. Through symbols and rituals each religious community tries to communicate to its members the meaning of man's attitude to ultimate reality and to his fellow men, and tries to impart the norm of social organization. But the maintenance of group solidarity is never an easy problem for any religious community, especially for the so-called founded religions which are based on the particular appeal of some man or some ideal and not on natural, social ties.[36]

The basis of the religious community, in Wach's view, is a rapport with ultimate reality which is reflected in religious experience. Ultimate reality is understood as transcendental power from which life is not set apart, but upon which it depends. The categories of religious thought and action are evolved in the encounter with this power in its cosmic order which is viewed as the norm of social and individual life. While ultimate reality may or may not be experienced in personal terms, any religious experience

tends to expression. The three main fields of expression are the "theoretical"—theology, cosmology and anthropology; the "practical"—cults; and the "sociological"—fellowship and community. In all three fields expression tends toward formalization and standardization. Thus, we distinguish (1) the mythical, (2) the doctrinal, and (3) the dogmatic stages in the theoretical aspect, to which correspond (1) simple, (2) complex, and (3) elaborate stages both in cultic forms and in the religious community.[37]

Wach's "sociology of religion" must be seen in the total context of his *Religionswissenschaft*. In his article, "Religionssoziologie," in *Handwörterbuch der Soziologie*,[38] Wach defined the task of the sociology of religion as the investigation of the relation between religion(s) and *Gesellschaft,* in their mutual ways of conditioning each other, and also of the configuration of any religiously determined social processes. He stressed the importance of both the empirical-descriptive and the phenomenological–a priori methods for this task, leaving the normative problem to ethics and the philosophy of religion. Wach was cautious to state that the subject matter of the sociology of religion is not a "pure" religion but an empirical form of it. In this sense, the problem of "religion and the world" is viewed as the relation between empirical religion and society. The sociology of religion does not evaluate society either as a "fallen state" or as a part of the divine plan. What interests the sociologist of religion is the analysis of social structure (cross section of society) and the movements and changes of social structure.

The influence of religion on society, according to Wach, is twofold. The first is a definite influence upon the form and character of social organizations, relations, and forms, for example: (1) the natural groupings such as family, clan, and nation; (2) associations such as vocational organizations or unions; and (3) the highest social organization, the state. The second influence is that of religion on society as seen in forming, developing, and determining new "specifically religious" groups such as the mystery group and the church, together with the possibility of transforming the total secular order and also creating new forms.

On the other hand, the influence of society on religion is equally complex. Wach was especially interested in the social factors which give nuance and differentiation to religious feeling and attitude within a certain social circle or group. It is well known that the sociological background of the founder conditions the initial character of a founded religion. The influence of socio-economic factors on the stratification and development of social relationships within the religious community cannot be neglected by the sociology of religion.

Elsewhere, Wach discussed the benefits and assets as well as the dangers and limits of the sociological study of religion. In his own words:

It was the mistake of the discoverers and pathfinders of the use of this method to believe that it represented the universal key to an understanding of religious phenomena. The ideologies of Comte, Marx, and Spencer shared in this error. Many of their followers were and are inclined to substitute for questions of meaning, value, and truth, an inquiry into the social *origin,* the sociological structure, and the social *efficacy* of a religious group or movement. . . .

Nevertheless, the sociological approach to the study of religion has its great rewards. After a period of unqualified individualism it has reminded us of the importance of *corporate* religion. It has helped to correct the rationalistic prejudice that it is the *intellectual* expression of religious experience alone which counts. The rediscovery of the central place of worship in all religion . . . was facilitated by sociological studies. . . . [Also] it was the merit of sociological inquiries to have opened up the wide fields of social grouping, of covenanting, and associating, in which religious motivation plays so highly significant a part. . . . "Religion," Liston Pope has written . . . "is neither simply a product nor a cause, a sanction or enemy, of social stratification. It may be either or both, as it has been in various societies at various times." [39]

It is virtually impossible to deal with all the important aspects of Wach's sociology of religion. Unfortunately, Wach's works have not been fully understood or appreciated by American sociologists of religion.[40] On his part, Wach was critical of many American sociologists of religion for viewing religion "as a function of natural social grouping"[41] or "as merely one more form of cultural expression."[42] His opinion was that "communion with the numen is primary and is basic in achieving religious integration" in any religious community.[43] To many American sociologists, such a starting point is not reconcilable with Wach's avowed principle that "the study of the sociological implications of religion requires an impartial and objective approach, with the facts studied without bias, *'sine ira ac studio.'*"[44] However, Wach was convinced that

We like to believe that, though there is a Catholic and a Marxian philosophy of society, there can be only *one* sociology of religion which we may approach from different angles and realize to a different degree but which would use but one set of criteria. Divergence of opinion is caused not so much by the variety and difference of the views on society as by those on religion. . . . [But] objectivity does not presuppose indifference. . . .[45]

Another criticism has been made concerning Wach's "descriptive" principle. According to him, the sociology of religion is a descriptive study of "religious grouping, religious fellowship and association, the individual, typological and comparative."[46] In so defining the task of the discipline, Wach's Kantian epistemology too clearly differentiated the descriptive and normative functions, and did not do justice to the "analytical" aspect of the *Wissenschaft*.[47] Wach would have acknowledged the truth in this criticism. Nevertheless, his careful discrimination between social philosophy (normative theory of society) and sociology made it imperative for his sociology of religion to be "descriptive," in his sense of the term, fully realizing its inevitable limitations.[48]

HIS CONCEPT OF RELIGION

Wach's diverse concerns, notably his philosophical interest in man and his sociological preoccupation with *Gemeinschaft*, found an integrating principle in religion. Indeed, to him religion was both the central intellectual problem, to which he applied all the critical faculties he possessed, and man's most supreme act of communion with the Divine Creator, to whom he offered unqualified faith and genuine commitment. Wach quoted Carlyle:

By religion I do not mean here the church-creed, which he professes, the articles of faith which he will sign, and, in words and otherwise, assert; not this wholly, in many cases not at all. . . . But the thing a man does practically believe and this is often enough without asserting it even to himself, much less to others, the thing a man does practically lay to heart, and know for certain, concerning his vital relations to (this mysterious Universe,) and his duty and destiny there, that is in all cases the primary thing for him, and creatively determines all the rest.[49]

Wach's understanding of religion was conditioned by his family background and his own personal experience. He inherited an irenic attitude in religious matters from his family and environment. The memory of Moses Mendelssohn was revered by his descendants. Even though his son, Abraham, had his children baptized in the Lutheran Church and Felix Mendelssohn, grandson of Moses and son of Abraham, married the daughter of a Reformed church minister, the spirit of *Nathan der Weise* lives in Wach's family to this day. The atmosphere of the University of Leipzig, the alma mater of Goethe, Klopstock, and Schelling, nurtured in Wach the gift of religious tolerance. One of Wach's favorite quotations was from William James: "The divine can mean no single quality, it must mean a group of qualities, by being champions of which in alternations, different men may all find worthy missions."[50] Religious tolerance, however, was never understood by Wach to be religious indifference. On many occasions he discussed his own religious faith. For example,

A genuine encounter with the redeeming love of God in Christ is . . . on the part of any Christian the presupposition for his testimony through act and word. Merely having been brought up in Christian ways is not sufficient. ("Fiant, non nascuntur Christiani"—"Let them become Christians, since they were not born thus.") Though it would certainly not be required of anyone to look back upon and give an account of a "conversion experience," a conscious decision and commitment to Christ, implicit in our life, explicit in our testimony is indispensable.[51]

It is extremely difficult to reconstruct Wach's religious development. He was raised in the Lutheran Church in Germany and although he later became a member of the Protestant Episcopal Church in the United States, Luther continued to be an important spiritual guide throughout Wach's life. Significantly, Wach's description of Casper Schwenckfeld reminds us of his own qualities—a Christian humanist and idealist, an ecumenically minded layman who was biblical and devotional, a true pupil and teacher in the school of Christ.[52]

Of paramount importance in his life and thought was his experience of the living Christ. Though deeply influenced by the Pauline interpretation of Christ, he belongs to the Johannine type of Christian piety. He learned more from St. Augustine than from any other of the Fathers . . . . we are reminded of the great masters of devotion of the Middle Ages: Bernard, Hugo of St. Victor, Bonaventura, whom he resembles in temperament and in the character of his spirituality. . . . He belongs with the leaders of the Christian Renaissance. . . . The first Epistle of John is the text which [he] interprets to us.[53]

It is fair to say that Wach's intellectual temperament was congenial to the Anglican emphasis on philosophical theology, an emphasis exemplified in William Temple. Also, Wach's profound appreciation of both Catholic and Protestant traditions and his love of liturgy made him feel at home in the Episcopal Church. Although he gave his time and energy very generously to his own church's work, he was also an enthusiastic advocate of the ecumenical movement. For example, as the chairman of the University Commission of the World's Student Christian Federation, Wach presided at the Study Conference on the *Meaning of History*, held at the Château de Bossey in the summer of 1949.[54]

This convinced Christian was also a firm believer in the principle of the plurality of religions. As such, Wach quoted Alexis de Tocqueville in his enthusiasm for America's great experiment of combining loyalty to religion with devotion to liberty:

Religion perceives that civil liberty affords a nobler exercise to the faculties of man, and that the political world is a field prepared by the Creator for the efforts of mind. Free and powerful in its own sphere, satisfied with the place reserved for it, religion never more surely establishes its empire than when it reigns in the hearts of men unsupported by aught beside its native strength. Liberty regards religion as its companion in all its battles and triumphs as the cradle of its infancy, and the divine source of its claims. It considers religion as the safeguard of morality, and morality as the best security of law, and the surest pledge of the duration of freedom.[55]

Wach advocated the principle of the plurality of religions on a global scale, too. In a real sense, according to him, Christ, the Buddha, and Mohammed are "universal options," [56] and a religious man must choose his faith despite the environmental factors. Thus, he argues that

It is wrong for a Westerner to say: because my forebears were Christians, I had better be one also. No less a theologian than Søren Kierkegaard has pointed out how difficult it is for a Christian, that is to say, for one brought up in and hence "accustomed" to Christianity, to become a Christian. Modern determinism assumes many subtle forms: one is cultural determinism. Many anthropologists, sociologists, and psychologists—even philosophers—regard religion merely as an expression of a function of civilization. That means I confess a religion because it happens to be the prevailing one in the culture or society to which I happen to belong. Should we not respect a Westerner who, out of conviction, turns Buddhist or Moslem higher than a *soi-disant* "Christian?" [57]

As a student of religions, Wach was deeply impressed by the "spirituality, faith, and devotion to the Divinity to which the words and lives of the Eastern masters witness." [58] Thus, he wrote:

The sheer intensity and burning zeal of Mohammed's religion, his powerful witness to the omnipotent God, the utter truthfulness, serenity, and peace which are radiated by the great Enlightened One, his insight into the human heart and its dispositions, his counsel to the lonely seeker; Confucius' sincerity and wisdom, his convincing rectitude and uncompromising moral courage; finally, the beguiling simplicity and profundity of the mysterious hermit author of the

Tao Te King—are all these witnesses to the highest spiritual attainments nothing?[59]

To solve this admittedly difficult question, Wach found three main alternatives: (1) to yield to historicism and relativism, (2) to revert to "classical" standards, or (3) to make new attempts at a constructive solution.[60] The significance of his last work, *The Comparative Study of Religions,* lies in the fact that here Wach attempts to combine the insights and methods of *Religionswissenschaft,* philosophy of religion, and theology. It is all the more regrettable that he did not live long enough to complete the task which he assigned himself.

In an earlier work Wach discussed the relationship between *Religionswissenschaft* and philosophy.[61] In his view, there is very little friction between the two, because "while the former investigates the individual, the specific, and the historical, the latter is interested in general and universal validity."[62] On the other hand, the relationship between theology and philosophy, or between theology and history (or science) of religions, is far more complex.[63] Rejecting the oft-repeated misconception that the task of the historian of religions is the study of non-Christian faiths while the theologian is concerned with what one ought to believe, Wach asserted:

Actually the historian of religions does not wait for the final quest for help from the theologian. Without pressing his material to conform to a framework and to notions which are alien to it, he will be well advised if he informs himself thoroughly about the work done in the various theological disciplines. But the theologian, the exegete, the church historian and, most of all, the systematic or constructive theologian can ill afford to neglect the material with which the historian of religion is ready to supply him.[64]

In stating this, however, Wach did not confine the task of the history of religions to historical and philological research alone.

Rather, the historian of religion must be concerned with the "meaning of all these expressions of religious experience, and the meaning and nature of religious experience itself." [65]

In *The Comparative Study of Religions,* Wach discusses the "Nature of Religious Experience" in the second chapter, and deals with the expressions of religious experience in thought, practice, and fellowship in the third, fourth, and fifth chapters, respectively. Utilizing a phenomenological analysis, Wach attempts to determine "if anything like a structure can be discovered in all these forms of expression, to what kind of experience this variegated expression can be traced, and finally, what kind of reality or realities may correspond to the experiences in question." [66] He explains how each religious group, with its own "intention" and "self-interpretation" of religious experience, develops its own unique forms of expression of religious experience itself. Numerous illustrations are cited; they are elucidated separately or comparatively, without value judgments. By this approach Wach attempts to demonstrate that "the forms of this expression, though conditioned by the environment within which [they] originated, show similarities in structure; there are universal themes in religious thought; the universal is always embedded in the particular." [67]

Discerning as this analysis is, it does not do justice to Wach's recent attempts at a constructive approach to the study of diverse religions, incorporating the insights of philosophy, theology, and *Religionswissenschaft.* Unfortunately, he did not leave behind him a systematic exposition on the subject, and we can only depend on his personal remarks, lectures, and fragmentary statements from his later writings to indicate the general direction of his thought. In all fairness to Wach, it must be made clear that in undertaking a new constructive effort he did not envisage the emergence of a new synthetic discipline, blending as it were *Religionswissenschaft,* philosophy, and theology, or another form of a Religious League of Mankind. His primary concern was to develop and articulate a general framework in which scholars of different disciplines interested in religions, as well as adherents of diverse religious faiths, could understand each other.

HIS "IRENIC EFFORT"

It is understandable that Wach's "irenic effort" was strongly preconditioned by his temperament, his academic training, and his religious faith. His intellectual principle was that the universal and the particular must be correlated, yet by temperament Wach tended to view the particular from the standpoint of the universal. This also explains, in part, why his methodology in *Religionswissenschaft* developed almost independently of his research in particular religions. In fact, his interpretation of specific religions—Mahayana Buddhism, for instance—was strongly colored by his systematic, methodological, and philosophical interests. Characteristically, one of his favorite quotations was taken from Max Müller's letter to Renan: "Before we compare, we must thoroughly know what we compare." [68]

Methodologically, Wach's constructive attempt depended largely on the perspective of Max Scheler, who inquired into the nature of the divine, revelation, and the religious act. In the first chapter of the present book, Wach commends Scheler's effort to let religious data speak for themselves rather than to force them into any preconceived scheme. This did not mean, however, that a study should be undertaken without any presuppositions. Much as Scheler did earlier, Wach accepted Rudolf Otto's phenomenological analysis of the experience of the Holy.[69] After the nature of religious experience is articulated, one can proceed

LIFE AND THOUGHT OF JOACHIM WACH

with the investigation of phenomena called religious, taking into account the widest possible range of historical phenomena. In this task, Wach suggested the use of the "concept of the classical"[70] and the typological method. Wach was under no illusion about the scope of such a method and approach by the historian (scientist) of religions. In his own statement:

Are types . . . the last word which the historian of religions has to contribute? Very possibly, yes; *qua* historian he cannot go further. . . . The historian *qua* historian will examine the sociological forms under which religiously motivated groups have organized, and he will inquire into the underlying theological assumptions. He will show parallels between different types which belong to different historical contexts. But he cannot *qua* historian go beyond this *descriptive* task to answer the *normative* quest.[71]

While he fully recognized the limitations of the methodology of *Religionswissenschaft,* Wach nevertheless insisted that a historian of religions, in order to help develop a common basis for the study of religions, must be concerned with the question of "truth."[72] This is the underlying thought in the second chapter of the present book. Wach's thesis is that a historian of religions has to approach the question of truth phenomenologically, that is, relating the question of truth to the nature of religious experience. In so doing, he feels that *Religionswissenschaft* can contribute something to the question of truth without absolutizing any one religion's interpretation of it. Rejecting the view of some of the dialectic theologians, Wach insists that religious experience presupposes a capacity on the part of man to respond to divine instruction. He affirms Von Hügel's conviction that there is only one ultimate reality, but that the modes of human apprehension result in a multiplicity of religious experiences. It follows, then, that while the truth is the maximum God can give, it has not been adequately apprehended or expressed by man's religions. In this connection, he agreed wholeheartedly with Farquhar:

Neither is any one religion alone true in the sense that all others are merely so much sheer error; nor, again, are they all equally true; but while all contain some truth, they not only differ each from the other in the points on which they are true but also in the amount of importance of the truth and power possessed.[73]

This perspective, Wach was convinced, is a necessary corrective to both Christian and non-Christian assertions on the question of religious truth.

Wach wrote only one article concerning the claims of non-Christian religions,[74] although he voiced general views on them elsewhere. In the main, he held that a sincere effort to understand religions other than our own is imperative, "yet we do not feel that it is all said with the simple formula: let us share."[75] Unfortunately, in this article Wach used the first person to refer both to Wach the historian of religion and Wach the Christian, thus blurring his main thesis. Also confusing was his use of Christ as an example in the discussion. Nevertheless, Wach took pains to articulate the difference between the perspective of the "comparative study of religions" and that of an "apologetic theology of a particular religious faith." The former must apply a universal method of study, which cannot do full justice to the self-interpretation of any religious faith. Even then he felt that the comparative study of religions must exert every effort to understand correctly the "intention" of each religion. Wach was disturbed by the fact that too often the comparative study of religions is colored by the apologetic interests of a particular faith. Thus, despite his high regard for Hinduism and Radhakrishnan, Wach had four main criticisms of Radhakrishnan: (1) he interprets all of Hinduism in terms of only one of its aspects, namely, Vedanta, at the expense of earlier and medieval developments of Hinduism, and thus distorts the history of Hinduism; [76] (2) Radhakrishnan's description of the "pure and simple teachings of Jesus" as the "intuitive realization, non-dogmatic toleration, insistence on non-aggressive virtues and universalist ethics," without any reference to the passion and crucifixion, is a very one-sided view of the Christian understanding of Christ; [77] (3) Radhakrishnan's oversimplified insistence on religious tolerance does not do justice to the difference which exists, for instance, "between the Indian concept of Avatars and the Christian notion of 'the Son of God' "; [78] and finally, (4) Radhakrishnan's favorite thesis of "religious tolerance," which is often accepted as a desirable and necessary attitude for the comparative study of religions, is unmistakably based on the Hindu dogmatic interpretation of "tolerance," which is used by Radhakrishnan for an "apologetic" purpose. While a spirit of tolerance is desirable, Wach asks: "in which spirit, and why not in the Spirit of Christ?" [79] Ideally, however, the spirit of tolerance must be implemented by a practical methodological framework, which is not colored by any one religious view of tolerance.

Wach suggested the following three main principles for the comparative study of religions: first, it must recognize the existence of an apologetic element in each religion, but the discipline itself cannot be influenced by that apologetic interest; second, it must regard all religions as universal options, not subject to cultural determinism; third, while it must recognize that "every living religion has its part in the spiritual education of the race," it cannot be blind to the qualitative differences of various religions.[80] In other words, the comparative study of religions must be aware of the philosophical and theological problems involved in the formulation of its own general perspective.

More important is Wach's attempt to relate the insights of *Religionswissenschaft* to Christian theology. In this attempt, Wach was compelled to deal with the problem that has been known historically as "general revelation." His perspective is not that of a theologian who is interested in the history of religions, but of a historian of religions who is interested in establishing a theological basis for his study.[81] Affirming William Temple's famous statement that "unless all existence is a medium of revelation, no particular revelation is possible," Wach held that "genuine religious experience is the apprehension of the *revelatum wherever it occurs,* that is, within whatever ethnic, cultural, social or religious context."[82] In so stating, Wach rejected David G. Moses's view that general revelation is revelation in the world of nature, in the conscience and reason of man, in contrast to special revelation which is given in the events of history and in prophetic individuals.[83] But, in Wach's view, the more crucial question is "particular revelation." He rejected on the one hand the views of the *religionsgeschichtliche Schule* which recognizes only general revelation, and on the other hand the views of those who insist that there can only be one particular revelation, because "every instance of general revelation is a particular one."[84] However, Wach as a phenomenologist distinguishes between a genuine and a non-genuine revelatory experience.[85] Thus, Wach was not disturbed by the question of "continuity *vs.* discontinuity," or the "points of contact" between Christianity and other religions, which is debated by missionary thinkers. Rather, he was interested in the notion of "phenomenological preparation" as a necessary corrective to "chronological preparation," in regard to the question of *praeparatio evangelica*.[86]

Wach did not think of the new constructive solution for the study of religions as a simple division of labor among the various disciplines, such as a gathering and registering of facts and phenomena by the historian of religions, and an evaluation by the theologian and philosopher. He was convinced that the history of religions must evaluate apprehension of the Divine by non-Christian religions. He recognized the legitimate use by Christian theologians of Christian revelation as the normative standard; however, he did not think the Christian should "examine non-Christian expressions of the experience of God, by viewing them under categories borrowed from Christian dogmatics and the Christian doctrine of God." [87] Rather, Christian theology must depend on the history of religions to interpret the implications of these non-Christian apprehensions for thought, life, and conduct in the various non-Christian communities, because, as Brunner states, "The Christian faith does not criticize from its standpoint the quest for God in non-Christian religions which it can only perceive and clarify but rather the *answer* which is given by non-Christian religions." [88] Wach as a historian of religions offered the following principles to be taken seriously by Christian theologians in their evaluation of non-Christian religions.[89]

1. There is a genuine experience of ultimate reality in non-Christian religions; finite values such as blood, soil, class, *et cetera* are not the primary concern of these religions.

2. Where a genuine revelation is present the Divine is experienced under the categories of *mysterium tremendum* and *mysterium fascinosum,* using Otto's terms, even though these two aspects are not always equally represented in non-Christian religions.

3. The experience of the Holy is integrally related to ethics and morality in all religions.

4. Non-Christians, past and present, have had the "grace of God," to use Christian terminology, even though they may not recognize it as such.

5. There are various kinds and degrees of apprehension of the Divine represented in non-Christian religions. A criterion of the degree of these apprehensions must be articulated in non-Christian religious terms and not in Christian terms.

6. There is a genuine sense of "worship" in non-Christian systems.

7. Religious experience in all religions expresses itself in some form of "togetherness."

Wach's conviction underlying these principles is that there is a definite place for the history of religions in theology today, not merely in the theologian's apologetic task but in the "even more central concern of the theologian, namely, to determine the nature and extent of God's revelatory activity in history."[90] In this respect Wach was indebted to Rudolf Otto, to whom he pays warm tribute:

If a study of universal features in the expressions of the religious experience of mankind can supply us with a framework within which we can find this experience articulated, it must be possible to test the validity of this framework by applying it in the study of primitive cults *and* of the universal religions. It was just that which [Otto] set out to do. Whatever criticism might rightly be levelled at his epistemology, here is a successful attempt to combine appreciation based on the most thorough acquaintance with different types of religious experience with profound Christian conviction and commitment.[91]

Throughout his life, Wach never questioned the truth of Max Müller's words: "The real history of man is the history of religion: the wonderful ways by which the different families of the human race advanced toward a truer knowledge and a deeper love of God. This is the foundation that underlies all profane history: it is the light, the soul, and the life of history, and without it all history would indeed be profane."[92]

This brief account of Wach's life and thought cannot be complete without some reference to him as a teacher and master. In one of his early works, *Meister und Jünger*,[93] Wach characterized the relationship between teacher and student, and that between master and disciple. Between teacher and student the objective is the transmission of knowledge, which requires competence in subject matter on the part of both. Between master and disciple the importance lies in their personal relationship, based on the master's personality and his sense of vocation. After death, a teacher continues to live in his work, but the master lives in his disciples who can only witness to the master's character and personality as he experienced it. In a true sense, Wach tried to combine these two qualities. Thus, while his scholarship will continue to enlighten future scholars, the depth of his personality and character can be told only by those who came to know him as a "guru."[94] No disciple's characterization of his master's personality can do full justice to the master. This writer's description of Wach is no exception.

Permission to quote from C. C. J. Webb's *God and Personality* was granted by George Allen and Unwin, Ltd.; from William Temple's *Nature, Man and God* by Macmillan and Co., Ltd., and by St. Martin's Press; from C. C. J. Webb's *Religious Experience* by Oxford University Press; from Jean Daniélou's *Origen* (copyright 1955) by Sheed and Ward, Inc.

Grateful acknowledgment must be made to the American Council of Learned Societies as well as to many individuals who have read Wach's manuscript in various stages, particularly Professor Friedrich Heiler of Marburg University, Professor Mircea Eliade of the University of Chicago, Professor William Earle of Northwestern University, Dr. Wilhelm H. Wuellner, the

Reverend F. Dean Lueking, and the Reverend Herbert P. Sullivan. Much of the information concerning Wach's life and publication has been furnished by a number of Wach's family and friends. The editor, however, acknowledges full responsibility for any inaccuracies or misrepresentations in this account.

THE
COMPARATIVE STUDY
OF RELIGIONS

Le siècle présent n'achevera pas sans avoir vu s'établir dans son unité une science dont les éléments sont encore dispersées, science que les siècles précédents n'ont pas connue, qui n'est pas même définie et que, pour la première fois peut-être, nous nommons science des religions.

E. BURNOUF, *La Science des religions*
3rd ed., 1870, p. 1

(This present century will not come to an end without having seen the establishment of a unified science whose elements are still dispersed, a science which the preceding centuries did not have, which is not even yet defined, and which, perhaps for the first time, will be named science of religions.)

I

DEVELOPMENT, MEANING, AND METHOD IN THE COMPARATIVE STUDY OF RELIGIONS

There can be little doubt that the modern comparative study of religions [1] began with Max Müller, about a century ago.[2] His *Comparative Mythology* appeared in 1856, and in 1870 the *Introduction to the Science of Religions* was published. This was followed in 1878 by the lectures on *Origin and Growth of Religion as Illustrated by the Religions of India*. This first stage of study was characterized by a genuine enthusiasm, a sincere desire to understand other religions, and a measure of speculative interest. Among the various forms of expression of religious experience it was mythology which attracted special attention. Language study, history, and philosophy were blended during this era while theology receded. The term "science of religion" (*Religionswissenschaft*) was used to denote the emancipation of the new discipline from the philosophy of religion and especially from theology.[3] The historians of religion willingly cultivated their reputation as discoverers of a new and highly promising method of inquiry.[4] Everyone was looking for "parallels." There was a strong desire to make use of the sources provided by sacred texts in which the religious traditions of different tribes, nations, and peoples were written. The landmark of this endeavor was the publication of the *Sacred Books of the East* (begun in 1897).

The interesting Gifford Lectures given by the Dutch scholar Tiele from 1896 to 1898, published as *Elements of the Science of Religion*,[5] indicate the transition from the first to the second stage in the development of comparative studies of religion. The speculative element, although it frequently yields to historical interest, is still strong in Tiele's lectures. It is noticeable in his construction of lines of evolution,[6] which he discovered not only in the history of religions but also in folklore, sociology, and psychology—three fields which were to contribute heavily to our discipline. The works of Tylor[7] (*Primitive Culture*, 1871), Emile Durkheim (*Les Formes élémentaires de la vie religieuse*, 1912), and Wilhelm Wundt (*Völkerpsychologie*, 1906) illustrate the application of the evolutionary theory to the study of religion. This second period was dominated by philological and historical concerns and was characterized by a positivistic temper. Description was to take the place of evaluation. Norms and values were to be "explained" historically, psychologically, and sociologically. Important contributions were made to the exploration of the religions of man, past and present. Specialization was highly developed and "objectivity" was the supreme demand.[8] Great interest prevailed in the study of *origins*. While the mistake of the first stage had been neglect of detail, the second erred in its overestimation of detail. The scholars of the previous period had indulged in the search for parallels with the joy of fresh discovery; those of the second were prone to overlook dissimilarities in favor of similarities. Ernest Renan[9] was a great name of this era. Usener's *Götternamen*[10] (1889) and the works of his followers, especially Dieterich, Reitzenstein, Wissowa, and

Norden, are representative of this period's study of the classical religions of the Greco-Roman and Near Eastern worlds.[11] These efforts are related to those of the so-called *religionsgeschichtliche Schule* in general [12] (H. Gunkel, Bousset, Bertholet, Gressmann, Cumont, A. Reville, M. Dibelius, Eissfeldt).[13] In anthropology, Frazer [14] and Boas [15] followed similar lines.[16] The work of men like Clarke, Warren, Barrows, G. F. Moore, and Toy [17] represented American efforts in this phase of our studies.

With the First World War important changes again took place. The age of historicism [18] had come to an end, although philological, historical, and critical studies continued and the positivistic methodology persisted in many places. Ernst Troeltsch, regarded by many as the guiding spirit and leading dogmatist of the so-called *religionsgeschichtliche Schule,* clearly stated the problem in his great work *Der Historismus*.[19] The historic flux into which every phenomenon is dissolved cannot yield the *norms* for faith and action, yet life without such norms does not seem worth living.[20] That had been sharply and powerfully stated by the young Nietzsche in *Unzeitgemässe Betrachtungen* as early as 1873. With the turn of the century the two disciplines, philosophy and theology, which had degenerated into technical epistemology or historical research, began to reassert themselves. The beginning of a new and third era in our studies was made possible in philosophy [21] by the neo-Kantians, Bergson, and the phenomenologists; in Catholic thought by von Hügel and Scheler; and in Protestant theology by Söderblom, Barth, and Otto.[22] It is characterized by three things: the desire to overcome the disadvantages of exaggerated specialization and departmentalization by means of an integrated outlook, the desire to penetrate deeper into the nature of religious experience, and the exploration of questions of an epistemological and ultimately metaphysical character. Though in some quarters there has been a sharp reaction against the predominance of the positivistic temper, the majority of scholars believe that the results of the labors of the preceding generation should be preserved at any cost. The foundation upon which a fruitful comparative study of religions rests must always be historical and philological, or, in other words, *critical* studies. I think that the work of Rudolf Otto is characteristic of the third period of the comparative study of religions.[23] It lays powerful stress upon the objective character of ultimate reality and thus refutes all subjective and illusionist theories of religion. Von Hügel[24] and Webb[25] have shown a similar concern. By stressing the nonrational element in religion without neglecting the value of rational investigation, an exaggerated intellectualism and scholasticism are excluded. Although it may destroy a similarity, that which is dissimilar, specific, and individual is not overlooked. This rules out any superficial identification and parallelism on the part of the historians of religions.

There has been much international cooperation among scholars of Europe, Asia, and America throughout each of the three periods we have sketched. The historical surveys of the development of comparative studies in religion by Jordan, Lehmann, Pinard de la Boullaye, and more recently by Puech, Mensching, Widengren, and Masson-Oursel show the extent of this exchange.[26] Asian scholars have increasingly participated in this work and the names of Moslem, Hindu, Chinese, and Japanese scholars deserve special mention along with those of smaller nations (Burma, Siam, Philippines, the Arab States, Pakistan, Indonesia). Moreover, Western students have begun to show increased realization of the need for help from those who grew up in another religious tradition in order to do full justice to the *meaning* of the phenomena to be investigated. In the era of positivism a sovereign disregard for and suspicion of the

DEVELOPMENT, MEANING, AND METHOD

"native" commentaries was not infrequent. Only Western critical techniques could be admitted. There can be no doubt that the eagerness with which the techniques of Western critical studies have been appropriated by Eastern scholars promises highly significant contributions from them in our field.

This exchange has been fostered during the past fifty years by a number of International Congresses of the History of Religions. It cannot be denied, however, that political circumstances and the effect of two great wars have made it more difficult to maintain the standard which the earlier meetings had set in terms of universality and significance of the topics discussed. Since the end of the initial phase in which contact was established between scholars of different nations and faiths, it has become ever more manifest that the vague syncretism characterizing some of the gatherings of those of different faiths around the turn of the last century cannot fulfill the demands of the newly awakened religious consciousness nor stand the scrutiny of a strong constructive philosophical interest. Herein lies the danger. As both Christian and non-Christian religions reassert their convictions it becomes increasingly difficult to safeguard the positive results of the age of liberalism [27] in terms of scholarship and knowledge. The newly won freedom has to be guarded against any form of tyrannical authority; this was the dominant concern of the second period in our studies sketched above. But on the other hand, skepticism, relativism, and historicism have to be prevented.[28] This means that the problem of the relation of authority and freedom in religion has become of vital importance. The author of a recent survey of religion in twentieth-century America reminds us that "the reconciliation of the spirit of freedom with the spirit of religious devotion or commitment has become a serious problem of public morality." [29]

We spoke of certain basic methodological and epistemological problems which have to be raised and answered in this era of comparative studies. During the preceding period some of these questions were considered unanswerable and taboo, since raising them would have led to discussion and strife. But in this day and age there is no avoiding the challenge which the pluralism of religious loyalties and its relationship to the problem of truth poses for individuals, groups, and governments. As long as detachment was regarded as the highest virtue and commitment was looked on with suspicion, there was no great occasion for disagreement. There were no minorities to be protected and tolerance was no issue, inasmuch as the frequent presence of indifference made such "tolerance" possible at no high cost. To me there is something pathetic about the modern historian of religion who uses strong words only when he wants to convince us that he has no convictions.[30] His interest, so he says, is antiquarian or the result of sheer intellectual curiosity. He is "neutral" as far as religion is concerned. Nietzsche vehemently attacked this attitude in *Nutzen und Nachteil der Historie für das Leben*. Ernst Troeltsch has characterized an "unlimited relativism" by stating that a weakly constituted natural history has become identified with empathy (*Nachfühlung*) for all other characters together with a relinquishing of empathy for oneself, with skepticism and playful intellectuality, or with oversophistication (*Blasiertheit*) and a lack of faith.[31] It could be asked if an open hostility is not more appropriate to the subject of religion than this noncommital attitude.

All this is not to say that the ideal of objectivity should be abandoned by those engaged in comparative studies. It is rather to assert that it must be rightly understood. I have elsewhere indicated that "relative" objectivity is a necessary ideal in ascertaining the "given," the data, the meaning of which concerns us.[32] All philological and historical research must be determined by this ideal. Until recently no one in the East would have been

Confessional

interested in studying religion as some of the "scientifically" minded Westerners try to deal with it. Though the word was not known, an existential concern motivated those who were engaged in this work. Now the scientific idea has conquered the Near East as well as India, China, and Japan. The West had to relearn from Kierkegaard that religion is something toward which "neutrality" is not possible. It is true that dangers accompany the appeal to emotions and the arousing of passions. Yet emotions and passions *do* play a legitimate role in religion. It is precisely here that the *raison d'être,* the best justification, for the comparative study of religions can and must be found. It is an error to believe that comparative studies must breed indifference. They contribute toward the gaining of perspective, as well as of discernment and understanding.

If it is the task of theology to investigate, buttress, and teach the faith of a religious community to which it is committed, as well as to kindle zeal and fervor for the defense and spread of this faith, it is the responsibility of a comparative study to guide and to purify it. How can that be brought about? That which I value and cherish and hold dear beyond all else, I also want thoroughly to understand in all its implications. It is true that to love truth you must hate untruth, but it is not true that in order to exalt your own faith you must hate and denigrate those of another faith.[33] A comparative study of religions such as the new era made possible enables us to have a fuller vision of what religious experience can mean, what forms its expression may take, and what it might do for man. It could be argued that this would mean the subjection of one's religious faith to a judgment pronounced in the name of some generalized notions. But does a ruby or an emerald sparkle less if called a jewel? Not only different religious communities but groups within them develop certain emphases and neglect other aspects.

Next to reorientation to the primary norm of religious experience, what better way to understand religions is there than to study the notions and practices of others?

But can you understand a religion other than your own? [34] This question must be analyzed. There seems to be a sense in which the answer would have to be "No," and yet there are indications that in some sense a positive reply is possible. Undoubtedly it is possible to "know the facts" in the sense of gathering and organizing all the available information. As we have seen, that was and is the task of our field according to the positivistically minded scholar. Yet, is that enough? [35] Is it not necessary to be a member of a religious community to understand its religious notions and customs? But what does it mean to be a "member?" Could it be seriously maintained that a great scholar belonging to Group A would be less capable of understanding the religion of Group B than any ignorant and humble person belonging to the latter? Obviously official membership cannot be the criterion for the possibility of understanding. Could not one conceivably participate in the ritual performance of a cultic group, for example, and yet be unaware of the meaning of that which is said and done? Does that in turn signify that even a commitment would not be sufficient in itself, since such could also exist in the case of an ignorant and humble member? And how about the alert skeptic who may be nearer a "conversion" than he or anyone else may know? In all tribal religion the question of membership is a relatively simple one: it is conferred by birth and birth only, though there may be qualifications such as the fulfillment of duties, and so on. It is more complicated in specifically religious communities. Among these there are usually objective criteria of membership—*notae ecclesiae*—but the fideists, mystics, and spiritualists usually insist on additional and often subjective standards. An inner attitude alone can qualify one as a "true" member. It goes without saying that in the latter case it would be more difficult to indicate what "full understanding" would entail than in the former case where participation is regulated in a more automatic or mechanical sense.

There are definite stages of understanding. One stage would be partial, another integral, comprehension. Thus it is conceivable that we could do justice to a particular religious thought or act without being able to grasp others appearing in the same context or to grasp this context as a whole. Religious communities recognize this by stratifying their religious groups, especially those with an esoteric character such as mystery societies in which different grades correspond to varying degrees of "comprehension." In this problem of religious understanding there is also the law of irreversibility, according to which it is possible for the higher to comprehend the lower and the older (master) to perceive what is going on in the younger (disciple) but not vice versa. That brings us to the discussion of the conditions that must prevail if an integral understanding is to be achieved.

Let us turn first to the necessary equipment. We have seen previously that it will in part be of an intellectual nature. There is no hope of understanding a religion or a religious phenomenon without the most extensive information possible. We owe a great debt of gratitude to the painstaking work of the past one hundred and fifty years which has so increased the depth and degree of our knowledge of other religions. The most comprehensive survey of this development has been given by the French Jesuit scholar, Pinard de la Boullaye, in the first volume of his *Étude comparée des religions* (1922).[36] The student of religions is never well enough equipped linguistically. It is now desirable to know many languages and families of languages which were barely known by name fifty years ago. This is especially true with regard to the ancient Near East, Africa, Central Asia, and

South America. Yet we agree with Webb when he says: "I do not indeed suppose that it is necessary, in order to enter into the spirit of a religion, that one should be able to read its scriptures and its doctrines in their original languages. A man may be a very good Christian without Greek or Hebrew, and a very bad Christian with both."[37] It may not be necessary, but the chances of an adequate understanding are infinitely better where the interpreter is in a position to at least check on the translation of key terms, if he is not actually competent to read the foreign tongue. Yet this competence in and by itself does not guarantee positive results in the study of religion.

Secondly, a successful venture in understanding a religion different from our own requires an adequate emotional condition. What is required is not indifference, as positivism in its heyday believed—"Grey cold eyes do not know the value of things," objected Nietzsche—but rather an engagement of feeling, interest, *metexis,* or participation.[38] This is not an endorsement of the widespread notion that religion as such is an exclusively emotional affair (a notion held by Schleiermacher and Otto). As we shall see in greater detail, religion is a concern of the total person, engaging intellect, emotion, and will.

The realms of the human personality and human values are often invaded by a scientism which insists upon only one method of knowing and one type of knowledge. One of the weightiest arguments for those who want to preserve the human personality and its values against the imperatives of science is the demonstration that any form of reduction falls short of the aim of a student of religion, which is to do justice to that religion's true nature.

A third form of equipment, the equipment of volition, is therefore required for anyone who wishes to deal adequately with the religion of his fellow man. The will must be directed and oriented toward a constructive purpose. Neither idle curiosity nor a passion for annihilating whatever differs from one's own position is an appropriate motive for this task. Ignorance, uncontrolled passion, and lack of direction are enemies of that state of mind which alone promises success in the venture of understanding. There will never be a lack of those differences (difference in temperament is one example) which make it difficult even for the student of broad concerns and deep sympathies to comprehend various kinds of religiosity, types of religious thought, or devotional practices which differ sharply from his own.

But there is still something else that is essential equipment for the study of religion, and that is experience.[39] We use this term here in a wide sense, leaving the analysis of the nature of religious experience for the next chapter. We should like to define experience in the broadest sense, thus opposing all narrow concepts which separate and even isolate it as a province of life into which only the specialized professional can enter. In all likelihood there is no contact with any aspect of life which would not bear upon the problem of understanding another's religion. As the psychologists and sociologists of religion have told us, there are not only different religious temperaments (beginning with William James's "healthy-minded" and "sick-minded") but also different types of religious institutions.[40] Whoever has had wide experience with human character possesses one more qualification for understanding an alien religion, for such a person has thereby contacted the minds of people in the variety of their acting, feeling, and ways of thinking. It is important for one to realize that there are different ways to be "religious," to know and to worship God; for in the area of expression between man and man even the narrowest religious fellowships show differences.[41] The group as well as the individual will be religious in its own way. We are not talking here about "heresies" but about the legitimate range of psychological and sociological differences. This is not an endorsement of pluralism or relativism. Even if one holds fast to the belief that truth is one it is possible to concede that there are "many mansions" in our Father's house.

After dwelling upon the nature and the task of comparative studies in religion, we can now discuss the method to be followed. Much controversy has been carried on in the last decade between two schools of thought. One has insisted that the method of religious studies is totally *sui generis* and in no way comparable or related to methods in other fields of knowledge. The other school has maintained that, irrespective of the character of the subject matter to be investigated, the only legitimate method is the so-called "scientific" method. The term scientific is used here in a double sense: in the narrower sense it denotes the method used in the so-called natural sciences, and in the wider sense it refers to any procedure which works with logical and coherent discipline from clearly indicated premises. Both these approaches have been found wanting; in the present era of the comparative study of religions a new synthesis is being worked out. Beginning with the second school of thought, we see that there is good reason to oppose an unqualified pluralism or even a dualism in matters of method and of knowledge. Truth is one; the cosmos is one; hence knowledge also must be one. This insight is all important. Although we will not agree with the positivistic interpretation of this principle, we must incorporate it into our methodology, which will be based on a dual demand. The first demand is that the method be unified. Such is the imperative of Aristotle, Aquinas, Leibniz, and Whitehead. All idealism and all naturalism—including materialism—stand or fall with methodological monism. Yet to conceive of one truth is one thing and to possess or comprehend it is another. We should be realistic enough to see the profound wisdom in the apostle's words that here we know only in part, which is to say that only God himself can be aware of the whole. The second demand is that the method be adequate for the subject matter. This qualifies the first principle, that of a unified method.

Many theological and philosophical writers in the first half of this century have demonstrated the insufficiency of the narrowly defined scientific approach to the study of religion. Many distinguished scientists have questioned the applicability of the methods and techniques of experimental, quantitative, causal investigation to the world of the spirit. The philosophical vindication of the freedom of the spirit was ably pursued by Bergson, Dilthey, Balfour, Von Hügel, Troeltsch, Husserl, Scheler, Temple, Otto, Jung, Baillie, Berdyaev, and others. In order that the method be adequate for the subject matter, the phenomenon of individuality, the nature of value, and the meaning of freedom must be recognized. It has been rightly said that the whole realm of the personal, with which the religious quest is so indissolubly connected, must remain closed to the investigator who does not make concession to his method [42] as required by the nature of the subject matter.[43]

A positivistic age could cherish the notion of a universally applicable technique of inquiry. Religion was to be studied exactly as any phenomenon of the inorganic or organic world. With the above-mentioned qualification that the method must fit the subject matter, the new era has shown a growing demand for a metaphysical concept which would do justice to the nature of phenomena of the spiritual as well as of the physical world.

The tremendous success of the philosophy of Alfred North Whitehead [44] in the Anglo-Saxon world can be explained in terms of this need. It has been widely felt that he has provided a coherent system for understanding nature, mind, and spirit. This is the necessary successor to a prolonged preoccupation with technical problems of a primarily epistemological and somewhat esoteric character. With its appearance the school of emergent evolution [45] has been added to the two major systems, Roman Catholic and Marxian interpretation, which have survived the positivistic era in the West and which have maintained their formidable prestige among many systems of metaphysics. We cannot trace the development and fortunes of emergent evolution here; we can only indicate with a few quotations what its aims and conclusions are. The underlying metaphysical concept is described in the words of its founder, Lloyd Morgan: "Evolution, in the broad sense, is the name we give to the comprehensive plan of sequences in all natural events. But the orderly sequence, historically viewed, appears to present from time to time something genuinely new. . . . Salient examples are afforded in the advent of life, in the advent of mind, and in the advent of reflective thought. If nothing new emerges, if there be only regrouping of pre-existing events and nothing more—then there is no emergent evolution." [46]

Methodologically that meant that "the emergent entity is not to be accounted for in terms of antecedent stages of the process." [47] Hence allowance was made for recognizing the emergence of new and unpredictable properties. "Emergent evolution urges that the more of any given stage, even the highest, involves the 'less' of the stages which preceded it and continues to co-exist with it. It does not interpret the higher in terms of the lower only." [48] It is no accident that Morgan was himself religious. More than the somewhat abstract Alexander,[49] Whitehead himself has pointed out the implications of this philosophy for religion. The final word on this topic has yet to be said. A wholly satisfactory monographic treatment of the role of religion in the thought of Whitehead remains to be written. The best criticism and constructive interpretation from the point of view of Christian thought is still the famous Gifford Lectures of Temple, *Nature, Man and God* (1932–34).[50] Though there is little reference to non-Christian religions and their study, all the implications and consequences of the philosophy of emergent evolution are clearly indicated for the understanding of individuality, values, meaning, and freedom—in short, for the realm of the personal. Thus the demand for a unified method which accords with the exigencies of the subject matter is justified. It is therefore not surprising to see the influence of his thinking on some of the keenest students of these problems in our own day. It will be sufficient to name, besides Thornton, Richardson and Ferré.[51] Richardson's apologetic follows Temple's methodology,[52] particularly in the doctrine of revelation, and D. G. Moses's[53] penetrating analysis of the notion of religious truth proceeds along the same lines. While clearly stating his conviction that "ultimate truth is one,"[54] Moses holds that "the different aspects of reality disclose their nature only as we use different methods of knowing." He maintains that "reality" is an identity expressing itself differently in different parts.[55] "Matter, life, mind and self-consciousness represent different levels or orders of reality."[56] Here we agree wholeheartedly with Moses's distinctions, though we shall later take exception to his notion of the criterion of religious truth.

In a very provocative sentence in *Nature, Man and God*, Temple points to the fact that the mind itself emerges in the midst of the process which it apprehends.[57] This means that consciousness is not given priority as that which legislates the principles of possible experience. Rather we must look upon a mind as that which arises out of the background of its given world and progressively constructs its own concept according to the kind of connection which it finds or expects to find in its world. It tries to express this connection in symbolic form.⁵⁸ This is a hint as to how we have to understand the old saying (which dates at least from the time of Plato) that there must be a resemblance between the knower and the known. "We come back, therefore, to the Platonic principle that if any rational understanding is to be possible, the *logos* in us must be akin to a *logos* in things." ⁵⁹ This hermeneutical principle proves to be valid for the understanding of religion, too. A love letter will appear meaningless and silly to anybody not in love, though it may be appreciated aesthetically if it happens to be a work of art. As Richard of St. Victor says, "How then can a man speak about love who does not feel it? Only the one who composes his speech according to what the heart dictates can worthily speak of love." ⁶⁰ By the same token a religious utterance will bewilder, frustrate, or repel anyone whose religious sensitivities have not been developed.⁶¹

It is in this context that the Christian doctrine of the Holy Spirit and His inner testimony must be understood.⁶² Otto has said, "The mere word, even when it comes as a living voice, is powerless without the 'spirit in the heart' of the hearer to move him to apprehension." ⁶³ It was not by accident that Otto's first written study dealt with this subject.⁶⁴ This seems to me to be a more adequate statement than the notion of some "preunderstanding" (*Vor-Verständnis*) tied to the self-analysis with which a certain type of existentialism is so much concerned.⁶⁵ It is right to say that "no understanding and no interpretation of sources is possible without the *inter esse* of the scholar. He must engage in a dialogue with the past, but not primarily because it is a part of his own history." ⁶⁶ Schleiermacher was right in pointing out that the realm of the understandable extends between the utterly foreign and the totally familiar.⁶⁷

Interestingly enough there is a close parallel between the thought of the Anglo-Saxon philosophy of emergence and that of the new theory of ontological stratification of Nicolai Hartmann.[68] His conception of reality as a structure (*Gefüge*—that same mode of being or reality which encompasses everything from matter to spirit) [69] involves four separate levels (*Schichten*). He distinguishes between the material, the organic, the psychic (*seelisch*), and the spiritual (*geistig*) without assuming that they have evolved from each other or from "below" or "above." Each of these strata has its own peculiar ontological categories.[70] In every instance some categories characteristic of the lower stage recur in the next one. Certain fundamental ones such as unity, temporality, and so on, apply to all of them. New categories, as in the realm of the mental (psychic) and the spiritual, constitute a superstructure [71] and hence necessitate different methods of approach for study. "The categorical laws teach the dependence of the higher ontological strata on the lower strata, the former being supported and partly determined by the latter." [72] Because the higher depend on the lower and not conversely, the latter are the stronger ones.[73] "Strength and height in the order of strata stand in an inverse relationship." [74] "The center of gravity of the higher stratum is in the laws of novelty and freedom." [75] There is freedom in the "novelty" which the higher level represents in comparison to the lower. "Anthropology has room for the autonomy of spiritual life but it also knows how to unite it with the organic stratum of the human being." [76] Yet Hartmann tends to ascribe the greater power to the "lower" levels as Marx and Scheler did before him.[77]

As is the world, continues Hartmann, so also is man an ordered structure of body, soul, and mind which is reducible neither to the merely biological nor to the spiritual.[78] However, body and spirit do not shade off into each other. There is no continuum between them. The spirit has its own kind of power, but it is a limited one. It is a power different from everything that opposes it; it is based upon the unparalleled singularity of the categorical novelty of the spirit.[79] It presupposes the whole stratification of the lower powers with which it has to deal in life, and at the same time it rests upon them.[80] Body and spirit do have a connection in the third intermediate and distinct ontological stratum called psychic being.[81] "The nature of man can be adequately understood only as the integrated whole of combining strata, and, furthermore, as placed within the totality of the same order of strata which, outside of man, determines the structure of the real world."[82]

We have mentioned the resemblance of the knower and the known and the implication of this principle for the study of religion. We feel that it is here that the Western understanding of religion has a great deal to learn from the East. Until recently at least, there has been little inclination in the East to admit that perception and inference are the only legitimate ways of knowing. The Eastern sages have always insisted that there is an immediate awareness of and inclination toward truth,[83] although the sources of religious insight have been differently conceived in different communities of faith.[84] Datta[85] has shown us how knowledge (prama) and the true source of knowledge (pramana)[86] are conceived in different schools of the Vedanta. (True knowledge is defined as cognition of an object neither contradicted nor already known.)[87] In Hinduism the true method of knowing reality must be based upon the revealed texts, and this knowledge is identical with liberation. Metaphysics precedes epistemology. For some the only pramana is perception. Others add inference, comparison, postulation, and "non-perception." "Authority" or "testimony" (*sabda*) is finally recognized as an independent and ultimate source of knowledge by almost all Indian thinkers except Carvakas, Buddhists, and Vaisesikas.⁸⁸ The fact that authorities may disagree does not invalidate this source of knowledge since this may be the case with the other pramanas as well.⁸⁹

The West, however, rightly conceives of knowledge in terms which enable it to incorporate the information acquired into the various departments of scientific pursuits—scientific in the wide sense of the word—for thus it fruitfully relates knowledge and life. This does not put essential and nonessential knowledge on the same level; rather does it attempt to overcome indifference toward all that does not immediately pertain to salvation. It is also an effort to avoid a pluralistic epistemology according to which there is no relationship between different levels of inquiry. The East may profit by pursuing this aim instead of copying Western positivism, for the ancient and noble tradition by which the East has always lived is that the highest goal for man is realization of the truth. In this Western incorporation of knowledge and life, Christianity is not in league with those for whom religion is "a sense of scruples which impede the free exercise of our faculties" (Salomon Reinach).⁹⁰ It is not contrary to, but rather in harmony with, the Christian gospel which teaches that truth is God's truth and hence one truth. To know this truth is to be free, yet one can know it here only in part. This truth is that there is an order in man's cosmos of knowledge even as there is order in the universe.

Actually there is a variety of ways to study religion and religions.⁹¹ First there is the historical approach. This is the attempt to trace the origin and growth of religious ideas and institutions through definite periods of historical development and to assess the role of the forces with which religion contended during these periods. This study must begin with the earliest accessible epoch in the history of man, which James has reconstructed in his study of the beginnings of religion.⁹² In the last half-century great strides have been made in the investigation of early civilizations in the Near East, India, East Africa, Africa, and Europe, which were inaccessible to previous historians. There is now no religion which has not had its historical development illumined by the work of several generations of scholars trained in the techniques of the historical craft. Not only has the study of the past itself been pursued, but thoughtful attention has been directed to the inner forces, phases, and aims of historical development. Troeltsch has suggested a distinction between formal and material philosophy of history:[93] the former is concerned with the logic of historical knowledge and the latter with the aforementioned forces within the history itself.[94] Strangely enough, the highly important contributions to the formal theory of history made by Bernheim,[95] Croce, Simmel, Collingwood, and especially Dilthey, which have centered upon the exceedingly important problem of understanding, have aroused much less interest in the Anglo-Saxon countries than have the writings of those treating the material philosophy of history, such as Spengler, Toynbee, Löwith, and Reinhold Niebuhr.

The work of the historian is frequently based upon previous archaeological and philological research. Through a careful study of the monuments and literary evidence of the past, material necessary to reconstruct the past is collected.[96] Only in a few instances has the study of non-Christian documentary sources reached the level of Old and especially New Testament research. Source criticism and stylistic analysis (*Formgeschichte*) will remain basic for all future work.[97] Throughout the nineteenth century, archaeological and philological hermeneutics produced an elaborate theory of understanding[98] which was formed for classical studies but which soon expanded to include Oriental and preliterate civilizations as well. Although the anthropological study of preliterate societies developed its own techniques,[99] at least part of its task was to construct man's history. Without the painstaking work of linguists and archaeologists the early and much of the later religious history of man would have remained unknown or would be inaccessible to us. Philological and historical interpretations will always remain an indispensable element in the study of religion when we try to approach it through the past. But they do not constitute the only avenue of approach.[100]

The quest for knowledge of the interior aspects of religious experience wherever and whenever that experience may occur constitutes another legitimate approach.[101] Individual and group feelings, together with their dynamics, have to be explored. This is the task of psychological interpretation. Although the more recent decades have shown an appreciable cooling of the fervor once displayed[102] by the advocates of the psychology of religion[103] at the beginning of the twentieth century, today the various schools of depth psychology and psychoanalysis offer clues to the understanding of the unconscious and its workings. The writings of Grensted, Allport, Horney, Menninger, and Fromm—to mention only a few contemporaries—have applied Freudian and Jungian theories to the study of religion.

To these older methods several new ones have been added. In France and Germany the so-called sociology of religion has emerged.[104] At first the application of the methods of general sociology as outlined by Comte and Spencer[105] was closely tied to the economic interpretation conceived by Lassalle and Marx. It was later corrected by the founders of modern sociology of religion, Fustel de Coulanges,[106] Emile Durkheim,[107] Max Weber,[108] Ernst Troeltsch,[109] Werner Sombart,[110] and Max Scheler.[111] We shall speak again of this approach in Chapter Five of this work.

Finally, still another school emerged in this century which opened a new avenue to the investigation of religious phenomena. It was called phenomenology.[112] Edmund Husserl,[113] its founder, considered it a strictly philosophical discipline with the purpose of limiting and supplementing the purely psychological explanation of the processes of the mind. Soon the phenomenological approach was employed to illumine the fields of artistic creation, law, religion, and so forth.[114] The phenomenology of religion has been developed by Max Scheler, Rudolf Otto, Jean Hering, and Gerardus van der Leeuw. Its aim is to view religious ideas, acts, and institutions with due consideration to their "intention," yet without subscribing to any one philosophical, theological, metaphysical, or psychological theory. Thus a necessary supplement to a purely historical, psychological, or sociological approach is provided.

Since only scant attention has been given in America to the ambitious attempt to apply phenomenology to the study of religion, it might not be amiss to summarize briefly Scheler's ideas on the subject.[115] With Brentano and Husserl, he is concerned to let manifestations of the religious experience speak for themselves rather than to force them into any preconceived scheme. That means the safeguarding of their intentional character. Three tasks must be undertaken by the phenomenology of religion: it must inquire into the nature of the Divine (*Wesensontik des Göttlichen*); it must provide a theory of revelation; and, it must study the religious act. All this is neither positive theology nor "philosophy of religion." Hence Scheler is inclined to accept Otto's analysis of the experience of the Holy, but he rejects Fries's speculations on religion and his categorial scheme.[116] Otto's discovery of the "numinous" as a value category *sui generis* is regarded by Scheler as parallel to his own demonstration of the nature and apprehension of moral values. Neither history nor psychology can do the job of phenomenology. Neither deduction nor abstraction secures the "essence" (*eidos*) vouchsafed by the *Wesensschau*.

In a recent lecture on "La Structure de la Religion,"[117] Bleeker describes a double procedure characteristic of the phenomenological approach: the *"epoche,"* or temporary suspension of all inquiry into the problem of truth, and the "eidetic vision," which could be described as a search for essences. "The eidetic principle has the Eidos as the goal of inquiry, that is to say, what is of essence in religious phenomena."[118] However, in suggesting a distinction between "theoria" (the direct and impartial study of religious phenomena) and the search for their *"logos,"* he follows van der Leeuw instead of the classical interpretation of phenomenology by Husserl. He identifies the *logos* with structure. "This term," he says, "again emphasizes this truth: that religion is not an uncontrollable, subjective secret of the soul but an objective entity shaped by strictly spiritual laws with its own altogether logical, that is, phenomenologically logical, structure."[119] According to this theory, structure is revealed in four ways: through constant forms, irreducible factors, points of crystallization, and types. In a stimulating contribution to the *Festschrift* for Alfred Bertholet (1950), Alfred Jespers has reemphasized the fact that the real problems in a study of religion are raised by phenomenology.[120] We cannot follow this scholar in his stress upon the self-explanatory basis of religious experience ("es gibt soviele Religionswissenschaften als es Verständnismöglichkeiten für den Menschen gibt"[121]), but we agree with the attempt to describe an "original type" of religion as a permanent structure of religious experience.

Typology supplies still another bridge between empirical and normative inquiry. The endless variety of phenomena which the history, psychology, and sociology of religion provide us must be organized. Typological categories are designed to do that. "This construction of types is only intended for a better understanding of history from the point of view of life." [122] As long as this is borne in mind there is no danger that concrete individuality and historical variety will be slighted in favor of a typological approach. Types of mythical or theological notions, types of worship, types of religious charisma may be conceived. There also emerge types of religious leaders whose lives have been illumined by historians, whose intellectual and emotional make-up has been investigated by psychologists, and whose social role has been explored by sociologists. Types of religious grouping and religious authority also emerge. William James, Wilhelm Dilthey, Max Weber, and Howard Becker have masterfully employed this method. Finally, it may be used for the characterization of religions as wholes. Herder and Hegel began to do just that. Today there is no dearth of such typologies.[123]

II

THE NATURE OF RELIGIOUS EXPERIENCE

If we wish to determine the nature of religious experience, where shall we begin? In opposition to the popular preoccupation with the quest for the function of religion, it is necessary to stress the search for the nature of religion. A view sharply opposing this position has been recently stated by Wilfred Cantwell Smith: "It seems to me that progress in the study of religion can come when we can bring ourselves to forget about the nature of religion and attend rather to the process of its contemporary development."[1]

The opinions of the "functionalist" school of anthropology, represented by Malinowski, Radcliffe-Brown, and Evans-Pritchard, are not quite so outspoken, but they are similar in thought. Malinowski states: "Since we cannot define cult and creed by their objects, perhaps it will be possible to perceive their function," and in another place adds, "Religion . . . has no such simple technique and its unity can be seen . . . rather in the function which it fulfills. . . ."[2] Though Radcliffe-Brown does speak of a "real understanding of the nature of religions," he lauds Robertson Smith, Fustel de Coulanges, Emile Durkheim, and others for studying the effects of particular religions.[3] He is primarily interested in these effects, even when some reference is made to the nature of religion as a "sense of dependence."[4] (No reference acknowledges the author of this famous definition.)

There seem to be two ways to discover the nature of religious experience. One way is to appropriate the historical formulation of one religion, denomination, or school of religious thought. The other is to start from "where I am," that is, the potential range of personal experience. The "I" can be either an individual or a plural—a collective or corporate—"I." William James used the personal approach;[5] the collective approach seems to be the intention of Alan Richardson in his claim that "it is the actual faith and worship and experience of the living Church which must provide the data of theology."[6] This agrees with the so-called existentialist emphasis upon what is my own as opposed to that which is common, general, organized, or institutionalized.[7]

The approach which starts from one's potential range of experience is open to at least the two objections which Webb has designated.[8] First, the word "experience" seems to suggest human instead of any divine activity. It tends to focus on the experience instead of the experienced.[9] However, it also suggests the independent existence of the object experienced and thus subjectivism is avoided. The use of the term "my" or "our" experience by no means precludes the possibility that there may be divine revelation which is incorporated in this experience. The second objection is that the singularity of special revelatory events may seem to be consumed in the term "religious." This concern has brought forth the violent protests of Barth, Brunner, and Kraemer against any designation of Christianity as "a" religion. Yet we hope to prove that the specific can be more adequately apprehended and not obliterated if seen in the context of the whole religious experience of man. At this point we follow Rudolf Otto, and feel that it was his great merit to have based a theory of religion on this insight.

A third objection to this theory states that to begin with the experience of the individual renders it difficult or even impossible to do justice to the corporate character of religion.[10] But this objection is unfounded, because corporate and individual religions are not mutually exclusive. The Psalms illustrate the interpenetration of both.[11] Though individual experience may correct collective experience, the history of religions shows us that it is the exception and not the rule when individual experience presupposes and reflects collective experience.

There is definite merit to the emphasis upon an empirical approach and upon observation, which are characteristic of much of the American studies in this as well as other subjects.[12] However, there should be no denial of the reality contacted in such experience. As with any other mental act, it is the intention (*intentio* in the scholastic sense) which characterizes the religious act, as the phenomenologists since Brentano have told us.[13] This intention must be considered, and not neglected in favor of psychological circumstances or characteristics of the act.[14]

This manner of beginning makes it possible (in an analysis of the nature of religious experience) to raise the all-important question of truth without absolutizing one's own religion. The development of the discipline known as the comparative study of religion has been necessitated by the naive claim of religious communities to an exclusive possession of truth—a claim unhampered by any doubt as to the adequacy of its apprehension and understanding. Such a study has overstepped its limits whenever it has denied the claims to truth on the part of other Christian or non-Christian religious groups, churches, denominations, and sects. When it prepares the ground for the raising of the problem of truth by gathering necessary data, this discipline is not only within its legitimate province but also is performing one of its essential functions. The empirical approach which we have advocated will more easily do justice to the intimate relationship between religious experience and other kinds of experience, and at the same time will preserve the true nature of religious experience. To quote Paul Tillich: "Religious experiences are embedded in general experiences. They are distinguished but not separated." [15]

There seem to be four views on the nature of religious experience. The first is the notion that there is no such thing and that what passes for it is an illusion. This view is held by many psychologists, sociologists, and philosophical thinkers. The second view allows the existence of genuine religious experience but holds that it cannot be isolated because it is identical with general experience. Dewey, Wieman, Ames, and other European and American thinkers have expressed this opinion. The third view completely identifies one historical form of religion with religious experience, a procedure which is characteristic of a strictly conservative attitude in many religious communities. The fourth view is that there is genuine religious experience and that it can be identified by means of definite criteria which can be applied to any of its expressions. These criteria, enumerated below, will enable us to discover that religious experience is a structured experience. Far from being an inchoate and vague expansion of the emotions, it is an experience which is ordered.

The first criterion of religious experience is a response to what is experienced as Ultimate Reality.[16] By Ultimate Reality we mean that which conditions and undergirds all, that which, in the words of Dorothy Emmett, "impresses and challenges us." [17] Thus we can say that the experience of anything finite cannot be a religious but only a pseudoreligious experience.[18] (Symbols, as long as they are understood as such, may point to the infinite and hence do not necessarily fall under the category of the merely finite.) We define religious experience as response, and hence it is not merely subjective. We respond to something.[19] As Von Hügel once said, "Descartes starts with a subject only; *cogito ergo sum*—I think, not this or that, but *I* just *think*: and then Descartes ends somehow with an object as well. Yet our experience (which is our only satisfactory starting point) always gives us subject and object, the two together or neither of them."[20] And again, Von Hügel states: "All our knowledge is a process of discovery on the terra firma of experience, as it were, just as our spiritual knowledge is a process of discovery based on the *is*ness of the supreme reality, God."[21]

In our definition of religious experience as a response to what is experienced as Ultimate Reality,[22] the experience involves four things. The first is the assumption that there are degrees of awareness, such as apprehension, conception, and so on. "Consciousness," according to Whitehead, "presupposes experience." Second, the response is considered as part of an encounter. Genuine religious experience has been understood by *homines religiosi* of all ages and in all parts of the world and as such it has been described by Kierkegaard, Ebner, Scheler, Buber, Brunner, Baillie, Marcel (with his categories of "call" and "response"), and many others. Third, the "experiencing" of supreme reality implies a dynamic relationship between the experiencer and the experienced.[23] Genuine religion cannot and must not be thought of in static terms. Together with the *homines religiosi* of all tongues and ages, Mouroux asserts "God is never *possessed*."[24] Religious experience is continuous, though not without intermittences; it does not consist of unconnected "thrills." Finally, we have to understand the situational character of religious experience, that is, we must conceive of it in its particular context. When seen historically, culturally, sociologically, and religiously, our experience and its forms are always conditioned. An absolutely spontaneous religious experience is as inconceivable as is its counterpart, an absolutely determined one. This does not endorse relativism or determinism of any sort.[25] Rather is it a methodological caveat which should prevent us from absolutizing when we start—as we must—from where we are, from our own religious experience, our own apprehension.

We shall now turn to the second criterion which will enable us to determine what is and what is not genuine religious experience. The statement that experience must be conceived of as a total response of the total being to Ultimate Reality [26] means that it is the integral person which is involved, not just the mind, the emotion, or the will. Mouroux calls this experience the most unifying and the most "realizing" (*réalisante*), the highest synthesis of elements otherwise easily dissociated.[27] According to him, religious experience composes a hierarchy of three elements: the intellectual, the affective, and the voluntary. In this respect religious experience differs from experiences which are partial and concern only one part of man's being. Let me quote here the admirable statement of Webb:

. . . the religion of every religious man belongs to him not merely as a participator in an activity shared with others, but as being the individual person that he is. It belongs to him, indeed, not only as the person that he is but as being *all that he is;* with his bodily senses, his emotions, his interests, his social contacts, his affections, as well as with his understanding and with that instinct of curiosity and wonder wherein, when it is cultivated by the understanding with its power of analysis and discrimination, science and philosophy take their rise. To no part of man's life is religion merely irrelevant; only as his total response to what is by him envisaged as the ultimate reality, embracing, in Tertullian's phrase, *totum quod sumus et in quo sumus,* our whole selves and our whole environment, can religion be what it implicitly aims at being; and only as such must a Philosophy of Religion endeavour to interpret it.[28]

It has been rightly claimed that "religion is concerned with the whole man and with the whole of human life." [29] This truth of the involvement of the total person in religious experience has not only been stressed by all great religious teachers through the ages [30] but is also vindicated by modern psychological and psychopathological studies. It has come as a surprise to many a modern Westerner to realize how significant and indispensable the function of worship can be in preserving or restoring an individual's physical and spiritual health, a fact of which those adept in Yoga or its equivalent in Hinduism and Buddhism have long been conscious. "If we understand religion properly," writes one of the most experienced Eastern experts in this field, Swami Akhilananda, "we cannot help thinking that religion alone can solve the basic problems of mental ailment." [31] He quotes Jung to the effect that "there is no reason for the conflict between real religious leadership and real psychotherapy." [32] According to this author, Indian psychology places great emphasis on the study of religious experience and is able to make a therapeutic contribution through its understanding of different states of consciousness.[33]

Catholicism and the more conservative Protestant groups have never quite forgotten this connection between the physical and the spiritual, but the positivistic age allowed the different parts which make up the human person to become semi-independent and thus threaten the unity of the individual personality. It is permissible for us to dismiss the tiresome discussion about the "seat" of religion which was quite popular in the Protestant theology and philosophy of the nineteenth century. (From Schleiermacher to James, Whitehead, and Otto it was sought in feeling; from Hegel and Martineau to Brightman, in the intellect; and from Fichte to Reinhold Niebuhr, in the will.) [34] The great anthropologist, Marett, rightly observes that "in any such concrete phase, processes of thinking, feeling and willing are alike involved; and it may suit the purpose of the analysis to lay stress now on the ideas, now on the emotions, and now on the actions in which the religious experience finds expression."[35] In the same vein, Allport suggests that "subjective religion . . . must be viewed as an indistinguishable blend of emotion and reason, of feeling and meaning."[36] "Reason, the emotion, and the will," according to an outstanding classical scholar, "have no more separate existences than Jupiter, Juno, and Minerva."[37] In India a similar difference in emphasis is reflected in the classification of the major pathways (*marga*) along which man may tread and which may shape the religious life. These are *jnana* (knowledge, exertion of the mind), *karman* (work, exertion of the will), and *bhakti* (loving devotion, extension of feeling).[38]

Not only in a descriptive but also in a normative sense, it is the total being alone which confronts ultimate reality in religious experience. That is to say that religious experience forces me to be utterly myself as it reveals me to myself in my highest and in my lowest possibilities (Niebuhr). What Otto calls the sense of numinous unworth awakens in the realization that *Tu solus sanctus*. The East is very conscious of this relationship and has never erred quite as much as the modern West in its doctrine of man.[39] In the East anthropology has ever been considered closely related to cosmology and theology.[40] But the modern West sorely needs to be reminded that only the self which sees itself in the right perspective to the whole is safe, and that such "sight" is ultimately a religious perception. Philosophy as well as the sciences of man (anthropology, psychology, psychopathology) need the correction of the science of religion.[41] In religious experience the total man is engaged, in contrast to the philosophical pursuit which primarily concerns his mind, or the aesthetic[42] which has to do with his emotions. Yet one word of caution is necessary. Recently, Western psychology and philosophical anthropology have been much concerned with what is known as the integration of the human personality. It must be understood that this integration should not be viewed as a "purpose" of religion; on the one hand it should be regarded as a precondition and on the other as a result of religious experience.[43] Not the function but the nature of religious experience will concern us here.

The third criterion of religious experience is intensity. This is not meant as a descriptive statement. Potentially this is the most powerful, comprehensive, shattering, and profound experience of which man is capable. Tillich is right in saying that "gods are beings who transcend the realm of ordinary experience in power and meaning, and with whom men have relations which surpass ordinary relations in intensity and significance."[44] The great men of religion of all times and in all countries have given witness to this intensity in thought, word, and deed. In Judaism there have been, throughout the ages of its history, the moving expressions of the zeal for the Lord's house which inflamed the prophets, inspired the rabbis, and kindled the older and newer Hasidim to praise God.[45] In Islam the burning enthusiasm for Allah's cause which fired the Prophet is echoed by the traditionalists such as Ibn Hanbal, thinkers such as al-Halladj, al-Bistami and Rabi'a, reformers such as Ibn Taymiyah, al-Wahhab, and al-Afghani.[46] Who could match the rishis and bhaktas of Hinduism in religious and devotional intensity? We find this intensity in the alvars, the singers of Vishnuism,[47] and later on in Chaitanya and Tulasi Das. We find it in the bards of Shaivism[48] such as poets of the *devaram,* and especially in Manikka Vasagar. We find it also in the *acharyas*—the teachers—in both denominations and in modern saints such as Sri Ramakrishna[49] or the Maharshi.[50] Many Christian religious leaders from St. Paul on illustrate the intensity of religious passion which we have in mind. Augustine, Bernard, Bonaventura, Luther, John Donne, John Wesley, William Booth are only a few. In the modern West a great deal of religious passion is revealed in music, from

Palestrina to Bach to Bruckner and Vaughan Williams; in painting, from Rembrandt and El Greco to the Chagall of the Old Testament illustrations and to Rouault; and in literature, from Milton and Bunyan, through Blake and Dostoevsky, to Melville and Rilke—and none of these was a theologian.

IV The fourth criterion of genuine religious experience is that it issue in action. It involves an imperative;[51] it is the most powerful source of motivation and action.[52] "Our practice," according to William James, "is the only sure evidence even to ourselves, that we are genuinely Christians."[53] He quotes Jonathan Edwards: "The degree in which our experience is productive of practice shows the degree in which our experience is spiritual and divine." Either the lack of, or emphasis upon, "action" has played a large part in discussion between the West and the East, between European and American Christians, between traditionalists and modernists everywhere. An enlightened modern Hindu such as Sarvepalli Radhakrishnan admits frankly the past shortcomings of Hinduism with regard to social action and amelioration.[54]

It is not a question of whether religious faith should issue in action but rather a question of what constitutes the right, godpleasing "action" to which the faithful are called. The "Martha" aspect of religion has sometimes been slighted by contemplatives, just as the value of the contemplative life may have been underestimated by the activists.[55] There is much wisdom in Von Hügel's statement that "religion is, primarily, a need, an experience, and an affirmation of what is, and only in the second instance a command as to what ought to be. Because our Father is, and because the Blessed are and do His Will in Heaven, because of this . . . are we to do this same Divine Will as nearly as we can here upon earth."[56] "Action" should be understood, in a very broad sense, as opposed not to contemplation but to sluggish inaction or indifference. Not all mystical religion is of the quietist type; not all action in the name of religion is motivated solely by devotion.

The presence of one or even several of the four criteria is not sufficient for an unequivocal characterization of an experience as religious. All four have to be present. That implies that there can be no "godless" religion, and only a misunderstanding can make Buddhism or Confucianism into such. Buddhism and Jainism may have started as criticisms of the traditional or of any positive characterization of Ultimate Reality, but they soon developed into genuine religions. Confucius strongly affirmed a transcendental faith in his references to cosmic order (Tao) and to the ordinances of heaven.

Pseudo religion may exhibit features of genuine religion, but in it man relates himself not to ultimate but to some finite reality.[57] There are four major types of pseudo religion today. The first is Marxism. Of the two major elements in Marxism, chiliasm and economic theory, it is the first which gives it the semblance of religion. It is well known that communism is at least a pseudo religion since it transcends a mere materialistic creed with its sacred books, dogmas, rituals, and its fellowship, its insistence on the creation of a "new man," its possession of an impressive sense of justice and willingness to sacrifice.[58] Yet not only its methods but also its principles show that it is not a genuine religion. The basic difference is the lack of a satisfactory solution to the three kinds of quest central to genuine religion— the theological, the cosmological, and the anthropological. Because man is central, there is no acknowledgment of his numinous unworth (sin) and of the necessity for more than an economic liberation of man and society.[59] The second type of pseudo religion is biologism—the cult of life as such or of the sexual drive —of which Nietzsche, D. H. Lawrence, and Huysmans were the prophets. The third is populism or racism in which divine character is attributed to an ethnic, political, or cultural group instead of to its creator. Examples of racism can be found in Europe, America, Africa, and Asia. Finally there is statism, the glorification of the state, be it the German, American, Russian, Japanese, Chinese, or Indian version. Indeed, physical or economic well-being either of individuals or groups is a good. But it is a finite good which must be seen in perspective and not equated with an ultimate reality. All four are instances of what is known as secularism. It is secularism which represents the gravest danger in both the West and, increasingly, in the East.

Genuine religious experience, as we have tried to show elsewhere (*Types of Religious Experience,* Chapter II) is not limited to time or space; it is universal. The anthropologists, such as Marett and Malinowski, have proved that, far from being artificially induced ("invented," as the age of enlightenment believed it to be), religion is an ubiquitous expression of the *sensus numinis* (Otto's now-famous term). Henri Bergson has stated: "There has never been a society without religion";[60] and Raymond Firth confirms that "Religion is universal in human societies."[61] It was Marett who suggested that we might change the title *homo sapiens* into *homo religiosus*.[62] As the modern anthropologist, Evans-Pritchard, very well puts it: "If we are attempting to understand Islam ... or Christianity or Hinduism, it is a great help toward our understanding of it if we know that certain features of it are universals, features of all religions, including those of the most primitive peoples; yet others are features of certain types of religion; and yet others are distinctive of that religion alone."[63] Robert Redfield enumerates the following as "universal features": recognition of the self and others, groupings of people, ways of confronting the inevitable experiences of the human career, confrontation of Not-Me (including earth, sky, night, and "invisible beings, wills and powers") in some ordered relationship.[64] There is a disposition, a propensity—a nisus—in man to worship and to respond to divine self-disclosure.[65] As Webb has aptly expressed it: "Thus I would see in the religious experience of mankind as a whole a genuine unity and would consider it as the response of the human spirit to the Divine Spirit with which it is by the necessity of its nature in propositional contact." [66] This disposition needs development [67] and cultivation. In his very significant contribution to the *Festschrift für Karl Jaspers,* José Ortega y Gasset, in discussing the "birth" of philosophy, stresses the fact that man possesses an immutable structure which persists through history.[68] But he adds: "This structure is not real because it is not concrete but abstract." The capacity to respond to ultimate reality needs developing. Without cultivation the tender plant may wither.

There are different degrees in which the *sensus numinis* is present in individuals. Tor Andrae defines this propensity (*Anlage*) as "an inborn tendency which expresses itself in actions of very different kinds." [69] Radin has referred to the "formulators" who speak, as it were, for the multitudes, and whom the multitudes regard as their representatives.[70] The sociology of religion studies the various types of religious authority and the nature of the charismata to which they respond.[71]

However, there cannot be any doubt that religious experience is constitutive in the nature of man.[72] "Our common human nature, I believe, embraces a permanent possibility of religion," says Marett.[73] In another place, the same author states: "A man's religious sense is a constant and universal feature of his mental life." [74] This is not to say that what is revealed to him is his achievement, that the "permanent possibility" is a human possibility. Kierkegaard, and after him, Barth, Brunner, Kraemer, and others, have rightly warned against this "humanistic mistake." But they fail to appreciate what James, Söderblom, Otto, Hocking, and Hartshorne, as well as Catholic authors, have clearly seen; namely, that religious experience presupposes a capacity on the part of man to respond. The idea of God's self-revelation as an objective manifestation in nature, history, and the life of man, requires for its counterpart an "interior unfolding of man's powers of spiritual apprehension."[75] The Jews and Moslems, the Hindus and Buddhists, also had their Augustinians and their Synergists. E. L. Wenger, formerly of Serampore College in India, has stressed that revelation through divine activity needs a human receptivity and that receptiveness is not entirely a passive thing.[76]

All religions teach that the *sensus numinis* has to be developed through evocation, teaching, and even indoctrination. *Fiant non nascuntur Christiani*—Christians are not born but made. It has rightly been said by William Ralph Inge that true religion is not taught but caught from somebody who has it. One of the most moving experiences possible for the student of the history of religions is the realization of how universal is the insistence that instruction—above all, divine instruction—is necessary for any progress in spiritual growth. Such divine instruction is symbolized by figures such as Ea in Mesopotamia,[77] Toth in Egypt and Hermes in Greece, Shiva as Satguru[78] in Hinduism, the Bodhisattvas in Buddhism, the Confucian teacher,[79] the shaikh in Sufism, the *pater spiritualis*,[80] and so on. We meet two kinds of spiritual progress in the history of religions: sudden conversion followed by cultivation characteristic of Methodism, theistic Hinduism, Taoism, and Zen Buddhism),[81] and continuous growth involving a gradual development through stages.[82] Both the individual and collective growth of a religious personality have their dialectics.[83] The group is not as dispensable as some would think. Certain religious acts can be validly performed only if a quorum is present (such as in Jewish and Moslem prayers).[84]

Religious experience, then, is the inner aspect of the intercourse of man and the human mind with God. Why do religious experiences differ as much as they do, if ultimate reality is One? Von Hügel gives the answer to this question, which had also intrigued Schleiermacher:

The problem for us is not strictly one of truth but of reality; not of whether we think correctly, but whether there are subjects and objects corresponding, in any way and degree, to our speculations and thoughts. And it seems to me that this Ultimate Reality cannot be conceived (except with a sense, on our part, that we are deliberately using images and words that we cannot really apply), as in eternal movement or in eternal becoming. God *is,* overflowingly; and there is an end of that point. It is *we* who, moving necessarily in the category of time and space, but with a keen sense that there exists, and that we are influenced by, something other and better; it is we who are necessarily in movement and in becoming. Yet even we not altogether; even we not in the very best of what we are . . . I mean that, wherever we insist upon movement, we must also indicate the rest. Where we insist upon the necessity and right of change we should make clear the contrasting abidingness.[85]

What Von Hügel wishes to say is that being and becoming both can and cannot be rightly predicated of Ultimate Reality.[86] This point is also stressed by Hartshorne in his comment on the (Yogacara Mahayana) Buddhist doctrine of Suchness (*Ashvagosha*). He writes: ". . . interest in the concrete and individual exposes us to innumerable anxieties and conflicts, to all the tragedy of life. There is a real need to steady ourselves by some fixed love, by delight in some factor common to all changes and all differences, and hence indestructible." [87] Max Müller has said:

If the history of religion has taught us anything, it has taught us to distinguish between the names and the thing named. The names may change, and become more and more perfect, and our concepts of the deity become more and more perfect also, but the deity itself is not affected by our names. However much the names may differ and change, there remains, as the last result of the study of religion, the everlasting conviction that behind all the names there is something named, that there is an agent behind all acts, that there is an Infinite behind the Finite, that there is a God in Nature; that God is the abiding goal of many names, all well meant and well aimed, and yet all far, far away from the goal which no man can see and live. All names that human language has invented may be imperfect. But the name "I am that I am" will remain for those who think Semitic thought, while to those who speak Aryan languages it will be difficult to invent a better name than the Vedanta *Sakkid-ananda*. He who is, who knows, who is blessed.[88]

Because our relationship to Ultimate Reality antedates all other experiences, thus making them possible, John Baillie[89] is right in speaking of the continuous invasion of God's Holy Presence or of the "spiritual vulnerability of even the most self-enclosed human nature."[90] Man must experience himself and see himself in his relationship to Ultimate Reality in the depth dimension of this relationship. Von Hügel rightly insists that "this source and sustenance of the other realities is apprehended by us ever with, and in, and through, and over against those other various realities that impinge upon our many-leveled lives."[91] The great Chinese, Hindu, Buddhist, Moslem, and Jewish thinkers agree.

How is Ultimate Reality given? There is a widespread conviction among religious thinkers that Ultimate Reality cannot be fathomed, comprehended, or reasoned out: *finitum non capax infiniti*.[92] Not only is our language too poor, as St. Augustine says, but the same is true of the organs of our mind. "We can never attain to a completely synthetic view of what God has revealed Himself to be, for that would involve a level of unified knowledge which can belong to none but to God Himself."[93] The true figure of Vishnu remains eternally hidden, even to

NATURE OF RELIGIOUS EXPERIENCE

meditation.[94] "What God is in Himself," says Von Hügel, "we, strictly speaking, do not know. All our true knowledge of Him is limited to what He is to us and in us."[95] The very same idea is expressed in Hindu imagery by Sri Ramakrishna: "Once a sanyasin entered the temple of Jagannath. As he looked at the Holy Image he debated with himself whether God had a form or was formless. He passed with his staff from left to right to feel whether it touched the image. The staff touched nothing. He understood that there was no image before him; he concluded that God was formless. Next he passed the staff from right to left. It touched the image. The sanyasin understood that God had form. Then he realized that God has form, and again, is formless."[96] This story illuminates the relative right of all "negative theology." Yet Paul Tillich aptly says that every "symbolic" statement is affirmed and denied at the same time.[97] Charles Hartshorne has made the same point.[98] Ultimate reality does not remain completely aloof or hidden, nor does it persist in being "totally" other, as gnostics and agnostics, some fideists, and some mystics have claimed. Here "positive theology" comes into its right. Ultimate Reality does open itself, manifest, or reveal itself.[99] It never does this "objectively," but only in a close relationship or in the "encounter" of which more and more Christian and non-Christian theologians since Kierkegaard have spoken.[100] Underhill has put it very aptly: "That which we really know about God is not what we have been clever enough to find out, but what the Divine Charity has secretly revealed."[101]

It is the exception rather than the rule that an immediate apprehension of Ultimate Reality is granted to man. Von Hügel has said that "the knowledge of God is not during this life given to us in isolated purity but only through the humiliation of the natural order."[102] One of the most important differences between religions is found in their notions concerning the media of revelation.[103] Ferré very aptly reminds us that "what is revealed will always have to be seen in the total context of the being and doing of the revealer." [104] In the brilliant twelfth chapter of his treatise, *Nature, Man and God,* William Temple has put it very clearly:

We affirm, then, that unless all existence is a medium of Revelation, no particular Revelation is possible; for the possibility of Revelation depends on the personal quality of that supreme and ultimate Reality which is God. If there is no ultimate Reality, which is the ground of all else, then there is no God to be revealed; if that Reality is not personal, there can be no special revelation, but only uniform procedure; if there be an ultimate Reality, and this is personal, then all existence is revelation. Either all occurrences are in some degree revelation of God, or else there is no such revelation at all; for the conditions of the possibility of any revelation require that there should be nothing which is not revelation. Only if God is revealed in the rising of the sun in the sky can He be revealed in the rising of a son of man from the dead; only if He is revealed in the history of Syrians and Philistines can He be revealed in the history of Israel; only if He chooses all men for His own can He choose any at all; only if nothing is profane can anything be sacred. It is necessary to stress with all possible emphasis this universal quality of revelation in general before going on to discuss the various modes of particular revelation. . . .[105]

The history of religions tells us of various ways in which revelation has been received and apprehended by man.[106] Religious language gives the name of "sign" to such demonstrative actions and manifestations in which holiness stands palpably self-revealed.[107] Here is an enumeration of how such revelation may reach him—in dreams, in visions, in oracles, in the beauty and order of the world, in art, in history, in human character, in reason and in conscience, in the dialectics of the philosopher and the intuition of the saint.[108] In the provocative paper previously mentioned dealing with the problem of *Truth in Religion,*[109] Wenger has stressed the necessity of "testing the instruments" which men use in their religious utterances and thinking. "If somebody renounces reason," Hartshorne has remarked, "what are the grounds of validity for their faith? In answer to a claim to have received these insights directly from God, we should want to ask 'by what mode of human response to a divine message could the possibility of error be ruled out?'"[110] Wenger thinks that what gives a word its credit is not the fact that it is presented as divine revelation, but its content. It is also Ferré's opinion that "What God reveals is different," but he reminds us that all revelation is to be understood in the context of the nature of Ultimate Reality.[111] Wenger agrees with Temple that revelation is a relationship established, not knowledge communicated. Since men are different, what they receive of God is also different. Promulgation can only be in human terms. "The revelation in Jesus Christ was not the only one."[112] In a criticism of Brunner and Kraemer, Wenger asserts that "It is in loyalty to 'Biblical Realism' that we assert that God has been actively revealing Himself, not merely in a small circle in a small country, but universally. And . . . it is in loyalty to the fact that we can find men in all religions who bear unmistakable evidences of God's self-revelation to them, and no abstract argument concerning God's justice that leads us to the conviction that God is everywhere personally active." Because revelation is, first, made to man (adjusted to his state), second, humanly conditioned in its apprehension by man and, third, only expressible in human terms, we have to ask, with Wenger: (1) is the truth received the maximum God can give; (2) is it adequately apprehended; and (3) is it adequately expressed?

The problem of truth in religion is related to the conditioning factors in man's apprehensions of experience. Our religious apprehension is bound up with structures of our thinking. We do believe that the finite may become transparent for the infinite. "As one window stands out of a row if a face looks out, so one finite object becomes 'special' or 'holy' as it symbolizes Ultimate Reality," says Max Scheler.[113] That belief is held in widely differing civilizations and religious communities,[114] and it is at the heart of the Christian notion of the Incarnation.[115] It is evident that in other religions, especially in Hinduism and Buddhism, the principle of the Divine adapting itself to human forms is not unknown. In Vaishnavism there is a very old tradition concerning the modes of divine manifestation (going back to the early Pancaratra theology) [116] which in the theology of Ramakrishna, the great twelfth-century thinker, is developed into the doctrine of the five modes of Isvara's (the Lord's) manifestation.[117] These are manifestations as *para* or supreme deity; as *vhuha* (form) for the purposes of creation, worship, and meditation; as *vibhava*, which includes the *avataras* (theophanies) and the *arcas* (images).[118] In Buddhism, the Mahayana doctrine of the Three Bodies indicates a similar divine incorporation. Of the major religions, Judaism and Islam are most sharply opposed to any idea of "embodiment." We shall discuss the danger of idolization and demonization presently.

Let us turn now to the primary aspects by which we apprehend Ultimate Reality.[119] Above all, it should be said that its aspect is first that of *mysterium*—the *anyad*, the *alienum*—but not, as we saw, the wholly other. Though it is different from everything finite, it reaches us (the window) through finite mediation. None can contain it. Hence we understand why the *homines religiosi* of past and present have had difficulty in "naming" it. Rudolf Otto, in his *Idea of the Holy*, has very effectively pointed out the mysterious (he calls it the numinous) character of Ultimate Reality,[120] and has illustrated this feature with examples from different religious contexts. Marett, also, has stressed the "uncanniness" of the sacred.[121]

The second aspect under which Ultimate Reality presents itself is that of spontaneity, life, creativity, and energy. Here religious apprehension seems to be contradicted by philosophical reflection. While the latter stresses the immutability and immovability of the absolute, the *homo religiosus* experiences the "living God." Of great interest in this connexion are the recent studies in African religion (by Griaule, Deschamps, E. W. Smith, Parrinder) in which terms such as *force vitale,* "mystic energy," and so on, are central.[122] One of the leading students of the ancient Canaanite religion explains Baal as the personification of that "indwelling dynamic force," and as "energizer." [123] The Hebrew tradition in contrast with the Greek, Al Ghazzali in contrast with Ibn Sina or Ibn Rushd, Ramanuja or Manikka Vasagar in contrast with Shankara, share this emphasis upon life and energy. Among modern historians of religions, Nathan Söderblom has made much of it.[124] According to Thornton, the Christian's God is one who has to do with living man because He is Himself the living God.[125] He is self-directed energy, "love," according to Ferré.[126] Modern metaphysics, represented by such thinkers as Bergson, James, Whitehead, and Hartshorne, is turning toward a dynamic rather than a static conception of Ultimate Reality.[127]

Majesty and power are terms which can be used to describe the third aspect under which Ultimate Reality presents itself to religious experience. Rudolf Otto speaks of the *tremenda majestas* of that which impresses man as exalted above all finite might, [128] and Paul Tillich defines gods as "beings who transcend the realm of ordinary experience in power and meaning." [129] Or, as Amos Wilder, a modern New Testament scholar, puts it: "Here it is the nature of God not in respect of some attribute that has affinity with human virtues but in its essential and divine quality that is urged: in its majesty, sanctity, hallowedness, glory, power." [130] He calls an "overpowering sense of the august reign of God, of his glory and power" the central and essential source of Jesus' teaching and of his immediate religious experience.[131] Those centers of power which for pluralistic religions symbolize supreme reality are regarded as instances of the Divine to which man reacts with feelings of awe. In religions such as the African, the Mayan, the Aztec, the Canaanite,[132] the Assyrian and Persian, the Hindu and the Mahayana Buddhist, the Hebrew and the Moslem,[133] the *majestas dei* is given powerful expression. "In Vedic and Vedantic theology, in Hellenic, the Judaic, the Christian, the Islamic, and the Zarathustrian systems," says Farnell, "the multiplicity of divine attributes could be brought under the three great categories, Potentia, Sapientia, Bonitas—Power, Wisdom, and Goodness—which was the quasitrinitarian formula summing up the medieval schoolmen's ideal of God."[134] When some modern Christian theologians stress the love or goodness of God, rather than his power or righteousness, they can claim to focus upon that Christian apprehension which might be regarded as the most distinctive. In other religions this stress, though by no means absent,[135] is not central.

In our analysis of religious experience we have proceeded to a point at which the ways of metaphysics and of religion part.[136] Tillich has very aptly said that religion deals existentially with the meaning of supreme reality—"being" for him—and philosophy deals theoretically with its structure.[137] It is the experience of Ultimate Reality as holy which distinguishes the two. As we have indicated earlier, this apprehension requires the engagement of the total person in the encounter with the supremely real. Although the mysterious, spontaneous, and majestic character of Ultimate Reality is accessible to the reflecting mind, this is not true of its character of holiness. William Temple thus describes the marks of a true revelation: "a union of holiness and power, before which our spirits bow in awe, and which authenticates itself by continuous development to some focal point in which all preparatory revelation finds fulfillment and from which illumination radiates into every department of life and being."[138] And rightly does he observe that the spiritual authority of revelation depends wholly upon the spiritual quality of what is revealed.[139] We do not need special revelation for the apprehension of holiness in our religious experience, but we need it for interpretation. It is certainly correct to say that special revelation is not just an "illustration" of general revelation.[140] In Alan Richardson's words, it is both an affirmation and a negation of general revelation, a "correction" and a "translation."[141]

We shall turn now to an analysis of the subjective factor in religious experience. This response we have characterized as "total response of the total being to Ultimate Reality." We have stressed the dynamic and dialectical aspect of this confrontation. Awe, as distinguished from fear, is at the heart of it. There is always the danger of its degeneration into fear, but there can be no genuine religion without awe. Farnell believes that the "emotion of awe is likely to be less intense in the polytheist than in the monotheist."[142] This statement is open to question. As the "fruits of awe" Marett enumerates "respect, veneration, propitiation, service."[143] Significantly, Rudolf Otto, following Marett,[144] distinguished and determined the nature of Ultimate Reality as one making man stand in awe (*tremendum*), and simultaneously attracting him (*fascinosum*).[145] We have a self-devaluation, known in religious language as "sin," in the feeling of "profaneness" which marks the response to the Holy and which, according to Otto, the "natural" man, as such, cannot know. Marett compares it to the reactions of the frightened animal: it runs away (the sacred as uncanny); it cowers in its tracks (its secret); it prostrates itself in abject self-surrender (*tabu,* or a form of heart-sinking). Thornton states that "Contrasted attributes are really interdependent and are mutually necessary to one another."[146] There is an interesting parallel between the cabalistic speculation on divine attributes which incorporates the traditional notions of the *middath ha-din* (justice) and the *middath ha-rachamim* (mercy),[147] and the Sufi emphasis on the qualities of majesty (*djallal*) and beauty (*djamal*), or power and grace.[148] We can compare these to the pairs of *gunas* (qualities) which in Vaishnava theology represent the six members (*sadangani*) of God: knowledge (*jnana*) and strength (*bala*), lordship (*aisvarya*) and virility (*virya*), potency (*sakti*) and splendor (*tejas*).[149] Wrath or judgment is one of the two faces; love or grace, the other. "However grim and terrible the deity may be presented habitually in the popular mythology or theology, he is likely to be invoked in some occasional prayer or liturgy as 'the Merciful' or 'the Compassionate.'"[150] The moment of *tremendum* dominates almost exclusively in some religions, especially in the African and Melanesian, the Aztec, Tibetan, and Assyrian religions. In others, although still felt, it is balanced by its opposite. In the modern West, since the period of the Enlightenment, it has been all but eliminated among certain groups. Niebuhr had this radical development in mind when he spoke of "a god without wrath who led man without sin into a kingdom without judgment through the work of a Christ without a cross." Of the major world religions, it is Islam which stresses the *tremendum*—though not to the exclusion of the *fascinosum*.[151] The latter plays a large role in Hinduism, Buddhism, and Christianity. In the pietistic version of all three,[152] the *fascinosum* almost completely triumphs over the *tremendum*.[153]

One of the most important questions with regard to the nature of religious experience concerns its cognitive factor. We take exception to two extreme views, one which absolutely denies any cognitive value to religious experience,[154] and another which identifies religion with knowledge, as the gnostics in all faiths do. "An impartial observation of the phenomena of religion leads one to conclude that at no time in its history, even if we consider only the primitive forms of it, has it failed to include a theoretical or cognitive element," claims D. G. Moses.[155] John Baillie rightly holds that it is not as the result of an inference of any kind, whether explicit or implicit, whether laboriously excogitated or swiftly intuited, that the knowledge of God's reality comes to us. He reminds us of Cook Wilson's fine observation that one does not want merely inferred friends, so how could one possibly be satisfied with an inferred God? Ultimate Reality is not only inferentially known. In all non-Western civilizations we find that perception and inference are not the only recognized sources of knowledge, but Western "scientism" considers these alone as valid. Dhirenda Mohan Datta, in *The Six Ways of Knowledge,* provides us with a critical study of Vedanta epistemology by analyzing its six *pramanas* (perception, comparison, negative cognition, inference, postulation, authority) for the acquisition of true and new knowledge.[156] The Moslems have warmly debated the legitimacy of any knowledge acquired by *agl* (reason) beyond *taklid,* the acceptance in faith of what is revealed in the scriptures.[157] The Moslem theologians distinguish between the primitive "necessary" knowledge which God implants in every man and the "acquired" knowledge gained through *nazar* (discursive reflection). Gardet and Anawati have stated the three central problems in question form: (1) Is the use of reason legitimate and why? (2) Does the *nazar* produce genuine knowledge *(ibm)*? (3) How and by what guarantee does the *nazar* work?

Baillie's well-chosen phrase, "mediated immediacy," pertains to the nature of that awareness which is characteristic of religious experience. We saw previously that Ultimate Reality cannot be known as things are known, but opens itself only in an encounter. Now there are differences in the degree to which this communion or encounter implies "knowledge." The lowest degree is *awareness*.[158] Awareness of Ultimate Reality is the most general form of relationship between the experiencer and the experienced.[159] The term *apprehension* implies a certain articulation of content in the knowing act; thus power and spontaneity are apprehended as constitutive of Ultimate Reality. These qualities stand out and impress themselves upon the consciousness of those who find themselves in communion with Ultimate Reality. Each of the great religious communities possesses certain basic apprehensions which may or may not undergo revision and transformation due to the influence of seers and prophets, teachers and reformers.[160] Apprehensions are usually expressed in symbolic form, in words or acts.[161] The highest degree is *conceptualization*.[162] What the *homo religiosus* apprehends is clearly conceptualized and cast into a systematic whole. Here the term religious "knowledge" fully applies, and here the problem is posed concerning the relation of this kind to other forms of knowing.

Upon the initial encounter with Ultimate Reality, two ways are revealed: that of magic and that of religion. Each is the development of a basically different attitude. We should not think of the relation between magic and religion in terms of a chronological sequence, for both are always present. As it is possible to detect true religious elements in many a "primitive" cult, so we find magic at the highest level of cultural sophistication.[163] We term as "magic" the techniques which develop out of the desire to conquer, control, and manipulate the apprehended power.[164] The same motivation is at work in science, as the brilliant German physicist, Von Weizsäcker, has shown in *The*

History of Nature.[165] He contrasts "instrumental knowledge," the search for, and application of, means for a desired end,[166] and "insight," "that knowledge which considers the coherence of the whole."[167] Religion differs from magic in that it is not concerned with control or manipulation of the powers confronted.[168] Rather it means submission to, trust in, and adoration of, what is apprehended as the divine nature of Ultimate Reality. In this connection it is still very worth while to read Marett's inaugural lecture, "The Birth of Humility" (1910).[169] In speaking of the arrogance which characterizes magic, he says that it is not peculiar to primitive magic and defines it as "the nemesis attendant on all . . . output of vital forces which are not occasionally chastened and purified by means of pilgrim's progress through the valley of humiliation."[170] Jaeger has pointed out that it is in Greece that we first meet the philosophical personality that is considered the bearer of knowledge. "This is a real meaning behind the conception of 'the man who knows'; he is one who has come to share in a knowledge of a higher origin—an analogue to the 'knower' or 'mystic' of the religious initiation rites, who is thus distinguished from the uninitiated."[171]

The world is seen and evaluated in the light of religious experience as we have defined it—an intense response to what is apprehended as Ultimate Reality. Here a bifurcation takes place. The phenomena in which Ultimate Reality is primarily or exclusively revealed and manifested are set apart from those which are neutral, or actually obstacles, to the manifestation of its character. The areas of the sacred and the profane are thus set off, contrasting with each other.[172] The sacred is treated with awe, reverence, and care because of the "danger" of its invading the realm of the profane. "It may bless or blast" (Marett).[173] Callois has studied this phenomenon of bifurcation in his *L'homme et le sacré*,[174] where he has set forth the very important theoretical, practical, and sociological implications inherent in this conception. These implications are especially noticeable in the so-called primitive societies and religions—Mana, Joia, Hasina, Orenda, Wakanda, Söderblom and others [175] have pointed to corresponding notions in higher religions (*baraka, Hamingya, virtus,* and so on). The sacred itself (things, beings, places, times) is of an ambiguous character. That which indicates or manifests the presence of power may be decreed helpful or harmful; its "virtue" may repel or attract.[176] A great deal of what we call *virtue* is destined to intensify the characteristics of the sacred ("purification," "lustration," "consecration") and thus to restore the pristine wholeness of the cosmos. We are indebted to Mircea Eliade for a searching analysis of this complex of notions and practices in his *Le mythe de l'éternel retour*.[177]

From the discussion of the nature of religious experience we shall now turn to an examination of its context. Religious experience, without fail, occurs in a concrete situation;[178] that is, in a temporal, spatial, historical, sociological, cultural, psychological and—last but not least—religious context.[179] "Here then," says Evelyn Underhill in her moving book *Worship,* "is man, the half-animal, half-spiritual creature, living under conditions of space and time, yet capable of the conscious worship of reality which transcends space and time."[180]

Though some forms of religion aim at a maximal detachment from physical life, as in certain types of mysticism, spiritualism, and asceticism, this does not mean that there is not a *physical context* in which religious experience occurs and which, for that reason, deserves attention. In more recent years a great deal of work by Western investigators has concentrated upon the problem of this relationship. Doctors, biologists, physiologists, psychopathologists, and psychiatrists, as well as students of religion, have contributed to its investigation. While there is still a tendency among many scientists to conceive of the relationship only in terms of a determining influence of the physical upon the spiritual life of man, there is a growing number of scientific explorers and theorists who are now prepared to admit that there is interaction. Considerable attention has been devoted to the effects which the establishment or reestablishment of the religious relationship may have on the restoration of the individual to wholeness and health. Physical symptoms may tend to disappear with the right cure of the soul. All this has been well known in civilizations and societies which have remained intact, but these insights have to be regained in the modern West.[181] Here the dichotomy of body and soul (mind) had led to a complete diastasis, a dangerous isolation, of both fields of inquiry. The names of Jung [182] and Von Weizsäcker [183] in Europe, of Roberts [184] and Hiltner [185] in America, stand for an integration of psychology and psychotherapy on the one hand and theology on the other. Von Hügel has said that "God is the God of the body as He is of the soul;—of science as he is of faith; of criticism and theory as of Fact and Reality." [186] This insight has great significance for the practical expression of religious experience and the theory of symbolism. Two of the recent publications which have made inquiry in this direction are Pittenger's *Signs, Symbols and Sacraments* [187] and Watts's *Behold the Spirit*.[188]

Religious experience occurs also in a *historical context*. "The historical element in religion," according to Webb, "is primarily a sense of continuity with the past of the religious community of which a man finds or makes himself a member, and through which . . . his religious experience is mediated." [189] While this sense has been overwhelmingly strong in some groups, in fact strong enough to limit any spontaneity, it is weak in others. Many mystics and spiritualists do not value it highly. Yet even in the religious life of the great founders of religion, the historical element has played a highly important role. With the opposition to, and condemnation of, certain features of traditional religion, they have combined insistence on the value of inherited notions and rites. The conservative character of religion in general and ritual in particular has often been emphasized. While religion is the most powerful means to integrate culture and societies, by the same token it may become an obstructive and reactionary force suppressing emergent vitalities with the weight of the authority of the past.

The *cultural context* in which religious experience occurs can in many ways be regarded as an instance of the influence of the historical factor. It consists of the highly traditional customs, mores, and folkways with which the expression of religious experience has often been so intimately associated—"Custom is king." The sanction which the close relationship with cult bestows upon custom is bought at the heavy price of having this relationship changed into tyrannical domination.

This author has devoted a special study (*Sociology of Religion*) to the interaction of religious experience and societal factors composing the *social context*. He has followed the lead of the great German scholars—Max Weber, Ernst Troeltsch, and Max Scheler—who have paved the way for an understanding of the tremendous influence which religious motivation has exerted upon social grouping, and which counterbalances the effect of social conditions upon the religious life. By stressing the second and underplaying the first, Marxism, for example, reduces the interaction of religious and societal forces to a determinism which leaves little or no room for the spontaneity of religious experience. It has been the danger of an excessively spiritualistic (idealistic) interpretation, on the other hand, to overlook or to minimize the societal context in which religious experience occurs and by which its forms of expression are powerfully influenced.

In sum, religious experience, though related to the wide context in which it appears, is spontaneous, creative, free. This must be emphasized in contrast to all forms of determinism in which religion is viewed as a function, and in contrast to all forms of relativism in which it appears wholly dependent upon environmental factors.

In a recent volume of studies devoted to the appraisal of the thought of Radhakrishnan, we have stated our objection to a relativistic regionalism in the history of religions which would emphasize tribalistic limitations and skirt the problems of religious truth. As we said then: "Modern determinism assumes many subtle forms: one is cultural determinism. Many anthropologists, sociologists, and psychologists—even philosophers—regard religion merely as an expression or function of civilization. That means that I confess a religion because it happens to be the prevailing one in the culture or society to which I belong."[190]

This problem has been competently discussed in recent times by two scholars who live in India, Wenger and Moses.[191] Since we have made earlier reference to Wenger, a few words on Moses should be added. He gives good reasons why we cannot regard either external correlation with scientific truths or pragmatic value as criteria of truth. His point is that the criterion must be adequate for the essential nature of religion.[192] Though the formulation, "A religious truth is true when it satisfies the fundamental religious demands and needs of man" sounds tautological, it expresses a perfectly valid insight. It is with these fundamental characteristics of the nature of religious experience that we are concerned in these chapters. Without discussing them in full, we wish to agree with Moses's three specifications with regard to religious truths. The first is the understanding that religious truths are not immediately relevant to our animal existence. We can agree with this proposition in spite of what we have stated earlier about the biological context. The second specification provides for the recognition of the demand for an adequate moral preparation which is regarded as indispensable in at least all higher religions and for which specified provisions are made though the enforcement (discipline) may be lax. The third relates to the impossibility of imposing religious truth since it must be accepted voluntarily. The failure to act according to this precept has caused mankind great misery and has blackened the name of religion and its servants. But the important point is that ultimately there cannot be conflicting religious truths and also that truth is one though it be mediated in and through differing apprehensions. It is wrong to say that they are of equally great or equally minimal value. The term adequacy, also, can never be intended to fit a particular set of historical, cultural, and social circumstances; it is only measurable in terms of the profoundest religious insight yet revealed to man.

III

THE EXPRESSION OF RELIGIOUS EXPERIENCE IN THOUGHT

"There are not words enough in all Shakespeare to express the merest fraction of a man's experience in an hour," appears in the diary of the French-American novelist, Julian Green.[1] How true that is, especially of religious experience! It is true of the somewhat stereotyped experience of the average man, but it is eminently true of the paradigmatic experiences of the great *homines religiosi*. "In his religion," says Webb, "a man expresses his view, or the view in which he is prepared to acquiesce, of the ultimate reality and of his relation thereto."[2] The tremendous insight which accompanies religious experience at its most intense point manifests itself in the powerful movements which we call the great religions of the world. Like all kinds of experience, religious experience tends to *expression*. "The great experiences do not resemble each other only by their content but often by their expression," remarks Eliade.[3] These experiences exist for others only in the degree to which they are expressed and where there is genuine religion, it will necessarily be expressed.[4] Like the lover, the *homo religiosus* can never hope to communicate completely his feelings, thoughts, and intuitions,[5] yet it is correct to say that "the two most important external characteristics of human behavior are expression and communication."[6]

First, let us glance at the motivation for expressing the meaning of that confrontation of Ultimate Reality which we call religious experience. To begin with, there is an *explosive* quality. One must give vent to joy and pain. It is the same with feelings of awe,[7] fear, and jubilation which fill the heart of the worshiper.[8] The ejaculation of a numinous sound may serve as an example.[9] Furthermore, there is the urge to *communicate* with others in sound, word, gesture, or act, thereby sharing with them ecstasies or shocks, and painting for them a picture of what has been seen. As Hocking has put it: "He who has had a profound religious experience must become a teacher, or else a hermit or an outcast."[10] Finally there is the additional motive which might be called the *propagandistic*. A strong urge is felt not only to share, but to attract and invite others to see and hear as one has seen and heard. This urge has frequently been so strong that it has succeeded in swaying and overwhelming individuals and groups not by the force of the message but solely by the power of the messengers. The grave danger of false prophets which lies therein will become more apparent when, in the final chapter, we deal with truth and religious experience.

Next, a few words on the modes of expression are in order. We shall distinguish between endeictic and discursive modes.[11] *Endeixis* is the Greek word for "announcement." The endeictic form of expression by which something is pointed out, hinted at,[12] or expressed in veiled form,[13] plays an immensely important part in the history of religions. "There is a wealth of expression," says Hartshorne in referring to primitive religion, "often highly poetic, not wholly consistent, of feelings and imperatives of behaviour, with a relative absence of definition, analysis, or demonstration. But the dearth of logical technique is partly compensated for by a richness of insight into the fundamental experiences from which alone a meaningful idea of God can be derived."[14] As we shall see, it is difficult to find adequate vehicles of expression for the religious vision. What is impossible to couch in precise language may be communicated in visible forms. In contrast to these, the discursive mode (explicit rather than implicit, direct rather than indirect) is articulate and strictly defined.[15] Here language is the foremost if not the exclusive vehicle, for words permit the greatest amount of precision.[16] In this instance the ear is the receiving organ, as is the eye in the other case. Both modes of expression can be spontaneous, the endeictic as well as the discursive; both can also be standardized. The old distinction of things done (*dromena*) and things said (*legomena*) is related to but not identical with the division here proposed.[17] All too often in some Western circles, unfortunately, the discursive word has been regarded as the only legitimate form for the expression of religious experience. The East has always valued the endeictic media. No religion which does not know how to cast its message in such forms can ever be fully adopted in Asia.

The most important instance of endeictic expression is the symbol.[18] "The religious symbol," according to W. M. Urban, "shows the general character of all symbols. Images are taken from the narrower and more intuitable relations and used as expressions for more universal and ideal relations which, because of their pervasiveness and ideality, cannot be directly expressed."[19] The word "symbol," derived from the Greek *symballein*, indicates the spontaneous and permanent joining or uniting of two parts, a concrete physical part and a reality of the spiritual order. The latter is "meant" by symbolic expression. The symbol may be interpreted conceptually, may lead to action, and may fulfill an integrative function.

"The symbol," Underhill has stated, "is a significant image which helps the worshiping soul to apprehend [and we may add, express] spiritual reality."[20] A survey of even the major symbols in primitive and higher religions would be an enormous undertaking. E. Bevan has this to say in his careful study, *Symbolism and Belief*, one of the best monographs on the subject: "Our survey of symbols in religion showed that the symbols by which man has tried to express his idea of the Divine are taken partly from the material world accessible to his senses, partly from conditions of conscious life as he knows it from himself and others, that is, from human emotions, acts of will, values."[21] Susanne Langer, following the fruitful lead of Urban and Cassirer, has analyzed some of the major symbols in mythical thinking which are taken from physical life (celestial bodies, plants, animals).[22] And Ewer has given us a very revealing survey of mythical symbolism, discussing symbolic expressions derived from the language of the senses, directions in space, process and progress, and natural forces.[23] "A thing heard," the author of a monograph on Christian worship has written, "is more vivid than one merely described.... A groan communicates a feeling of pain more vividly than a careful description of pain in words. It is very difficult even to tell a friend exactly what we feel about him, and we can often do it more easily by grasping his hand than by stammering out words."[24] Some twenty-five years ago Quick, in one of the most competent treatments of the subject, presented an important insight when he distinguished the element of significance from the element of instrumentality in the relationship between the inner and outer, the interior and spatio-temporal, and the spiritual and material.[25] Pittenger has treated the nature of symbols in Christianity in concise form.[26] Quoting Pratt, he has pointed to the use of "such objects as the crescent, the trident, the stupa, the spire, the image of Vishnu, the lingam, the lotus, the mystic rose, the vine and the marble Buddha as typical of those symbolic representations among non-Christians."[27] One of the most learned students in this field, Mircea Eliade, has remarked that a rite could never reveal all that which a symbol reveals.[28]

It would be interesting to know what the relation between the various historical religions would have been throughout history if there had been only symbolic and not conceptual expression of religious experience. It is evident that the symbol permits great latitude with respect to meaning, since it provides wide scope for interpretation and reinterpretation.[29] In a statement that is at once provoking and correct, Hartshorne has said that "Christians have symbols which they even yet do not know the meaning of."[30] Symbols often have a long and involved history, yet, because of its wide margin of interpretation, symbolic expression is highly suitable for the communication of religious experience.

That religious experience tends to expression is one of its universal characteristics, true even of mysticism and spiritualism. But its forms of expression, as well as the relationship between that form and the experience, vary in different cultural, social, and religious settings. According to Webb:

In the history of religions the idolatry of today is often the true religion of yesterday, and the true religion of today the idolatry of tomorrow, but only if we look for the identity of a religion merely in the identity of the symbolism which it implies. But that religion which has its face set ever towards the Supreme Reality and which does not lower its thought thereof to accord with its symbols, but rather adapts its symbols, or replaces them by others better adapted to the highest and best that it can conceive, this is true religion, whatsoever symbols it may use.[31]

Different religious faiths judge differently the value of expression, or the definite historical forms of expression. "Expression," says Whitehead, "is the one fundamental sacrament. It is the outward and visible sign of inward and invisible grace."[32] Its value is higher in Hinduism than in Islam, in Mahayana Buddhism than in Hinayana, in Eastern, Roman, and Anglo-Catholicism than in Protestantism, in Lutheranism than in the Society of Friends. Nearly all religions possess extreme cases in which some forms of expression are completely identified with religious expression; but the opposite extreme, a radical criticism of all "forms," is but rarely found. The danger of the former is idolatry, that of the latter an arid intellectualism or airy spiritualism. If it is the total man who is engaged in the venture of religion, then it is with his body, mind, and spirit that he worships.[33] The German philosopher, Max Scheler, has rightly remarked that the religious act is not a purely internal affair (*rein psychisch*) but something which manifests itself psychologically. Von Hügel has expressed himself similarly in his famous essay, "On the Place and Function, Within Religion, of the Body, of History, and of Institutions."[34]

While mystical and spiritual religion at least theoretically implies criticism and frequent rejection of some or all forms of expression, an emphasis on specific types of expression is found in various religions. The Hindu notions of *karma* (work), *jnana* (knowledge), and *bhakti* (devotion) are examples of this emphasis.[35] The major expressions of religious experience are those seen in action (either in acts of worship or service), those of the intellectual field, or those of emotional utterance. As there is tension between endeictic and discursive expression in the history of various religions,[36] so there are conflicts within religious communities with regard to attitudes and preferences in expression. Here again the comparative study of religions can render some positive service in stressing the necessity of a balance between these different ways of expression.

EXPRESSION IN THOUGHT

In various publications we have suggested three means of expression of the religious experience: thought, action, and fellowship. It has been shown that the symbol is the matrix containing and integrating all three forms of expression *in nuce,* and that both endeictic and discursive means play their role in these forms. We shall discuss first the theoretical expression.

Religious experience as intellectually expressed may be spontaneous, transitory, or standardized and traditional. The primary theoretical expression of religious experience is in *myth*. After a long neglect of this important category of thought in the positivistic age,[37] a great interest in myth and mythology arose about twenty-five years ago.[38] Following the lead of psychological investigations (Wundt, Jung) and folklore studies (Lang, Frazer, and later, Malinowski), philosophers and students of religion (Cassirer, Urban, Langer, Tillich) have set out to explore the meaning of myth. They were influenced in part by earlier thinkers who were fascinated by this problem, especially Schelling and Creuzer. The change in the concept of myth[39] and in the appreciation of its functions is apparent in, for example, an article by the well-known student of language, Steinthal,[40] with statements by Urban and Langer.[41]

Urban has cited Berdyaev's statement in *Freedom and the Spirit*: "... we stopped identifying myth with invention, with the illusion of primitive mentality, and with anything, in fact, that is essentially opposed to reality. For that is the sense which we give to the words 'myth' and 'mythology' in ordinary conversation. But behind the myth are concealed the greatest realities, the original phenomena of the spiritual life."[42] The conviction that there is in genuine myth a reference to reality has become much more widely recognized since this passage was written. Nowadays many would agree with Urban's definition of myth as "a primary and unique way of apprehending reality,"[43] or with Malinowski, who calls myth "a statement of primeval and more relevant reality."[44] In a similar vein, Langer believes that myth should be regarded not as wishful distortion but as a "serious envisagement of fundamental truth."[45] According to Griaule, "Myth is, for the Negro, simply a method of explaining . . . it constitutes a kind of 'light knowledge' [*connaissance légère*] as the Bambara say."[46] Because myth is a category *sui generis,* the positivist notion of the three stages of the development of the mind (the mythical, metaphysical, and scientific) has been proved wrong. Since myth is a statement of fundamental truth, we cannot agree with the German theologian, Bultmann, who urges the "demythologizing" of the Christian message on the basis of the claim that the mythical language in which it is couched renders it unintelligible to modern man.

The kinds of question which myth attempts to answer are: Why are we here? Where do we come from? For what purpose? Why do we act this way? Why do we die? Myth is narrative: "Image-making is, then, the mode of our untutored thinking, and stories are its earliest product," says Langer. But Malinowski is correct in this emphasis: "Myth as it exists in a savage community, that is, in its living primitive form, is not merely a story told but a reality lived."[47] Langer further states: "It is in the great realm of myth that human conceptions of divinity really become articulated. A symbol may give identity to a god . . . , and what really fixes his character, is the tradition of his origin, actions, and past adventures."[48]

There are always shifts and changes in mythical narration, due in part to oral transmission and in part to the individual creativity of the narrator. In speaking of Greek religion, Jaeger states that rather than consisting of any revealed teachings, "It springs from a lavish profusion of mythical views of the world, the characteristics of which are constantly changed and revised with each new shift of perspective."⁴⁹ Through Cassirer we have learned that the mythical world has its own laws, its own notions of time and space and causality.⁵⁰ Myths refer to primordial events whose archetypal character Jung has untiringly stressed.⁵¹ The "Eternal Present" is conjured up by myth; as Eliade has shown, it is the *illud tempus* in which the foundations for everything were laid. He has reminded us of the reference to the passage in the *Shatapataka-Brahmana:* "We do what the gods did in the beginning."⁵² In recent years a great deal of work has been concentrated on the study of the myths and rites of the ancient Near East, such as New Year, Coronation, and so forth, in which the paradigmatic character of what is told and what is enacted is clearly revealed.⁵³ The basic phenomena of the physical world provide the imagery for myths as well as for symbols. "As the sun," writes Urban, "is the most appealing and significant center for the mythical organization of external cosmic experience, so the life functions, more particularly the sexual, afford the most powerful center for the organization of internal experience."⁵⁴ Langer has developed these theories and added an analysis of the myth of the culture-hero, which represents a third basic subject for myths.⁵⁵ In a survey of such themes, C. H. Toy has suggested a tripartite division into cosmogonic, ethnogonic, and sociogonic myths and has presented pertinent material to illustrate the different kinds of myths.⁵⁶

We need not dwell on the slowness with which mythical lore changes. We have shown elsewhere that at any early stage variants of mythical narratives coexist. This stage is followed, though not in every part of the world, by another phase during which the various traditions are unified and, possibly, standardized. This is often the work of generations of the guardians of tradition—priests and scholars in religious schools. If André Gide was right, then it is easy to see that as faith in a particular way of expression dies out, degeneration, secularization, and even prostitution of the myth can occur. The twilight of the Greco-Roman deities or the Vedic gods in India provides examples of this process. Long after its religious significance has waned, the myth may live on in literature; the poets, as the individual interpreters of these archetypal narratives, then claim the right to reinterpret them. Ulysses, Prometheus, and many others have provided modern German, French, and English literature with themes popular into our own day.[57]

The second way in which religious experience is intellectually expressed is in *doctrine*. What the symbol implies and the myth illustrates is, if the historical circumstances are favorable, systematically explicated,[58] established as normative, and defended against deviation.[59] A number of factors are responsible for this development. First, there is a desire for coherence, a systematic urge; second, the desire for the preservation of the purity of insight; third, curiosity, the desire to "fill in"; fourth, the challenge of the situation; and finally, there are sociological conditions, especially the existence of a center or seat of authority. The Greek term *theologia* is frequently used for doctrine.[60] Doctrine has three differing functions: the explication and articulation of faith,[61] the normative regulation of life in worship and service, and the defense of the faith and the definition of its relation to other knowledge (apologetics).[62] In this sense doctrine is binding upon and meaningful to only the community of the faithful, and not beyond. Hocking has discussed the "place of thought and doctrine" in different types of religions.[63] He has reminded us that the Eastern emphasis upon "realization" both honors and humiliates religious thought; it honors that thought because the emphasis is both essential and instrumental. According to Hocking, the religions which welcome reason are higher in this respect than those in which "only divine *dicta* are given out."[64] It is indeed important to remember the words of Richardson: "Theology and reasoning are not in themselves sources of our knowledge of God; they are only the intellectual means by which the truth about God is formulated and more clearly seen."[65]

The ambivalent role of reason as a means of support, a buttress, and a connecting organ on the one hand, and as a critical tool on the other—"creative criticism and creative formulation"[66]—has led to the emancipation of philosophy from theology in different cultures and societies. Dilthey has aptly described the process of the emancipation of philosophical speculation from theological thought. In a previously mentioned essay on the birth of philosophy,[67] Ortega y Gasset states that when Dilthey wanted to say what is meant by philosophy he had to describe forms of thought which were not a permanent possession of mankind but which originated at a given time in Greece and "for all we know, may at one time cease to exist." For Hartshorne, reason is either the tracing of consequences of ideas (deduction), or an attempt at estimating their truth—"the most accurate attainable estimation of pros and cons." He distinguishes two forms of this estimation: the inductive reasoning of science, and the "presumed reasoning in metaphysics and theology." He rightly points out that "what needs justification is only the choice of *which* faith, which . . . form of expression we shall seek to give the faith we already have."[68]

The Greek development of this reasoning which was to be of such great importance for the major monotheistic religions has been ably traced by Jaeger.[69] "While the philosopher must work with rational concepts of his own devising, theology always operates with the images and symbols of a living world of religious ideas firmly rooted in the popular consciousness. Even philosophy must fall back on such symbolism when it faces the ultimate enigmas."[70] In a very stimulating lecture, "Faith and Reason in Buddhism,"[71] De la Vallée-Poussin points to the element of faith always found in rational certitude and the ingredients of reason present in all belief. "If there is much faith in the adhesion to revealed truth, there is still more reason and dialectic in the adhesion to revealed truths." Though the old Buddhism pretends to be a creed, it considers critical inquiry "the one key to the comprehension of truth," and though it values observation highly, it stresses intuition and insight. In Buddhist teaching, faith in the Buddha and his word is the presupposition of all progress in understanding, but it is not enough.[72] Mahayana Buddhism distinguishes between the domain of faith and that of reason: "One must meditate and understand those points of doctrine which are intelligible, one must accept and confess others while saying: 'That is within Buddha's reach, not within mine.'"[73] Though the Buddha requires submission to his word, "he is not satisfied until his disciples recognize, by rational and experimental evidence, the truth of his word." Intellectual assent is not sufficient: insight (*jnana*) is necessary,[74] not only discursive intelligence (*vijnana*). De la Vallée-Poussin doubts if there is an enlightened Buddhist who is not "something of a mystic, a rationalist, and a believer."[75] Farnell has testified out of his extensive knowledge of classical religion that "the intellect has played a great and progressive part in the development of religious systems, comparing religious judgments and testing their coherence, clearly eliciting the assumptions on which they rest, and tracing religious institutions, judgments, and emotions to their discoverable origin."[76]

In a penetrating study,[77] Gardet and Anawati have recently examined the development of the *kalam* (theology) in Islam, the function of which is the distinct articulation[78] and demonstration of the rationality of the faith in contrast to the unquestioning acceptance of the *taklid* (authority).[79] Ibn Chaldun's well known definition reads: "The science of the *kalam* is a discipline which supplies the means by which to prove the dogmata of the faith by rational arguments and to refute the innovators who, with regard to beliefs, leave the doctrine followed by the ancients and the traditionalists. The essence of these teachings is the confession of the unity of God." [80] In orthodox *kalam* only the great sources (*quran, sunna, idjma*) count, while in the more liberal or "progressive" *kalam,* reason becomes an equally important, if not a primary, source.[81] According to the great Moslem Modernist, Shaikh Muhammad Abdu, "Reason examines the proofs for the beliefs and the rules of conduct ordered by the law in order to know if they really derive from God." [82] The main periods of the historical growth of the *kalam* are clearly set forth in this study. They proceed from the formative period in Medina through that of permeation (contact with Christian theology) and the heroic era in which the Mutazilites were pitted against the *mutakallimun,* to the Asharite triumph and the synthesis of Al Ghazzali. Then follows the conservative period and, finally, the modern.

While doctrines, even of a conflicting character, may be simultaneously held in one religious community, *dogma* represents a definite norm.[83] This brings us to the third form of the intellectual expression of religious experience. Dogma implies a decision between varying theologoumena. Dogma can arise only where the competence of an authority to define it is clearly established. In Greek, *dogma* denotes a definite result, as distinguished from the word *doxa* (opinion). Dogma as such has developed in Christianity, Islam, Zoroastrianism, Buddhism, and Manichaeanism.[84] Harnack lists ten factors which contributed to its rise in Christianity: (1) concepts and sayings in canonical writings, (2) earlier tradition misunderstood, (3) *cultus,* (4) desire for harmony with the outside, (5) political and social factors, (6) changing moral ideas, (7) logical consistence, (8) harmonization of tendencies within the church, (9) refutation of erroneous doctrines, and (10) customs.[85] Dogma is meant to give greater certitude and finality to religious convictions, but it is not difficult to see that with precision and strictness, the dangers of rigidity and immobility arise.[86] While legitimate opposition within a religious community is possible where doctrines are concerned, submission or exclusion (automatic or by decree) comprise the only alternatives where dogma is involved. Criticism and opposition—both of which may be empirical as well as matters of principle—will be discussed presently.

The theoretical expression of religious experience can also be found in other forms: it may exist for a long time orally,[87] and only much later be put in writing.[88] The sacred word or sacred tale, the chant, the prayer, all mark stages which may or may not lead into a succeeding one, as in the development of the epic, lyric, and dramatic literary forms. Next there are writings which we call *classical,* exemplified by the works of Homer, the Edda, the Kalevala, the Gilgamesh Epic, the Mahabharata and Ramayana, the Chinese and Japanese classics, the Sybilline books, the Egyptian Book of the Dead, and sacred books in the stricter sense.[89] These are writings of a binding (and normative) character in a sense in which the classical texts are not. The latter are to entertain, to edify, and to educate, but sacred writings such as the Christian Scriptures, the Quran, the Avesta, the Veda, the Ginza, the Grath, the Tripitaka, reveal a norm of life. What we have here is a canon of texts, an authoritative collection of inspired writings which is the one and undisputed source of knowledge for the regulation of life. The enormous importance which is attached to the right understanding of sacred writings explains the growth of a secondary literature of an interpretive character ("tradition").[90] Some of these works may enjoy a semi-canonical authority. Illustrations of such abound: the Talmud, and the Pehlevi writings known as *Zand;* in Islam, the *musnads* of Al Bikhari and Al Muslim. In India, this type of literature is known as *smrti* and is represented by such writings as the Vedantas, the smarta-sutras, dharmashastras, bhakti-sutras, puranas, and tantras, as well as the great commentaries (*bhashyas*).[91] In Protestantism, finally, we may refer to Luther's and Calvin's writings as examples of this class.

Because of the trend outlined above, interpretation accrues vital significance. "A sacred book, like a legal code, calls for interpretation as a means of bridging the chasm which, in religion as in law, exists between the progressive development of life and the fixed letter." [92] In a famous study, Goldziher has reviewed the whole Mohammedan tradition from the viewpoint of exegetical principles.[93] According to him, the Mohammedan tradition started as a technique to ascertain the true and authentic meaning of the text and eventually developed into a complete theory (hermeneutics).[94] "In religions whose creeds and practices are derived from definite sacred texts, the legal and dogmatic development is illustrated in the exegetic work related to the sacred texts. The history of religions in such circles is also the history of the exegesis of the Scriptures." [95] Especially where the authority of tradition is challenged, as in Protestantism, it assumes the greatest theological importance.

We now turn to a consideration of confessions of faith and creeds in our study of the forms of the intellectual expression of religious experience. All great religions of the world have brief statements of faith which may be quotations from the sacred writings, as the Jewish *Shema*. Similar "confessions" have evolved in Christianity, Islam,[96] Zoroastrianism, and Buddhism. A further step is represented by statements growing out of, as well as serving, catechetical purposes. The most comprehensive and most articulate form of these affirmations is the creed. All major religions of the world have produced creeds. It has been well said by Temple: "The faith of a Christian is not set upon the creeds, nor even fully expressed in the creeds; but the creeds bear witness to it and safeguard it." [97] There are various sets of credal statements within Christianity according to the principal "families" of faith. Besides ecumenical creeds, there are Greek, Roman, and Evangelical creeds; the Evangelical are divided into Lutheran, Reformed, Anglican, Presbyterian, and others.[98]

Jaeger states that "an established confession of faith never played any part in the veneration accorded to the deities of the Greek cults." [99] He continues: "Their significance and their nature fluctuated with the universal change; and as life and human experience advanced from one stage to another, there were always new ways of discovering the divine presence in reality." Some statements of the great medieval teachers in Judaism (Moses ben Maimum, Chasdai Crescas) have something of the prestige of creeds, if not of full-fledged authority.[100] For Zoroastrianism, confessions of faith summarize the Parsee beliefs. These are recited at the initiation ceremony (*Naojote*): "Praised be the most righteous, the wisest, the most holy and the best Mazdayasnian Law. . . ." [101] The importance of the Islamic creeds of both Sunnite and Shiite traditions has been increasingly recognized by Western scholars.

In a classic study, Wensinck has pointed out that use of the first person plural pronoun "we" distinguishes creeds from personal confessions of faith. He has translated and analyzed three early creeds, the *Fikh Akbar I,* the *Wasiyat Abi Hanifa,* and the *Fikh Akbar II* (of the ninth and tenth centuries), and given a brief history of later developments which shows his view of a growing intellectualism. His study concludes with a translation of the creed of Al Sanusi, the *Ummal-Barahin* ("Mother of Arguments").[102] We are indebted to MacDonald for translations of al-Ashari's famous *Ibana* and al-Nasafi's creed.[103] Among the catechisms which became popular and concise statements of faith, we have translations of those of Al Taftazani (1413), the commentator of al-Nasafi (1159).[104]

Reviewing the variety of forms which the intellectual expression of religious experience may assume, we realize that a tension exists between the urge to express what is experienced and the limitation to which this expression will be subjected. In other words, there is a double restriction imposed: one is due to the confining character of *all* thinking and reasoning about spiritual realities; the other is due to the empirical tensions which will sooner or later develop between the thinking nourished by the particular religious experience and the general thought-climate which prevails in the given culture or society. Friedrich von Hügel has written: "Religion will be conceived as a thing fixed in itself, as given once and for all, and to be defended against all change and interpretation, against all novelty and discrimination; conceive it as a paste, and all yeast must be kept out, or as wine, and fermentation must be carefully excluded."[105] The same thinker has very rightly said that the religious temper longs for *simplicity*.[106]

The history of religions shows the frequently dramatic spectacle of conflict between those animated by a genuine desire to establish beyond doubt, to justify, and to explain what is apprehended as religious truth, and those who are moved to protest in the name of religious experience. Thus, protests against the mythical expression may be motivated by a rationalistic concern, for which the imaginative narrative is inferior to the logically coherent articulation.[107] Protests against *doctrinal* statements may arise from fideist, rationalist, or skeptic criticism.

Fideist objection is caused by the fear that vital insights accruing from the basic religious experience may be slighted in the doctrinal exposition, while rationalists and skeptics are reluctant to acknowledge any sources or standards of truth but those of an exclusively intellectual character. Protests against *dogma* may arise from at least four different sources. The mystic and the spiritualist shrink from the recognition of dogmatic statements because of a profound conviction of the ineffability of religious experience; the fideist may criticize the attempt to buttress religious convictions by rational argument; the rationalist will feel that he is expected to assent to formulations referring to rationally inaccessible truths; and the skeptic will be moved to protest out of his customary suspicion of any definite affirmation going beyond the most elementary facts. All this indicates the existence of a double protest: an empirical protest directed against any *one,* definite, historical expression of religious experience, and a protest based on principle, directed against *all* expression in general and, in particular, against any to which a normative character would be ascribed.

Now that we have reviewed the forms of intellectual expression of religious experience, we next turn our attention to its content. In his method of "correlation" Tillich has recognized that theological statements are always to be understood as answers to questions. "The method of correlation explains the contents of the Christian faith through existential questions and theological answers in mutual interdependence."[108] As the history of religions proves, the basic questions are eternal, but the modes in which they are asked and the terminology which is employed vary. We have mentioned earlier some of these questions which the intellectual expression of religious experience is meant to answer. The first and most fundamental theme in any statement of faith concerns the nature of *Ultimate Reality.*

EXPRESSION IN THOUGHT

That which is living and vivid in religious experience expresses itself in some concept of the nature of the deity. The second theme is that of the nature of all which is not ultimate—the *cosmos,* and within it, the *world.* The third singles out one phenomenon within this world—*man.* Theology, cosmology, and anthropology are central subjects in all religious thinking. The relationships between the Deity and the world and between God and man are of great importance.[109] These basic apprehensions are formulated in myth, doctrine, dogma, sacred writings, confessions of faith, and creeds. The formulations are doubted, attacked, and disputed as they are explained, commented upon, and defended.

Today these three great questions still haunt modern man, although more and more people follow the doubtful example of the West and look to science for an answer. Physicists, chemists, and biologists are expected to deliver the new cosmogony, cosmology, and anthropology. The more "progressive" have understood that study of these three subjects means metaphysical speculation; the most "progressive" see that the ultimate questions can only be answered by religion.[110]

Voluminous works have been written in recent years on the meaning and development of the idea of God. Pringle-Pattison, Von Hügel, Söderblom, Pettazzoni, Schmidt, Webb, Hocking, Temple, Wieman, Baillie, Gilson, Tillich, E. O. James, and Widengren are a few of the authors of monographs on this subject.[111] The pertinent paragraphs in general histories of religions such as those of Otto, Van der Leeuw, and Eliade suggest a typologically arranged survey of notions of God. Tillich has said very aptly that "historical forces determine the existence of the idea of God, not its essence; they determine only its variable manifestations."[112] And the same author has stated that "nothing can be said about God which is not symbolic."[113]

We propose to examine the notions of God as they occur in myths and in theologies the world over according to a threefold scheme which provides for a pair of polar concepts in each case. We used this scheme before the publication of the florilegium compiled by Hartshorne and Reese, *Philosophers Speak of God*,[114] which confirms our notion of polarity and suggests bipolar instead of monopolar understanding of the nature of Ultimate Reality. Hartshorne makes a good case for the notion of categorical supremacy as well as for the fact that there is difference not only in degree but in principle of whatever is predicated of the Deity. Hartshorne thinks it is sufficient to say of God simply that He is holy, good, wise, or powerful.[115] Thornton has rightly reminded us that the limitations of the human mind and the facts of revelation alike require that the content of the idea of God should be formulated under a variety of aspects.[116] Webb brings out one of the bipolar notions concerning the relation of God and man very beautifully in this passage:

It is indeed true that genuine religion involves a paradox, even if we do not care to call it a contradiction: On the one hand, worship is ever full of insistence upon the vast distance between the divine majesty and the worshipper who humbles and prostrates himself before it; and yet, on the other hand, it is of the essence of religion that this vast distance is annihilated, that the worshipper comes to live in God and God in him, so that it is not to himself but to God in him that he attributes the acts wherein he expresses the life which through his religion he is enabled to live.[117]

Following our tripartite plan, we propose to consider the various concepts of the Deity to which the comparative study of religion introduces us, first under the heading *Pluralism* or *Monism*, second under *Personalism* or *Impersonalism*, and third under *Distance* or *Nearness*.

We have previously referred to Tillich's definition of gods

as "beings who transcend the realm of ordinary experience in power and meaning, with whom we have relations in intensity and significance surpassing ordinary relations." [118] The power mentioned here may, in a pluralistic religion, appear diffused as "power-centers" in various phenomena. Many primitive religions, especially the Melanesian, African, and American Indian, exhibit the polydemonism to which polytheism corresponds (according to the personalist view). The panthea of ancient Europe, "the deeply rooted pluralism of Greek religion," of which Jaeger speaks,[119] Hinduism, the religions of the Near East,[120] Indo-Europe, and East Asia—all show that in no one of the manifestations of the Divine is the fullness of the Godhead vested. "Everything great and useful—everything strange, monstrous, and unusual, whether good or evil, is held to be permeated by the presence of divinity.[121] It is not merely all the mighty phenomena and forces of the universe—all the most striking manifestations of almighty energy—that excite the aims and attract the reverence of the ordinary Hindu. There is not an object in earth or heaven which he is not prepared to worship . . . ," Monier-Williams has written.[122] Because of this lack of a unifying principle, Tillich calls polytheism a qualitative, not a quantitative, concept.[123] Of the universal religions, Mahayana Buddhism [124] and some forms of Catholic Christianity have reintroduced the pluralistic aspect of divine reality in practical devotion. "So . . . the mythic mind finally reaches a point where it is no longer contented with the variety, abundance and concrete fullness of divine attributes and names, but where it seeks to attain through the unity of the word, the unity of the God-idea. But even here man's mind does not rest content; beyond this unity, it strives for a concept of Being that is unlimited by any particular manifestation, and therefore not expressible in any word, not called by any name." [125]

In certain parts of the world (Polynesia, Africa, India, China, Peru, Egypt, Greece, among the Turks and ancient Semites) this search for a unity has resulted in a tendency toward monolatry. Political, social, and intellectual factors have joined with the purely religious ones in contributing to this development.[126] As was first pointed out by Lang and Schmidt, the notion of a *maker* found among Australians, Africans, American Indians, and other primitives appears as a preparation for a High God concept. In a recent monograph, Widengren has studied this concept in Africa and the ancient Near East.[127] *Monotheism* emerged in Iran, Israel, Christianity, and Islam. Here the unifying tendency has more or less successfully prevailed. Still, throughout the history of Mazdaism in Iran, a dualistic qualification limited the monotheistic doctrine.[128] The difficult problem of the relation between Ahura-Mazda and the Amesha-Spenta is posed thus:[129]

Ahura Mazdah remains a god without visage, since he is a god without statues. They are, in a sense, only *aspects of God,* modes of his action. After all, the existence of entities does not limit the character of the 'only God,' of the Wise Lord. Certainly, Zarathustra did not insist on this Oneness, as Mohammed, for example, did for Allah.

Judaism and Islam have tended toward a radical (abstract) monotheism, while in Chrisianity the divine has been regarded as a dynamic unity which, in the words of Hodgson, actively unifies "in the One Divine Life the lives of the three divine persons."[130]

The discussion of the second set of polar concepts, personalism and impersonalism, may be introduced by this quotation from Hodgson's treatise on the Christian doctrine of the Trinity: "The ultimate reality in a conscious, intelligent, personal life of God, revealed to us as the life in mutual love of Father, Son and Spirit, and the reason for this universe is to be found in the councils and purposes of the Godhead."[131] All this illustrates the concrete meaning of Tillich's somewhat abstract but apt statement: "the trinitarian problem is the problem of unity between ultimacy and concreteness in the living God."[132]

Throughout the longest period of the history of the comparative study of religions there was no question of whether the Godhead carried *personal* features as far as most tribes, nations, and religions were concerned. According to Temple, "The event in which the fulness of Revelation is given, must be the life of a person, for the revelation consists in the unveiling of a person to a person."[133] Only the god of some of the philosophers represented an exception.[134] Around the turn of the last century a different notion prevailed, namely, that at least in its early stages the idea of God was identified with neutral, impersonal power. The third phase in the history of the study of this concept is characterized by a reluctance to think of its development in unilinear terms. The proponents of *Urmonotheismus*[135] have not succeeded in convincing the majority of investigators of their solution to the problem. There are reasons to assume that on very primitive levels both impersonalist as well as personalist concepts are to be found, the latter prevailing. In personalism, the ultimate nature of man's contact with ultimate reality is stressed; in the terminology of Buber this is the "I-Thou" relationship.[136] In the impersonalist notion, however, the emphasis is on the remoteness of the ultimate source of all existence. Webb has shown how the problem of the personality *in* God, stressed originally in the West in contrast to all tritheism, has since the sixteenth century turned to that of the personality *of* God. He has shown that a God with whom personal relationship is allowed to exist can only be described as personal, and that this notion excludes extreme emphases both on His transcendence and His immanence.[137] Studies have revealed how natural it has always been for the ancient Near Eastern man to think in personal terms while confronting Ultimate Reality.

The impersonalist tends to regard all personalist notions as anthropomorphic archaism, while the personalist understanding is that it must be in terms of the highest (that is, personal) values that we conceive of the nature of supreme reality. "The heart of religion," writes Temple in *Nature, Man and God,* "is not an opinion about God, such as philosophy might reach at the conclusion of its argument; it is a personal relationship with God. The closest analogy is not found in our study of astronomy or any other science, but in our relation to a person whom we trust and love."[138] Here the great difference between Temple and Whitehead becomes visible; in contrast to the latter's identification of the process with God, the former has emphasized that "He guides the process; He guides the mind of men; the interaction of the process and the mind which are alike guided by Him is the essence of revelation."[139] In the same sense, Tillich has stated that "God is not a person but not less than a person, the ground of everything personal, the principle of the participation and individuality."[140] Webb has demonstrated how much the personalist understanding of God has added both to the intelligibility and to the normative power of such important religious concepts as Sin, Forgiveness, Justice, Sacrifice, and Union.[141]

While in Judaism and Islam impersonal notions have at certain periods enjoyed considerable popularity, especially among philosophers and mystics, they have not prevailed except in the cabala and in Sufism. In ancient India and Persia, the respective notions of *Brahman* and *Hvarenah* stand for impersonal power, and in Hinduism the central theological problem since the Middle Ages has been the relationship of the two modes under which Ultimate Reality can be viewed. Its most representative expression is the controversy of Ramanuja with Shankara regarding the interpretations of the Vedanta. While the impersonal aspect prevails in the majority of the Upanishads and in the interpretation of the Brahmasutras by Shankaracarya, the bhakti religion of Vishnuism and Shaivism is devotion to a personal god.[142] Different answers to the same question have been given by Mahayana Buddhists, who worship one or several Buddhas as personification of the dharmakaya, and by Hinayana Buddhists.

The third set of polar notions, *Distance* and *Nearness,* is well represented in primitive as well as in higher religions. Instances of the remoteness attributed to Ultimate Reality can be seen in the *deus otiosus* characteristic of so much of African religion, the Gnostic "alien" god, and the terrible majesty of the deity in some of the prophetic religions. It has been rightly said even of Greek religion that "the very fullness with which the personality of the Olympian God is imagined tends to make personal sympathy, and still more, personal intimacy out of the question between the worshipper and such a different kind of person from himself as the God he worships." [143] "The Olympian God is too transcendent, the 'mystery' God too immanent, to be precisely what is meant by a 'personal' God." [144] Near, very near, on the other hand, appears the deity which some primitives address in prayer, manifesting itself in the helping, mediating, and saving figures of many religions representing the grace and love of the Divine.[145] Hinduism has developed the notion of *shakti* (divine energy) to bridge the gulf between God and man. Especially in Shaivism and Shaktism the problem of the relation of God and shakti has been of paramount importance. It is characteristic that God's energy (*shakti*) and his grace (*arul*) have been identified by the Tamul theologians, for in their case grace is one of the various "aspects" of divine operation.[146] Mahayana Buddhism has given powerful expression to man's longing for divine grace and aid. The notion of the *bodhisattva,* not unknown in early Buddhism, is central in the Great Vehicle (Mahayana and Tantrayana).[147] In discussing the Moslem concept of God, Hocking has pointed out that remoteness does not necessarily follow from transcendence, but that in their withdrawal from the world God and man may paradoxically move very close.[148] Allport has ably discussed the psychological relevance of the desire to find meaning in the universe and the differences which it assumes in different individuals according to the capacity for comprehension.[149] Brightman and the Whitehead school (especially Hartshorne) have argued that the Deity not only sympathizes, but actually suffers, with man.[150]

After the nature of the Godhead, the *world* is the second great topic with which myths and doctrines have been universally concerned.[151] The origin, structure, and destiny of the universe expressed in cosmological theories depend upon the apprehensions of Ultimate Reality.[152] If the latter is spiritually conceived, this feature will be reflected in all speculation on the nature of the universe.[153] With regard to the origin of the universe, there will be an understanding that a spiritual principle or agent has been involved in its coming into being with the result that a purpose is envisioned and thus the ultimate destiny of the universe will be conceived in terms of the relationship which the idea of the origin implies.[154]

The theory of emanation or emergence corresponds to an impersonal notion of Ultimate Reality, while a personalist view suggests the activity of a creative agent in whatever form or shape this agent may be envisioned.[155]

In Polynesian cosmology, which was probably influenced by Hindu thought, we find an elaborate cosmic genealogy which accounts for the development of powers of a gradually more material character which come into being from non-being. "The Maori believed that the original state of the universe was *kore*, a condition of chaos or nothingness permeated with generative powers. From this arose a yearning and immeasurable darkness, *po*, which was blank and uninformed, but carried within itself the potency and essence of all life."[156] It is significant that the cosmology of the Chinese [157] and of the Tai show many parallels, as Maspero has indicated.[158] The primordial sea is also found in Sumerian cosmogonic concepts.[159] Frazer has collected a great many variants in the accounts of creation and evolution among primitive cosmogonies.[160] A series of creations are assumed to have followed each other, according to Mexican, Hindu, and Rabbinic theories. The theories of the Shaiva and the Vaishnava, which depict the world as having passed through the stages of evolution, maintenance, and dissolution,[161] state that the purpose of the periodic reproduction of the world is the freeing of souls.[162] The Jains and Buddhists hold similar theories: "The whole development of the world is pictured perfectly steadily as a process of evolution and involution which persistently proceeds developing the same results; there is here no room for visions of a golden age to be attained on earth, nor material on which a reforming spirit could arise."[163] According to the Vaishnava, the Lord Isvara has five aspects.[164] He is supreme, unfolded, special, the inner ruler, and the *arca*.

Following the origin of the universe, the second subtopic of cosmology is the *cosmic order*, which is meant to reflect the character of that Ultimate Reality which itself guarantees this order.[165] Every important feature of the natural, social, and ceremonial order of both tribal groups and more civilized social systems is meant to mirror the order of the cosmos.[166] "What is new in Heraclitus is the way all this juridical symbolism is summed up in the conception of a single all-embracing cosmic law. A 'law of nature' is merely a general descriptive formula for referring to some specific complex of observed facts, while Heraclitus' divine law is something genuinely normative."[167] We can follow this coordination in even the smallest details of the lives of individuals and groups.[168] Its great psychological and sociological importance[169] is reflected in the work of several European scholars in recent years, such as Durkheim, Granet, Callois, Eliade, and Leenhardt.

The evaluation of the "world" differs considerably with different basic theological and cosmological assumptions. The world may be regarded as a play or phantasmagoria (*lila, maya*), or it may be considered "unreal," as it is in the Vedanta (*sesha,* rest), Buddhism, and Jainism, as well as in Neoplatonism and its offshoots.[170] According to Otto, India does not attribute value to the world because it does not know any *telos* for it.[171] In Gnosticism, Manichaeanism, and Mandaeism, the world was regarded as a prison which was predominantly evil, but the Greeks looked upon it as a work of art (*cosmos, telos*). The view common to Zoroastrianism, Islam, and Judaism was that the world exhibited a divine plan which was good and necessary for man as a school, a discipline, and for service. When the world is regarded as a divine creation, the problem of evil and its origin assumes great importance.

"History" may mean cosmic history or it may mean the chronological history of rather narrowly defined groups and societies,[172] peoples and civilizations, and individuals. Different religions conceive of history and evaluate it in different ways.[173] An acosmistic world view such as is found in the Vedanta attributes no meaning to the sequence of happenings in the indifferent sphere of this phenomenal world. An archetypal meaning may be ascribed to certain events of the "mythical past," as in the ancient Near East. History might be regarded as an aspect of the predetermined universal order, as in China, Babylon,

Egypt, Greece, and Rome. There may be a division according to which the *gesta Dei* would constitute a sacred history as distinguished from the "profane," [174] thus indicating a purpose and meaning in certain historical happenings, as in ancient Israel. Finally, supreme significance may be found in a single event in history [175] such as the Christian doctrine of the Incarnation,[176] which illumines the concepts of redemption,[177] the "Kingdom," the Church, and the end of all things.[178]

Eliade, in his brilliant analysis of the attitudes toward time in various cultures and religions, has indicated two types of notions: [179] one is *cyclical* (held by those living and wishing to live in an eternal present and illustrated by primitive and some Eastern civilizations), and the other is *linear* (starting, after some preparation in ancient Near Eastern thought, in Israel). In the latter, Abraham's act of faith meant the begining of a new religious experience—*par Dieu tout est possible*—[180] and Messianism added the anticipation of future fulfillment. This was developed in the Western philosophy of history from St. Augustine to Bossuet. Whereas the cyclical concept is an expression of the desire to annihilate time by means of ritualistic repetition of primordial events,[181] the linear attitude sees an irreversible course pointing in a definite direction, serving a definite purpose, and hence perceiving a spiritual and religious sense in history rather than a merely biological meaning. Eliade finds that the terror produced when a highly secularized world faces time without genuine (historical) meaning, a situation characteristic of "modern man," causes that man to resort to cyclic views such as those of Spengler, Toynbee, Sorokin, and Jung.[182] Modern man seems prepared to take the risk of a reversion and reintegration of man into a historic "nature"; [183] that is, he is prepared to make the sacrifice of consciousness, and thereby of freedom (*être libre, créateur d'histoire*) [184] as it has come to be understood in modern times.¹⁸⁵ Because the majority of people in the modern world have only the illusion of freedom to make history, it does not seem to be so difficult a sacrifice. It is Eliade's view that religion does not accept the destiny of man as definitive and irreducible because it believes in the possibility of regeneration which works toward a truly creative liberty in the collective and individual sense.

Finally, cosmological thinking will include some speculation on the eschatological theme. The problem of the meaning of history as it is posed and answered under the inspiration of religious experience implies notions concerning its end. "Eschatology is a symbolic way of expressing the reality of God's purpose with history." ¹⁸⁶ The myths and doctrines of the primitive and higher religions envision catastrophes which are brought about in varied ways and assume different forms. The difference between apocalyptic and eschatological vision and thought is that the apocalyptic concentrates upon prediction and portrayal of external events accompanying the end, and the eschatological interprets the end in the light of the central religious apprehension and hence gives it ethical meaning.¹⁸⁷ The interpretation of this catastrophe as a punishment or judgment plays a role in some of the major religions, especially in the four monotheistic systems. Anthropologically speaking, the end means the revelation of man's true nature in confrontation with Ultimate Reality or in the sight of God. "Eschatologies will vary with the power and truth of the religious institutions that create them." ¹⁸⁸ "As a man's faith, so is his eschatology." ¹⁸⁹ Christian eschatology believes both that the end has been realized and that it is still to come. "The Age to come is a present experience; and yet it is a future consummation, in that it is the paradox of New Testament eschatology." ¹⁹⁰ The numinous character of the "kingdom" has been stressed by Otto.¹⁹¹ He contrasts Christian and Hindu notions in interpreting the petitions of the Christian Lord's Prayer.[192] The *"telos* of creation" is to become the place and scene of God's glory in "His Kingdom." [193]

The nature of *man* is the last of the three major topics—theology, cosmology, anthropology—in intellectual expression of religious experience. Religious or theological anthropology is less known in Anglo-Saxon countries, whereas on the continent of Europe it has recently become a subject of heated debate. The present author, following some of Scheler's suggestions, published his *Typen der religiösen Anthropologie* in 1926.[194] In his *Nature and Destiny of Man*,[195] Niebuhr has given us a monograph on Christian anthropology, and in this same area, we may mention Hilliard's study, *Man in Eastern Religions*. Very recently a cooperative effort has been made to study the doctrine of man according to different religions.[196]

The position ascribed to man in myth and doctrine has to be considered in the light of a general theological and cosmological framework. Though there will be differences in the role assigned to him by different faiths, man is a *part of the cosmos*. This conviction is strong in primitive society, where the term "magic unity" was coined to designate the intimate relationship between man and all that lives.[197] There are notions which conceive of the nature and rhythm of human life as one phase within a great circle of life. The Sudanese Bambara, according to a recent study, sees man as a principle of nature; [198] he is the "grain of the world" and thus reflects the totality of all beings and things. There is life both in man and in the universe. Such conceptions are characteristic of higher civilizations and religions as well as those of Western Asia, India, and China. In a fascinating work, Leenhardt has studied the anthropology of the Melanesians,[199] and Elkin has contributed especially stimulating studies of the view of man in native Australian religions.[200]

It is highly significant that even primitive anthropology envisages a complex structure in which physical, mental, and spiritual elements are combined. Werner, in his study of the ideas of primitive man on personality, has stressed two things: on the one hand there is the *diffuseness* or lack of discrimination between the categories of human, animal, and other forms of life, between constant and transitional elements and the postulate of a multiplicity of "souls," and between transmutability and an extension of the self into its possessions; and on the other hand there is a *syncretism* or minimal differentiation between inner and outer, physical and spiritual, characteristics of the personality, as well as between individual and individual, and individual and group.[201] The primitive personality is less differentiated, in the psychological sense:[202] the idea of embodied and disembodied spirits appears in conjunction with that of power and power-centers such as rocks, trees, plants, animals, and human beings. In the human body there are a number of such centers of power (breath, shadow, hair, genitals, heart, liver, and so on). The concept of soul and souls has been thoroughly studied by Wundt, Frazer, Marett, Toy, van der Leeuw, and others.[203] Recent studies analyze carefully the African concept of the body, "personality-soul," spirit, over-soul, and the destiny of these entities.[204] Nearly all parts of the body have been regarded as connected with the soul,[205] but the soul has also been viewed as independent, arbitrarily leaving the organism to which it was attached temporarily—as in dreams, sleep, and ecstasy—or else leaving it permanently. Even in higher religions (Iranian, Gnostic, Mohammedan, and Christian), journeys of the soul[206] are not unknown, and this idea plays an important part in Shamanism.[207] Related to these concepts is that of the guardian-spirit of which primitive religions, especially American Indian beliefs[208] and Zoroastrianism,[209] are illustrative. As we have seen, belief in the preexistence of the soul is anticipated in primitive cults. According to Elkin, some Australian aborigines believe that the maker creates and occasionally replenishes the souls which are incarnated and later return to the spirit above. This belief may develop into a theory of reincarnation (migration of souls) as in Egypt, India, or Greece. With a clearer distinction between soul and spirit, a trichotomy is established (body, soul, mind or spirit), as it was in ancient Greece and Israel and throughout Christian anthropology.

Although there are considerable differences within various philosophical and religious schools, in Hinduism we have a concept of man which differs from the Greek and the Hebraic-Christian. What matters in man is his self (Atman) which is an aspect of Ultimate Reality. In the older Upanishad several *pranas* compose the self; in the later one the unified concept of Atman prevails. Shankara teaches that the *uphadis* (elements of the body in crude and fine form) cause the appearance of a soul; the idea of plurality is a result of ignorance (*avidya*).[210] Ramanuja postulates the coexistence of three principles, God, life (soul or thought), and matter. Only the first truly exists, while the second and third are dependent upon it. They form the Lord's body and as God is the guide (*antar-atman*) of souls, so the souls are the guides of their bodies.[211] Shaiva theology conceives of the relation of *pati* (Lord), *pasu* (souls) and *pasa* (matter) in a very similar manner.[212] However, Samkhya philosophy is dualist in its anthropology as it is in its metaphysics: the grasp of matter (*prakriti*) upon soul (*purusha*) is to be broken cosmically as well as individually. The answer to the question, "What keeps the soul from reaching redemption or reunion?" is rest, or material imperfection, rather than radical evil.[213] The Jaina teaches a similar doctrine.[214]

According to Buddhist anthropology it is impossible to demonstrate that there is a self (*atta, atman*). In his famous sermon of

Benares, the Buddha himself expounded the doctrine of the non-self. Neither material form (*rupa*), nor perception (*sanna*), nor feeling (*vedana*), nor disposition (*samkhara*), nor intellect (*vijnana*) are truly the self, since they are nonenduring and full of unhappiness.²¹⁵ Man is ever "becoming." What appears as a self, such as the combination of the *skandhas,* is unreal, impermanent, painful. There is only the *samtana,* or stream.²¹⁶ Even *Pudgaluvadin* and *Skandavandin* in the earlier times did not really postulate anything corresponding to the Western notion of personality. Trying to combine the idea of responsibility with the notion of *karman,* they conceived of a potency of control (*prapti, pudgala*). The doctrines of the Mahayana-Buddhist schools, though they may be more metaphysically oriented, (e.g., *Yogacara*) are even more radical in the denial of the reality of an individual self (*pudgala nairatyma*) as well as in the denial of the elements (*dharma nairatyma*).²¹⁷ In Buddhism there can be no other aim or goal of life than the striving after extinction achieved by the annihilation of desire (*tanha, trishna*) and *karman.*

The Christian doctrine of man, so convincingly presented by Niebuhr, has been influenced by the Hebrew and Greek anthropological heritage.²¹⁸ Man is believed to be both a child of nature and a transcendent spirit. He is believed to be equipped with a reverence for the majesty of God who created him and endowed with a sense of obligation as well as a longing for forgiveness. Man is a sinner not only in the sense of his finiteness but by an act of the will.²¹⁹ Sin is inevitable, and yet man is responsible both as an individual and as a member of collective society. But the Christian also believes, in Niebuhr's words, in a resource in the heart of the Divine which overcomes sin; this is the belief in God's love which transcends His judgment.

Generally speaking, in all religiously determined doctrines

of man an imperative will be recognized according to which man is called upon to realize his highest possibilities—whether they be conceived of as perfection or as redemption.[220] Religions differ in what may be regarded as the major *hindrances* in achieving this goal. "Among the American Indian peoples there is no conscious demarcation of classes of offence with respect to responsibility and object, such as is represented by the civilized man's conception of crime as offence against law, vice as offence against society, and sin as offence against the divine in nature or in human nature."[221] Among the primitives, there is no clear distinction between the notions of spiritual and material, psychical and physical. The history of religions shows us gradations of recognition of hindrances: from awareness of pollution to the ideas of vice (offense against society), crime (offense against the society or state), and finally, offense against the Deity. The Greeks made a distinction between the written law of the state and the unwritten law of the gods. "All which is not according to the will of Ahura Mazdah" is sin in Iran.[222] There is also a gradation from collective to individual consciousness of guilt. There may be accidental factors and physical limitations, and there may be basic defects, such as matter, body, and karma [223] ("the Buddhist would equate the abstraction 'sin' to every kind of collision—individual and social—with the cosmic moral law").[224] And finally there are such things as one's own failure, ritual offenses,[225] offenses against the cosmic or divine order, moral offenses, and the realization of numinous unworth (sin).[226] The hindrances may be cognitive (false opinion, ignorance), affective (inordinate affections), or emotive (rebellious will).[227]

The question is, then, Can these hindrances be overcome and if so, how? If they can, is man capable of achieving this end on his own strength or does he need help?[228] The availability of divine grace will be assessed and its nature conceived according to the basic experience of the nature of God.[229] There are two extremes: one represents a total and exclusive reliance of man on divine grace without any cooperation on his part, and the other represents the confidence of man in his own efforts. The problem of grace has been heatedly discussed in all major religions, especially in Christianity, Islam, Hinduism, and Buddhism.[230] Some elements in each of them hold that man is incapable of contributing anything to his own salvation,[231] but in all of them the conviction is also held that in spite of his dependence upon divine reality, man is called upon to exert himself.[232] A modern philosopher writes:

> The recognition that God requires freedom of the creatures for his own life is the best way to insure against a false conception of omnipotence as suppressing that freedom. Divine power is an ability to deal with free beings, not an ability to suppress or avoid their existence that they would not be free.[233]

Generally speaking, three different ways can be distinguished with regard to human activity. Salvation may be attained first by knowledge and contemplation (*marifa, jnana, muragaba, dhyana*); second, by good works (ritual, moral, social) and austerities (asceticism, training, yoga); and finally, by an attitude (faith, trust, love, surrender, *sola fide, tawakkul, bhakti, prapatti*). Among those of the first category, the Shaiva know of four steps by means of which the soul becomes prepared for release: temple service (*carya*), worship (*kriya*), spiritual training (*yoga*), and knowledge (*jnana*).[234] The Vaishnava have five, according to Pillai Locacarya.[235] There are eighteen differences between the Northern and Southern schools.[236] The Triratna of Jainism includes right faith (*samyagdarsana*), right knowledge (*jnana*), and right conduct (*caritra*).[237] Gnosticism, Brahmanism, and Mahayana Buddhism of the Tendai school are illustrations of the way of knowledge and contemplation. The religion of the Romans, Confucianism, and Shintoism represent the second way of good works. Protestantism, Vaishnavism, Shaivism, and, finally, Amidism offer examples of the third attitude of trust and love. Within different religious communities there are various conceptions of the relationship between the attitudes (*mahabba, isq, bhakti, prapatti*) toward works and ordinances; the extremes vary from repudiation (*malamatija, be-sharia, faqir's, aghoris*) to affirmation and integration into the "path" (Al Kushairi, Al Hujwiri, Al Ghazzali). Jaeger says of the mystery religions: "The experience of the Divine in the initiations is characterized as a true passion of the soul as contrasted with mere intellectual knowledge, which needs no special qualifying relationship with its object."[238] While there is little inclination to conceive of man's part as that which earns his salvation, the Qadarites in Islam have given expression to so-called synergism. Their conception of man is *chalq al af al* (partner in his deeds), and in this respect they have a kinship to the Vadakalai in Vaishnavism,[239] and the non-Augustinians in Christianity known as Semi-Pelagians. There are differences which exist among the Madhvas as well as the Ramanujas on the question of syncretism.[240]

Finally, we must mention some prevailing notions on the final goal of human life. It is universally felt that the end of human existence does not mean the end of its goals. Primitive peoples such as the Australians believe in the pre- and post-existence of souls. Some have elaborate ideas as to the dwelling place, occupation, and final destiny of souls. In Egypt the faithful expected to live with Osiris; in Persia they hoped to reach blessedness with Ahura Mazda in the house of song, after enduring great trial.[241] Immortality in India, according to the Upanishads, was the return into *Brahman,* while in Jainism the Siddhas could enjoy the condition of *moksa* or absolute freedom of the soul from matter produced by *karman* (*ajiva*). In Buddhism, *moksa* means the destruction of the *skandha* and the annihilation of the *dharma*—and this is *nirvana*. For the *bhakta* religion the goal is union with the Lord (*nistha*). To the shaiva this means the release of the soul from matter (*pasa*) and "attainment" of Shiva;[242] to the Vaishnava it means "attainment of Bhagavant."[243] To Madha's followers the highest aim is union with God, *aparoksajnana*.[244] Such union (*tawhid*) is craved in Islam.[245] The highest good for the Christian is the *visio-beatifica* —though it may have been conceived of as a different state of blessedness in different times. Far from regarding the past as gone and void, the Christian knows that it lives on in divine memory.[246]

IV

THE EXPRESSION OF RELIGIOUS EXPERIENCE IN ACTION

The wide range of expression of religious experience may be divided into expression in thought, in action, and in fellowship. It is with the second that we are here concerned. We have defined the true nature of religious experience as the confrontation of Ultimate Reality by man. The religious act by which this contact is established and preserved must be seen in the light of our previous discussion.[1] "The first and central act of religion," wrote Von Hügel, "is adoration. . . ."[2] *Cultus* may, in a sense, be defined as a *reaction* to the experience of Ultimate or Supreme Reality. "God comes to man while man approaches God."[3] In his religious experience the humbling awareness comes to man that it is not he who establishes a relationship or communion but rather that he is established by and through performance of the religious act. As we have said previously, man becomes man only by these acts which restore him to his true nature and destiny.

Cultus, then, or practical expression of religious experience, is a total response of the total being—intense and integral—to Ultimate Reality, in *action*. According to Scheler, "Religious cognition is an understanding which does not exist fully prior to its cultic expression."⁴ He has seen deeper than Burnouf who believed that "the dogma always precedes the rite, as the idea precedes feeling and as feeling precedes the external act."⁵ We should not think of practice as something tacked on to a correct theoretical expression of religious faith. Hocking errs when he calls "ritual" the "least significant" of the three aspects of religion —creed, code, and ritual.⁶ Rather we agree with the author of one of the most important treatises on Christian worship, Robert Will, for whom *cultus* as such is *the* symbol of the religious fact.⁷ Mowinckel confirms our view in his attempt to give a review of the manifestations of religion oriented toward *cultus*.⁸ The religious act takes place in time and space, in a context whose various positive forms we have discussed earlier. It is an act both free and yet possessing form; it is at once standardized and spontaneous. The act may be exceedingly simple, and again, it may be highly complex and composite; yet it will always be somebody's act.

The two principal forms of the practical expression of religious experience are devotion and service. They are closely interrelated: that which is apprehended as Supreme Reality is worshiped in an act of adoration, and is served in response to the invitation and obligation to enter into communion with the Divine. "Worship, then, at every level, always means God; however thick the veils through which He is apprehended and however grotesque the disguise He may seem to wear."⁹ Will writes: "Terrified by the sanctity and majesty of God, by rites man tries to neutralize the deficiencies of his profane nature."¹⁰ The spontaneous urge prompts expression; the desire to curb and correct this expression later is usually the result of a long development.

Two dangers are entailed when all the stress is upon expression: on the one hand, externalization, materialization, and institutionalization may occur; and on the other hand, an extreme spiritualism may result if the outward form is spurned because of a preoccupation with the purity of the experience.[11] Underhill has given us this excellent characterization: "Habit is a ritualist. Attention is a pietist. But it is the beautiful combination of order and spontaneity, docility and freedom, living humbly—and therefore fully and freely—with the agreed pattern of the cultus and not in defiance of it, which is the mark of genuine spiritual maturity and indeed the fine flower of a worshipping life."[12] Each of the religions with various schools within it represent different emphases in this respect.

In our discussion of the nature of religious experience, we have seen that it is the whole man and not just the inner man that is engaged in the experience. Body, mind, and soul are involved. Von Hügel, Underhill, Scheler, Will, Guardini, and Pittenger have insisted on this point. "I cannot accept as the really highest a spirituality which does not recognize and utilize the sense stimulations—indeed the whole man," Von Hügel has stated, and Ferré has reminded us that the body is our way of being related to the outside, that it exists "for the sake of communication and manifestation."[13] "To be human is to be a soul incarnate in corporeality and a body permeated by spiritual life."[14] These words of Will describe the balance of interior and exterior which ought to characterize the practical expression of religious experience. Because a person is not made of pure mind or spirit, material forms (images, sounds, gestures, rites, guilds, organizations) are necessary. Among the more developed non-Christian religions, the Hindu[15] and Iranian[16] stress this interrelation of spiritual and material. It has been rightly stated that these forms objectify what otherwise might remain as subjective and individual aspirations, and that they render concrete—as well as channel—the graces from above.[17]

Embodiment (that is, a medium perceptible to human senses) is indispensable in order to give precision to our concepts and persistence to our feelings which are subject to continuous oscillation.[18] While in some religions genuine devotion seems threatened by the weight of public rites through which it is supposed to be expressed, in others the lack of a concrete vehicle suggests the possibility that there might not be much to express. The symbol, a major form of expression of religious experience, represents the union of the intellectual and the emotional life of man inasmuch as it appeals to both.

We shall now turn our attention to the two major forms of the practical expression of religious experience, devotion and service. "Worship is the supreme act of a man's life," Underhill quotes from William Penn.[19] She writes further: "There is a sense in which we may think of the whole life of the Universe, seen and unseen, conscious and unconscious, as an act of worship, glorifying its origin, sustainer and end." Worship is, as is all religious experience, a *response*. In confronting Ultimate Reality there is but one thing to do: adore. A recent study on Christian worship has this to say: "Adoration is a response of our feelings . . . the characteristic religious feeling. . . . Adoration is reverence raised to its highest point and it is a complex state of mind compounded of wonder, fear, and love."[20] Praise, thanks, judgment of one's self, penitence—all these acts of worship are reactions. But as reactions they are action. According to Underhill, "All worship has a creative aim, for it is [also] a movement of the creature in the direction of Reality; and here, the creative aim is that total transfiguration of the created order in which the incarnation of the Logos finds its goal."[21] Worship aims at consecration, that is, at the transformation of all existent things and beings into harmony with the divine order and will. Ultimately, worship means nearness, union. "Adoration," Kay has written, "is at the same time a consciousness of our difference from God, and a uniting of ourselves in affection with Him, but the first is all the time swallowed up in the second. . . . Insofar as worship is a response of our feelings it is therefore a uniting ourselves with Him in heart." [22] For worship everything is needed and nothing (no thing) is needed. It is true that God wishes to be worshiped in spirit, but it is not necessarily a contradiction to say: *per visibilia ad invisibilia*. Will asserts that "The reality of the senses is indispensable to the expression of religious fact." [23] The children of Israel say—in this order—"we do and we hear" (*naaseh wa neshmah*). Worship also has a pedagogical significance: "Bow thy knee and become religious" (Pascal).

The religions of the world differ widely in their worship practices.[24] Permit us to quote again the beautiful statement of Underhill, referred to in our earlier work: [25]

Man, incited by God, dimly or sharply conscious of the obscure pressure of God, responds to Him best not by a simple movement of the mind; but by a rich and complex action, in which his whole nature is concerned, and which has at its full development the characters of a work of art.

Highly intricate patterns of worship are found in Polynesia and among the Indians of the Southwest of the United States. A long development must have preceded these formal patterns.[26] And just as we meet highly standardized expressions in primitive societies, so at the highest level of cultural growth we encounter the most immediate, spontaneous, and even inarticulate expression of religious experience. A very significant change is indicated when worship becomes restricted to specific forms carried out vicariously and with severe limitations, instead of blending easily with the total life and activity of a people. Theoretical concepts and notions generally play a less important role in primitive religions than they do on other cultural and intellectual levels. According to the psychologist Werner, "Primitive reality is above all a world of behaviour, a world in which everything is seen as gesture, as it were—physiognomically—and where everything either personal or thing-like exists in action. It is not a world of knowledge, but one of deed; it is not static but dynamic; not theoretical but pragmatic." [27] There is hardly any activity which may not pass as cultic.[28] Eating, sleeping, fighting, mating may be regarded as acts in which man relates himself to the Divine, as Marett has convincingly shown.[29] He has suggested that religious activity is but vital activity raised by spiritual intensification to a higher power.[30] But even at the simplest level we find certain acts which may be called specifically religious. As we have indicated elsewhere, it is the intention rather than the act in itself which is distinctive (as in the Hebrew *Kawannah*, or the Moslem *niya*). Dedication of an act may lift it into the sphere of that which is hallowed or sacred in the presence of the Divine. Individual acts may create a worshipful mood or may strengthen the receptivity for the gift of divine self-communication.

It is in this sphere, rather than in the intellectual expression of religious experience, that we notice a great difference between ethnic and universal religions. The ethnic religious emphasis is upon the performance of the act itself, the *opus operatum;* whereas universal religions place all value upon the individual intention as the measure of the genuineness of faith.[31] The Hasidim have always prized most highly the *Kawannah* (intention). One of their rabbis is said to have exclaimed that if he knew that he had pronounced "Amen" as it ought to sound, he would have no worries.[32] Divisions have occurred within the major religious communities (Hindu, Buddhist, Moslem, Jewish, Christian) because of the insistence of prophets and mystics that without the right *attitude* the performance of an act is without value. This is the watershed between Protestantism and Catholicism,[33] Christianity and Judaism, Buddhism and Hinduism. But in each case there have also been powerful movements within each group, which are similar to the religion's paired opposite. Such are monasticism within Catholicism, all forms of Hasidism within Judaism, and various "prophetic" teachings within Hinduism.

Where, when, how, and by whom is worship performed?[34] Originally, any place or height marked by a tree, rock, well, or river might serve temporarily or regularly as a site for worship. Such a spot, often the scene of an epiphany, can be further marked and its numinous character and power increased by sprinkling it with blood, rubbing it with oil or ashes, or decorating it with garlands. The ancient Greeks called such a consecrated spot *temenos*, the Romans, *sanctum* (from *sancire*, to make "taboo"). A rope may be used to fence it off. A hut may be erected and eventually an edifice, a chapel, or a shrine. Wissowa has this to say of the Romans:

The notion of sacredness is primarily attached to the soil; the form of the cult place on this soil is of secondary importance. It can be a grove, a fountain, a hollow (*mundus*), a cave (*faunus*), a gate (*Janus*), a fireplace (*Vesta*), but also an altar (*ara*), a niche or a chapel (*aedicula*), a shrine (*aedes Sacra*), according to the nature of the deity worshipped there, according to the means of the worshippers, the occasion and the taste of the period. . . .[35]

A special section is warded off, a *sanctissimum*, a holy of holies. Images (*eikon, pratika, arca*), special emblems, and cult utensils (*tjurunga*, "medicine bundle," *shintai*) may be kept there. Tables or altars are erected. The sanctuary may resemble a natural site, perhaps a forest or a mountain such as the ziggurats of Mesopotamia.[36]

Eliade has added greatly to our knowledge of the "heavenly prototypes" of countries, cities, and temples in the religions of the Near East, India, and East Asia; he has also discussed the symbolism of the center as well as the notion of the *axis mundi*. The sanctuary is dedicated with solemn rites and attended by special persons who perform functions, and may reside, in the sacred precinct. The sanctuary is carefully "oriented," and as a protective measure gates or moats are erected. Because much depends on the right selection and construction, elaborate procedures are used to insure felicitous choices. In ancient Rome, Palestine, Babylonia, China, and Mexico such practices were brought into an intricate system.[38] The numinous character of any place is believed to be greatly enhanced by the presence of objects or persons in whom numinous power is supposed to reside. Symbols, images, emblems, and relics are expected to insure the dispensation of special favors on the part of the deity for whom they stand. In most primitive and higher cultures not only the site destined as a place for worship but any settlement or dwelling is laid out on the basis of divinatory practices. The building of houses makes orientation and the performance of certain rites necessary, as does the establishment of towns and cities. Van der Leeuw has shown that several locations are especially powerful in the domestic realm. The threshold, the door, the hearth are so regarded.

When do men worship? In every cult there are times, sacred times, which are better fitted than others for the performance of an act of worship. Hours, days, months, seasons, or years are set aside as dedicated to the deity, to be observed with care.[39] These are "propitious" times. Morning or evening hours, the *horae* (of prayer), the *dies dominica,* the Sabbath, Eastertide,

Holy Week, the month of Ramadan, and the jubilee year are examples of special periods reserved for worship. *Ferias observare* is the Roman term for observance of special occasions.⁴⁰ There were *feriae publicae* and *privatae* even *feriae singulorum* to be observed in case of individual transgressions, *dies fasti* on which business could be transacted and *nefasti* on which it could not, and *dies religiosi* or *vitiosi*, officially taboo. Eliade has reminded us of the significance of *illud tempus*, the time in which the mythical, the primordial events took place, which are repeated in the act of ritual.⁴¹ In order to give to each time its due, the calendar was introduced.⁴² Through reconstruction of their calendars, we have come to know the religions of the Canaanites, the Romans, the Mayas, and the Babylonians. Each cultic act is like a minor feast, an occasion in which life is re-dedicated. The feast has been called the *tempus par excellence*, that period of time which is lifted out of its course as being especially powerful.⁴³ The feast is marked by a rich variety and combination of acts of worship: The word, music, dance, processions, songs, dramatic performances, and games all make it an occasion of great social, cultural, and religious significance.⁴⁴

How do men worship? By silently concentrating and meditating upon the divine presence, or by acknowledging it in sound or word, we render homage to a power which invites adoration.⁴⁵ It is moving to see how a simple sound—a whistle, noise, or the ejaculation of a word or two—suffice for the most primitive men to dispel evil spirits and to attract the attention of, as well as establish communion with, the deity. The simplest means, according to Marett, consists of making solemn mention of that with which communion is sought.⁴⁶ Numinous sounds are not unknown in higher religions, as Otto has shown. "Worship may have originated in the sacred cries which primitive cults emitted for the purpose of inviting friendly forces and warding off demonic forces."[47] A few humble words or sentences may make a prayer or an invocation; standardization and incantations may then develop.[48] The word hymn is derived from *hymnein,* to repeat,[49] and the Indian *kirtan* consists of such repetition.[50] Gestures are used, such as the kiss and folding of hands; body positions such as standing and kneeling are also known. (The Hebrew *brk,* "knee," also means "blessing.") Gesture and posture are employed either independently or as accompaniment to the spoken or sung word. The conjuring power with which the cultic word may be credited corresponds to the magic character[51] which, as we have seen, the encounter with Ultimate Reality may assume.[52] Silence, or the use of a numinous word, may be the profoundest acknowledgment of the divine presence. Gestures, postures, and movements contribute to the development of the pantomime and the sacred dance, universally used as a major part of the ritual.[53] "Dance is always sacred dance . . . the dancer while he dances, transcends himself . . . he dances in order to overcome his empirical self."[54] In most primitive religions the deity is worshiped by dancing, either in the spontaneous (ecstatic), or more frequently, in the patterned dance. In the words of the prominent anthropologist Marett, "The savage does not preach his religion, but dances it instead."[55] The sacred dance is found among Amerinds, and in Australia, Polynesia, Africa, Southeastern Asia, Northern Asia, the Near and Far East.[56] The place of the sacred dance among the ancient Semites has been studied by Oesterley.[57]

The combination of such elements as sound, word, and gesture have produced the elaborate ritual which has been the heart of the religions of all great civilizations. And it has been out of the ritual that various activities and systems of culture have developed which, in time, assumed a more or less high degree of independence and autonomy. Science, education, economics, law, and the arts originally represented one aspect of the *cultus* of the gods. In order to ascertain the appropriate time and place (geometry, astronomy) and the most efficacious formula (grammar), in order to give the sacred text the most efficient contour (music) [58] and to prepare the most worthy to serve the deity (education) all these activities were employed. It is the glory of the Eastern civilizations to have demonstrated to what extent the activities of man in even the minutest details of life can be made to reflect the central religious apprehensions.

Van der Leeuw [59] and Will [60] have stressed the observation that in worship man *gathers himself together,* as it were. In the act of confronting Ultimate Reality he becomes more truly himself than he otherwise is. He gives *himself*—his greatest gift.[61] As he invokes the deity, he relates himself to the center from which he seeks strength, sustenance, and inspiration. Two acts more than any other are meant to serve this end: *sacrifice* and *prayer*. It is exceedingly difficult for modern Westerners to understand the meaning of sacrifice.[62] Underhill is correct in stressing that "Sacrifice is a positive act. Its essence is something given, not something given up." [63] Kay also insists that "in all religion, including the Christian religion, the essential act of worship is the bringing of a gift." [64] In large sections of Protestantism the term sacrifice has become virtually obsolete. Van der Leeuw has reminded us of the nature of a true gift: [65] "To offer something to somebody means to offer something of oneself; to accept something from somebody means to take over—assume—something of his own essence." [66] The one who gives and the one who receives commune with each other by participating in the giving. "Giving" is so central to the followers of the Buddha that the whole message of the Enlightened One has been called *dana-katha* (giving sermon).[67] "Mention is often made of two sorts of donation, spiritual and temporal, the one meaning 'preaching the doctrine' or spiritual guidance, and the other 'giving requisites of life' or support of livelihood."[68]

It is a profound truth that no gift, however precious, could match the gift bestowed upon the worshiper by the divine source of his being. Nothing that man can give can measure up to the continuous favors which he knows in his heart of hearts he receives with every breath. There are three major reasons for making gifts to God: propitiation, expiation, and gratitude.[69] Man finds many substitutes for the supreme gift that he may offer, namely himself: a physical part of himself, part or all of his property as an "extension" of his self, or a living being (captive animal) as an object which he has reason to regard as welcome to the higher power. A recent study by Hooke teaches us how manifold were the "aspects" under which ancient Mesopotamian offerings were made to the gods.[70] They could be regarded as food, as rent paid for the use of land owned, as appeasement for pains in the liver, and finally as a substitute for the person of the sacrificer. When man comes to identify himself with his "soul" or "heart" or any other invisible entity, this alone may represent an adequate gift.

While the dedication of tangible offerings is open to general inspection, the gift of a person's thought, sentiment, or will is known to the gods alone. All these sacrifices are symbolic in the sense in which we have previously defined the term. In a lecture entitled "Myth and Ritual in Hinduism," given at the Seventh International Congress of the History of Religions, Mahadevan said:

The sacrifice is the external form of the inner relation between the gods and men, for it is through the spirit of sacrifice that one grows in spirit. It is true that in several of the hymns the aims sought after are materialistic but often the words for "horses" or "cows" have a double meaning, so that the Vedic poet offers the inner sacrifice to the gods in order to acquire the horses of spiritual power and the cows of the heavenly light.[71]

The sacrifice of intangibles is symbolic in a double sense, representing in the offered "heart" the person of the giver and symbolizing as well this total person's total surrender to God.

The intimacy of the communion established or strengthened by the sacrificial gift is expressed symbolically in the language of physical life. Sexual union, the common meal, and the maximal exclusion of all secular relationships become indications of both the negative desire to remain oneself, to retain one's own identity, and the positive desire to enter into closest conceivable association with the Divine.

The history of religion tells of rites in which the god through a substitute becomes the recipient of a woman's gift of her virtue.[72] In certain circles of left-hand tantrism, the sacrament of *maithuna* is practiced. On a spiritual plane, male and female mystics have experienced and celebrated their intimacy with the divine consort in terms of physical love. Robertson Smith, the great student of the Semitic religions, as well as Reutersköld, Mauss, and others have stressed the importance of the sacrificial meal. Here, a twofold symbolism can be traced: eating together is symbolic of the communion existing between the participants and the deity, and the animal eaten or the wine drunk stand as symbols of sacrifice. The Greek *thusia* and the Hebrew *zebach* consisted in the offering of a part of an animal, while the *holocaust* and the *olah* were its wholesale destruction by burning in honor of the gods.[73] Three main types of sacrifice are ordained in the Old Testament: (1) the burnt offering, or total gift consumed by God's fire, is an oblation to the deity; (2) the peace offering, culminating in the sacrificial meal of communion, which represents a covenant with the deity; and (3) the sin offering, a sacrifice of reconciliation and atonement, given in propitiation and penitence to the deity. Underhill sees in these types the universally accepted forms of ceremonial worship in the ancient world.[74]

Friedrich Heiler's great monograph, *Prayer,* deals exhaustively with forms which this means of strengthening and supporting the communion between God and man has produced throughout the history of religions.[75] He has shown how the depth of religious experience is revealed in even the simplest of prayers. To the *do-ut-des* principle with regard to gift and sacrifice corresponds the utilitarian type of petition found in both the highest and the most primitive religions. That the making of requests to God is a necessary element, and that it is a constant element in all the worship of the Christian church, is stressed by Kay.[76] Two conditions for Christian prayer are here stipulated: that the request be for what God desires us to do and that it be made in faith (and follow praise). More often than not, sacrifice will be a collective act. At the same time, individual prayer is possible within the context of group worship.

In prayer man communicates with a deity symbolically conceived in terms of finite relationships (lord-subject, judge-offender, father-child, beloved-lover, friend-friend). This dialogue in which man hears more than he speaks is meant to insure the continuity of the life-giving contact. The shortest prayer, with the exception of simple utterance of a numinous sound, might well be the exclamation of the divine name by which the presence of God is invoked. It may be taken also as the epitome of the ritual or the standardized, in contrast to spontaneous or free prayer. Heiler has indicated the enormous range of the variety of types of prayer very well: the lonely and solemn liturgical, the creatively original and plainly imitative, the "delight of the heart" and the fulfillment of the law, the explosively affective and the disciplined, the shouting and the silent, the artful and the stammering. As the apprehensions and conceptions of Ultimate Reality grow more dim, abstract, and impersonal, prayer becomes less vivid, sustained, and spontaneous. When used for apotropaic purposes, prayer may well degenerate into magic or other debased forms of spiritual life.

In addition to sacrifice and prayer, both of which are ultimately acts of standing in the presence of, and presenting oneself to, Ultimate Reality, there are other religious acts such as divination [77] and a variety of so-called rites. General divination, that is, exploration and interpretation of the will of the Godhead, need not be magical if it is done in the spirit of devotion and submission rather than coercion and manipulation. Elaborate techniques and systems of divination were developed in the primitive religions of Polynesia, Africa, and Mexico, in the religions of Israel, Greece, Etruria, and Rome, in Babylonia, India, China, Japan,[78] and among the Celts. The Etruscans inherited the Mesopotamian and Greek notions and practices of divination. These were bequeathed by way of the Roman world to medieval and modern Western civilization. The Etruscans made these practices so much a part of their culture that the discipline has been named after them (*disciplina Etrusca* or *auguralis*).[79] Different phenomena and objects were used as media to ascertain the desires of the gods (regular and irregular celestial events, lightning, fire, and earthquakes, the shape or utterances of animals, flights of birds, movements of serpents, barking of dogs, forms of liver or entrails). Both in Etruria and Rome a numerous and well-organized hierarchy of functionaries existed for the practice of the sacred arts.

Lustration [80] and purification [81] are rites of a preparatory character, frequently preceding central acts of worship such as prayer, sacrifice, and sacramental acts. Mensching [82] enumerates *eliminatio* (of demons), *purgatio* (by water),[83] and *expiatio* (by blood) as such cleansing rites. It is rewarding to compare, with Modi,[84] the elaborate Parsee purification ceremonies with those of the Hebrews and Romans;[85] or, as Tachibana has done, with those of Zoroastrianism, Brahmanism, and Buddhism.[86] To the followers of Zoroaster, the giving of the name, the introduction into the sacred tradition of the community, and certain domestic rites are solemn acts. Circumambulations and processions are acts of homage, combining the use of gesture and movement with prayer and incantation. Attending the deity would include the "opening of the mouth," feeding, painting, dressing, bathing, and promenading of the sacred images. They were thus cared for in Egypt, Rome, India, and China.[87]

By contributing to the gathering and expanding of the divine powers, the worshiper expects to share in the blessings of the numen. Again, religion and magic move very close to each other. The culmination of all acts of worship, and hence of religious life and experience, can be seen in the partaking of sacraments by members of a group sharing in a particular religious experience. A sacrament is not unlike a symbol in that both consider physical phenomena or objects as representative of spiritual reality. But while the symbol is a significant image, the sacrament (washing, eating, drinking) is, in the words of Underhill, "a significant deed." According to Quick, "A sacrament is a ritual act, using a certain form and matter, which both represents some universal relation of human life to God through Christ, and also, in thus representing all life, makes life worthy to be thus represented."[88] In the materials used and even in the actions themselves, there are many resemblances between the sacraments of simple folks (as discussed by Marett)[89] and those of higher religions.[90] But the decisive factor is the nature of the spiritual truth represented in the sacramental act.

Whereas the notion of the sacrament might be extended widely enough to include a great variety of forms—Hugh of St. Victor knew of thirty sacraments—it might also be limited to a few or even to one. "The Seven Sacraments," says Bulgakov, "are only the most important manifestations of the sacramental power in the Church."[91] The great Cardinal Berulle called Christ the major sacrament of the Christians. His sacrifice on Golgotha has thus been regarded as the sole actual sacrament; it is continued in the eucharistic service. Thus Canon Quick, of the Church of England, could say, that "as Jesus Christ Himself is the perfect sacrament of created being, so in the light of that one sacrament the Church appears as the sacrament of human society, Baptism as the sacrament of man's spiritual birth to God, Holy Communion as the sacrament of human fellowship in Him, holy days as sacraments of time, and holy places as sacraments of space."[92] The Christian sacraments can thus be regarded as the extension of both the Incarnation and the Atonement. Again quoting Quick, "All divine goodness, as it comes into relation with our world, must be conceived either as expressed or as actively operative in it."[93]

For this view of the sacraments it is decisive not only that something be mirrored but that something be actually effected by the sacrament. "A sacrament is actually an instrument whereby God's power operates upon us, not solely through the medium of a meaning apprehended by our minds."[94] The Christian believes that in receiving the sacraments with "pure faith and right intuition, God will use them to bestow upon him infinitely more than at present he can feel and know."[95] The sacrament is an instrument rather than a sign. There were "sacramental acts" in Judaism as well as in the Hellenistic-Oriental world in the days of Christ (Serapis, Attis, Mithra, Dionysius), but in none except Judaism is found reference to a historical figure and a historical fact.[96]

Kay quite correctly conceives of one type of response in worship as an act of receiving.[97] Instruction in divine truth would be one of the principal responses. Scripture reading, homilies, and sermons are a part of the worship service in many religions, especially in the higher ones such as the monotheistic faiths,[98] Hinduism, and Buddhism.

We have recognized devotion and service as the two major forms of the practical expression of religious experience. Service should be understood in the broadest sense of the term.[99] Then it can be said that "a specific act of charity may become an adjunct of worship if not worship itself."[100] In confronting Ultimate Reality man realizes the obligation which his true nature—understood in terms of this confrontation—imposes upon him. As we read in a comparative study of Christianity and Hinduism by McKenzie, "The ethical problem is inseparable from the more general problem of the nature of reality and of the relation of the individual to what is ultimate in the Universe."[101] Wilder says, "It would be true to say that the experience of God itself was both the ultimate sanction of ethics and their inspiring source,"[102] and "the essential sanction for righteousness is the nature of God."[103] To live in harmony with the Tao,[104] to follow God's commandments, to aspire to universal Buddhahood—these are formulas in which this objective has been couched.

"That which distinguishes practical activity from all other worlds of experience is that in it the alternation of existence is undertaken. . . . It is both the production and the prevention of change, and in either case it is not merely a program for action, but action itself. Practice comprises everything which belongs to the conduct of life as such."[105] In no other religions except those of the modern West is there a genuine discrepancy between religion and ethics, between devotion and service. A neutral analyst, Oakeshott, states the matter neatly: "The business of ethics, it is said, is to tell us what is intrinsically good and to indicate the means by which it may be attained; it is to tell us what we ought to do and to furnish us with a practical criterion of right action; it is to determine what is valuable, and to set about its realization.... Ethics, in short, is an attempt to decide what we shall do and how we shall live." [106]

It is a profound religious conviction that God's command can only be expressive of his nature, and it is in the light of the eternal order that man can understand what he is called to be and what he is capable of becoming. In other words, there is a close relationship between theology, anthropology, and ethics. "Religion, according to the savage, is essentially something you do." [107] To recognize an order in the universe (as profound religious experience would prompt man to do) means that in his every act man would strive to sustain that order. Where this order is interpreted as an expression of a divine will, the divine commands will have to be obeyed. They may be obeyed because they are commands, because they promise rewards, because they are believed to be conducive to well-being, success, or happiness, and finally because they are deemed to be expressive of the nature of Supreme Reality. Marett has spoken of the social habit of obedience bred by association with the sacred which "by steadying the nerves and bracing the will becomes a spiritual relief, and rises from subservience to a freshly-according respect toward the sacred powers." [108]

What does it mean concretely to serve God? The nature of that service will be conceived of according to what is apprehended as the character of Ultimate Reality. It may imply asceticism, either in solitude or in a select company (brotherhood); here the idea of withdrawal from the world means the withdrawal from that which would interfere with man's realization of his

true nature. Or it may consist in fully living "the ordinary life
... religiously," in which the divine purpose is believed to be
articulated.[109] Thus the ethics of the various religions of the
world show great divergences.[110] Otto has pointed out that
while both Hinduism and Christianity believe in the idea of
service, there is a basic difference in their conceptions of it.[111]
The Christian's need of an object (neighbor) to serve and a
sphere (world) in which to serve is in sharp contrast with the
exclusiveness of the God-soul relationship of the Hindu.

Whereas it may appear to be most pleasing to the deity for
man to perfect himself (the Greek *téleios* and the Hebrew
tamīm) and thus serve God, many religions regard this aim as
insufficient. Their criterion is a more transcendent one, such as
preparation for a state governed by divine rule alone. In this
case, the goals may be to obey the law perfectly, to become absorbed in the experience of oneness with the infinite, to acquire
much knowledge, to earn reward or survival, to be one with the
ground of things, and so forth. In Judaism,[112] Zoroastrianism,[113]
and Islam,[114] the highest aim of life is to glorify God by obedience; in Hinduism it is to prepare oneself for the final liberation by observance of the divine Dharma; in Buddhism it is to
become redeemed from life and to enter the state of perfect
peace by following the dharma of the Buddha.[115] Finally, in
Christianity the aim is to be filled with the spirit of God and
to obey the divine word in full communion with the living
Christ, to anticipate life in the Kingdom which is redemption
from sin and guilt, and to hope for forgiveness and for the peace
which passes all understanding.

In some religions a formal principle (an *ethos*) such as harmony with the Tao, surrender to the divine will, or love, is
stressed; whereas in other religious communities an intricate
system of casuistry has evolved in which the right way of act-

ing or serving is defined for every conceivable situation. Examples of the latter can be found in Judaism (Talmudic ethics), in Zoroastrianism (Dinkard), in Islam (*sunna, fiqh, sharia*),[116] in Hinduism (the system of dharma),[117] and in the Catholic forms of Christianity.[118] A middle way is indicated by the definition of so-called middle principles which would make certain types of behavior correct for certain types of situations, thus steering a middle course between the extremes of an ineffectual utopianism and a rigid nomism or legalism.[119] In higher religions, the principle of *imitatio* is of special importance.[120] This would correspond to the stages of the path of mystical search and spiritual perfection. The ideal of service is typified in the attitude and conduct of a man of God, a prophet, a saint, a mediator whom to emulate is the royal path to perfection or salvation.[121] Von Glasenapp, in his monumental work on the cult of the Jaina religion has said: "Experience tells us that nothing kindles the zeal of the faithful quite as much as the example of a great one whom the individual emulates as much as is possible for him, who serves as a paradigm for his endeavours . . . whom he venerates as master, and to whom he is dedicated with all the ardor of his heart."[122] The Siddhas, Acaryas, Upadhyayas, Munis, and especially the Tirth-mkaras are regarded as such. Two great texts in two great religions, the *Imitation of Christ* of Thomas à Kempis[123] and Santideva's *Bodhicaryavatara*[124] are illustrative of this ideal, an ideal which is by no means unknown in Hinduism and in Islam.

While it is possible to conceive of serving God in terms of a paradigmatic figure (the ideal Jew, Mohammedan, Hindu, Buddhist, or Christian), a more abstract canon of virtue may be established. This has been formulated in the ethical systems of all major religions.[125] Both in Buddhism[126] and Christianity, love (charity) is central,[127] but the differences in emphasis should not be overlooked. Tachibana calls the well-known five precepts—abstinence from destruction of life, from taking what is not given, from fornication, from lying, and from drinking— "the compendium of Hinayana-Buddhist virtue."[128] As a rule, the Buddha did set forth vices more vividly than virtues. Self-restraint, temperance, contentment, patience, chastity, purity, humility, benevolence, liberality, reverence, gratitude, toleration, veracity, and righteousness are, according to Tachibana, the virtues of a Buddhist of the Small Vehicle.[129] In Mahayana Buddhism the six cardinal virtues culminate in wisdom (*prajna*) and love (*karuna*).[130] The teachings of Confucianism are very explicit on the virtues expected of a *hsun-tse,* a "gentleman." These include kindness, justice, reverence, wisdom, good faith, and, of course, filial piety.[131] In Taoism all virtues are encompassed in the *wu-wei,* the contemplative "non-activity."[132] Greek notions have influenced philosophical ethics in Judaism, Islam,[133] and Christianity, especially in the concepts of virtues and vices. Two examples of important differences within these canons of virtue are conceptions involving the relationship of active and passive virtues and the stress on "transcendent" and "immanent" values. There are important differences even within Christendom. According to Bulgakov, each of the historical branches of universal Christianity has received a special gift: Roman Catholicism has the gift of organization and administration; Protestantism has the ethical gift of probity of life and of intellectual honesty; Orthodox Catholicism has the gift of perceiving the beauty of the spiritual world, a vision which expresses itself in the Orthodox Church, "a heaven on earth which is the manifestation of the beauty of the spiritual world."[134] The basic question is, however: what is right and what is wrong?[135] And how is the former to be realized and the latter eschewed in individual as well as in collective conduct?

EXPRESSION IN ACTION

We have previously seen that a profound religious experience leads to the desire to share it as well as to lift all existence to the point where life is illumined by religious experience. All universal religions testify to this desire. The propagation of the faith is regarded as the supreme act of service, more essential than any care or help in physical or material need could be. But it is just here, in the area of spreading the faith, that the greatest errors and blunders have also been committed.

The worst has been the use of violent means (persecution, coercion) in the service of religion with a total disregard for individual conscience. It is well to ponder Jeremy Taylor's famous words:

But whatever you do, let not the preference of a different religion make you think it lawful to oppress any man in his just right; for opinions are not, but laws only, and "doing as we would be done to," are the measures of justice; and though justice does alike to all men, Jew and Christian, Lutheran and Calvinist, yet to do right to them that are of another opinion is the way to win them: but if you, for conscience sake, do them wrong they will hate you and your religion.

Only little better has been the indirect method of forcing people to abandon their faith in favor of advantages which are not spiritual in character, and not much better has been the lack of tact with which the privacy of individuals has been invaded over their protest. These methods have brought untold misery for many and they have blackened the reputation of those who have acted in the name of religion and the propagation of the faith. The conviction that truth will prevail cannot excuse one from active service in helping it to win out; but it should prevent one from using means which are not compatible with the loftiness of the nature of religion. Between the skeptic and the zealot there is the man of conviction, who, because he is anxious to serve the truth and to make it known, extends to the other person all the consideration which is his due. Only too often the propagation of the faith is thought of solely in terms of verbal proclamation or exclusively in terms of deeds. Deeds are more than words, yet not even such deeds may suffice.

That which is of the essence is the disposition. The great medieval Christian mystic, Meister Eckhart, said: "Men should not think so much of what they ought to do as of what they ought to be. Think not to lay the foundation of thy holiness upon doing but rather upon being. For works do not sanctify us but we should sanctify the works. Whoever is not great in his essential being will achieve nothing by works whatever he may do." There is nothing offensive or coercive in such a method of demonstration.

V

THE EXPRESSION OF RELIGIOUS EXPERIENCE IN FELLOWSHIP

There are three traditional ways in which religious experience has found expression: in thought, in action, and in fellowship.[1] It would be a great mistake to look upon expression in fellowship as one which may or may not be added to expression through belief and through *cultus*.[2] All three forms are constitutive, yet only in the context of communion can the intellectual and the practical attain their true meaning. Myth and doctrine comprise the articulation in thought of what has been experienced in the confrontation of Ultimate Reality. *Cultus* is the acting out of this confrontation in worship and service. Both give direction to and "center" the community formed by those who are united in a particular religious experience, while the community cultivates, shapes, and develops in thought and action the expression of its religious experience.[3]

The religious act will always be *somebody's* religious act. Modern Western man is all too prone to think of the solitary individual first and last, yet the study of primitive religions shows that, individual experiences notwithstanding, religion is generally a group affair.[4] Marett puts it thus: "Primarily and directly, the subject, the owner as it were, of religious experience is the religious society, not the individual,"[5] and "the religious society rather than the religious individual must be treated as primarily responsible for the feelings, thought and actions that make up historical religion."[6] A Hasidic rabbi once said that a prayer which is not spoken in the name of all Israel is no prayer at all.[7] In most important religious ceremonies a large number of people participate in order to make them possible. Even the highly individualistic sectarians of Scandinavia believe that conversion can only be experienced in the cult-community of the brethren.[8] There is no denying that on a higher level of civilization a more strongly individualized attitude developed. Not only the outstanding individual (king, priest) but also the average devotee will cultivate his communion with the numen, say his own special prayer, and perform his personal worship.[9] This is eminently the case in the great world religions. The Christian theologian Ferré says that man, being God's creature and child, is "by nature more of a *socius* than of an individual."[10] Throughout the history of religious thought, the action of one man has been indissolubly tied to the thought and action of another. The old phrase *unus Christianus nullus Christianus* ("One Christian is no Christian") is true of all other religions as well. The French scholar Mouroux has stated it well: "In union with his brethren, a person gives himself to God who is the Father of all. The religious relationship which is profoundly individual cannot be individualistic."[11] And he has added that one can seek and find God only on the condition of helping others to seek and find Him jointly.[12] In this respect contemporary attempts to recreate religious fellowship in modern industrial societies and large urban areas are very significant. "The new *community,* built on a religious basis, about a 'charged' symbol, is the important thing." [13]

Numerous minds of many generations help to weave the fabric of myth, and doctrine is often the result of the reflection and deliberation of a long line of religious thinkers. It takes equally long until, through the cooperation of the members of a group over many generations, the ritual which both creates and directs action and interaction has evolved. Frequently a group is considered indispensable for a valid religious act.[14]

In and through the religious act the religious group is constituted. There is no religion which has not evolved a type of religious fellowship. Hocking asked why the *homo religiosus* tries to build a group; he answered it by saying that "the presence of his group is the continued experimental corroboration (and development) both of his truth and of his way of putting it to work." [15] From the point of view of the anthropologist, Malinowski and Radcliffe-Brown have stressed the role and particularly the effect of religion on society.[16] In several other of my works, I have stressed the double relationship which characterizes the religious group, as distinct from other types of grouping. The collective and individual relation of its members to the numen is primary and the relation of the members of the group to each other is secondary. In personal experience the latter relationship comes first but it is ontologically dependent upon the orientation to the numen. In another context we have said that "the nature, intensity, duration, and organization of a religious group depends upon the way in which its members experience God, conceive of, and communicate with Him, and upon the way they experience fellowship, conceive of it, and practice it." [17] We further stressed that "the religious group more than other types of association, presents itself as a microcosm with its own laws, outlook on life, attitude and atmosphere."[18] Except for certain developments in the modern Western world, there has always been a consciousness of the numinous character inherent in the religious communion, in the primitive cult-group,[19] in the *ecclesia*,[20] the *Kahal*,[21] the *ummah*,[22] or the *samgha*.[23] Only where historical developments have led to a degeneration in the life of the fellowship and hence to a weakening of this feeling will the rationalist or the mystic or the spiritualist protest against the actual manifestation or even the idea of a communion and community in religion. The numinous character of the fellowship which might be reflected in myths or formulated in doctrine is not necessarily the result of a venerable age, as some think, but is due to the "power and glory" which the fellowship assumes as a divine foundation. It is important to realize that there is this dimension to the notion of the religious community, because the secularized minds of many modern Westerners cannot understand it except in purely sociological terms.[24]

The first important concern for the student of religious groups will be to do justice to the self-interpretation of a religious communion. Full meaning is not gained where only the outward and measurable "behavior" is taken into account without regard for the meaning which concepts, attitudes, and acts are meant to convey. The actual performance in the past and in the present will have to be understood and judged in terms of this intention. How does a cult-community see itself in the light of the central religious experience which created it and which sustains it? In what sense is the religious experience which takes place within a religious community genuine and fruitful? What is revealed concerning the nature of Ultimate Reality, and how does that revelation move man? How does it influence his attitude toward the world and the major spheres of activity within it? What does it mean in terms of his relationship to his fellow-man? Are there distinctions and qualifications, and upon what grounds are they made and justified? Answers to these questions will tell us a great deal about the prevailing spirit and fundamental attitudes of a group. Religious communities vary not only with regard to their apprehension of the numen or the content of the theoretical expression of their religious experience, but also in the degree of their religious fervor or intensity. The intensity of religious feeling and the urgency of the religious concern differ greatly from group to group. On both lower and higher cultural and religious levels we find lively, intense, and strong attitudes as well as those which are perfunctory, weak, and indifferent.

As far as the relationship of the members of a religious group to each other is concerned, we may well expect to find a dimension of depth to which a nonreligious association will not always aspire. In most primitive religions a strong tie binds the members of a tribal cult together, and on the level of the great religions, spiritual brotherhood surpasses physical ties between brothers. A "father or mother in God," a "brother or sister in God," may be closer to us than our physical parents and relatives. There is no stronger tie possible between human beings than their being related to each other in God. It may consecrate the bonds of blood, neighborhood, and cooperation—and it may cut them. Alongside blood relationships and marriage, both involving physical ties, the religious life has given rise to the relation between master and disciple which has no physical bond but which is perhaps the profoundest and most fruitful relationship between men.[25] It is easy to see how in this cosmos of relationships and interrelationships an order is necessary in which participation itself will insure a minimum of recognition and dignity, but in which the more endowed will take precedence over the less endowed. The concept of the nature and function of the members of the community will vary according to the nature of the basic religious experience. Age or insight, power or skill, attitudes or deeds, may be regarded as criteria for the possession of grace. Thus a spiritual order will become manifest which may or may not coincide with any other competing order.

The use which some languages make of personal pronouns is interesting in this regard. Where the normal way of address may be a formal use of the second person plural, religious language favors the second person singular for intimacy. The first person singular is often circumscribed by expressions denoting humility while the first person plural ("we") serves to indicate —often in sharp opposition to the outside—what the sociologists call the in-group. In a genuine religious community the satisfaction of becoming a part, however insignificant, of that community will be outweighed by the member's humble realization of his shortcomings. The presence of unmitigated pride, ambition, and hypocrisy indicates the lack of genuineness in the character of the basic experience and in those who stand for it. Genuineness and intensity of religious experience are, as we have seen, even clearer indications of the character and value of a religious group than is size or structure.

The size of the group is important, and this is true in a sense which goes deeper than mere quantitative measurement. As long as it is a small, intimate group in which each member is known to the other (a situation which rarely exists beyond the early stages), the members are characterized by great intensity of feeling, great solidarity, and great activity. Where the size is greater but not yet limited by criteria such as birth, locality, and so on, the character of the community will be different. What may be spontaneous in the smaller unit must be organized in the larger; instead of intimacy there may be impersonal relations, and individual initiative may be replaced by representative action. The process of crystallization may begin anew and gain special significance where the religious community is established on the basis of universality, without any restrictions or limitations. The history of all major religions presents many examples of the formation of new and vital centers of brotherhoods in which we may see renewed attempts at the realization of the ideal fellowship.[26]

The integration of the religious group has been the subject of some study in the author's *Sociology of Religion*.[27] We have seen earlier that symbolic expression may be regarded as a primary means by which the members of a religious communion are united. As far as the various forms of intellectual expression, such as myth or doctrine, are concerned, a double effect can be noticed: they may well increase the feeling of solidarity of those bound by them, but they may also act divisively. While some religious groups desire precision of doctrinal statements in order to enhance the cohesion of their members and are only secondarily concerned with the effect of such regulation upon the spontaneity of their members, other communities value latitude without being disturbed over the vagueness and atomism which may result from an exaggerated breadth and width.

With regard to the practical expression of religious experience we have already noted that common acts of devotion and service provide an incomparable bond of union between the members of a cult-group. Praying together is the token of the deepest spiritual communion. To join in a specific act of devotion may constitute a permanent association. A brotherhood develops out of the common veneration of any number of people for a prophet or saint. The act of sacrifice might serve as an example for many other cultic acts which have a socially integrating effect. "Festivals and pilgrimages," we have said in another context, "are outstanding occasions, for here we find a close interrelation between different cultic activities such as purifications, lustrations, prayers, vows, offerings, sacrifices, and processions, all of which are of particular interest both to the historian of religion and the sociologist of religion." [28] Thus we observe a strengthening of cohesion at all levels of social grouping—in the family or in the house, in marriage or in friendship, in kinship or in the regional group, in village or in city, in a nation or in a specifically religious community. It illustrates the integrating function of a common religious experience.

But is there not another side to the picture? History tells us not only of the socially constructive but also of the destructive power of religion. Have not the closest ties of blood friendship been destroyed in the name of religion? The history of the universal religions seems especially to illustrate this contention. Indeed, in order to create a new and profound spiritual brotherhood based on the principles enunciated by the new faith, old bonds have to be broken. This break of sociological ties becomes one of the marks of the willingness to begin a new life. To become a disciple of the Buddha means to leave parents and relatives, wife and child, home and property and all else, as flamingos leave their lakes.[29] It is the cause for the sincerest rejoicing when those lost are found again in a new and consecrated bond of union, but for those who cannot be reunited with their natural brothers and friends, the spiritual family of brethren and sisters is waiting. Even the apparently socially destructive forces of religion turn out to be creative and beneficent.

As we have seen earlier, the religious group speaks its own language. It may use the phraseology of the outside world to express experiences, thoughts, and feelings to which there is no analogy, or new terms and constructions may be employed to do justice to these experiences. New and unaccustomed ways of communication are sought and found. New symbols will arise. The outsider may or may not find easy access into a group thus integrated. Even if there is no desire on the part of the participants to stress differences, these differences will make themselves felt in contacts with the "outer world."

A very important subject of study is that of the structure of religious groups. This structure is determined by two sets of factors, namely those of a religious and those of an extra-religious nature. Spiritual gifts such as healing and teaching are examples of the religious; age, social position, ethics, and background are qualifications of a nonreligious character. The pattern of structure might follow completely that of the natural order: where the family or the tribe or the people functions as a cult-group, the natural and the religious orders are identical. If the pattern of religious organization is altogether independent of the natural, the organization can be kept at a minimum or developed maximally. In this case the structure of the religious group will at no point coincide with other orders such as the social, economic, or political. As examples of this, there is the *ad hoc* kind of community which is little more than an audience gathered quickly and just as quickly dispersed; there are solid and lasting institutions which have survived millenniums; and there are fellowships which are more or less ephemeral and less tightly knit.

With regard to differentiation the variety is equally great: many, if not the majority, of cult-groups show little differentiation, but some exhibit a high degree of it. There seem to be four major factors which create differentiation within a religious community. First there is differentiation in *function*. Even within a small group comprising only a few members who are united by the bond of a common religious experience a certain degree of division of function will exist. While it behooves only the aged or the most experienced to lead in prayer or chant, some of the younger members may be charged with the provision of the material to be used for sacrificial purposes. While one will be a teacher, another will serve as deacon or deaconess. The enormously complex ritual of some of the higher religions presupposes an extreme degree of specialization on the part of those who function in these rites. We have examples of differentiation in cultic functions as well as social differentiation in ancient Mexico and Polynesia, in West Africa, Egypt, Rome, in Babylon and in Israel, in Hinduism and Confucianism, in Mahayana Buddhism and in Catholic forms of Christianity. We have elsewhere pointed out that the degree of differentiation of functions in the religious group does not necessarily depend upon the general cultural level. We find elaborate specialization in southeastern American Indian cults, in Shinto, and in modern Western secularism, just as we meet a minimum of it in the highest forms of religious group life. Some of the basic differences between kinds of functions are those between permanent and temporary, personal and hereditary, and actual and honorary, functions.

Second, in religious groups there is differentiation based on *charisma*. Even in the most egalitarian communities there is recognition of a diversity of "gifts" which explains the differences in authority, prestige, and position within the community. In speaking of hierarchies, Max Weber has widened the use of the distinction between personal and official charisma. The highest conceivable charisma possible for a person is constant and close communion with the numen or deity. Extraordinary powers are granted to one thus blessed, and there is no limit to the expectation of demonstrations of miraculous deeds. The honor in which such a man of God is held may be expressed by a position of influence, power, and wealth or, inversely, in the complete absence of prestige—weakness, poverty, and persecution being that man's lot. Next to this primarily charismatic type there is a derivative type. It consists of those who by a possibly long and close contact with the "friend of God" have acquired a charisma which places them in a category different from that of an ordinary member of the community. The apostles, companions, and first disciples of the great charismatics are of this type.

The "gifts" of the charismatics may differ in kind, but all indicate a high degree of spiritual power. The gift may be that of insight into divine mysteries such as the nature of Ultimate Reality and the laws governing the existence of the cosmos, of society, and of individual lives. It may be the gift of restoring to wholeness those broken in physical or spiritual health. It may be the ability to develop hidden possibilities of one's fellow-man by teaching or in other ways giving direction and purpose to their lives. It may be physical strength or intellectual power, moral goodness, skills, or exceptional faculties. Viewed sociologically, the possession of such charisma has a double effect: it may isolate its bearer to a greater or lesser degree, or it may become the focus of a process of social crystallization—thus having an integrative effect.[30] Let me quote here a beautiful passage from Jean Daniélou's book on Origen and his notion of a Christian order of spiritual charisma:

The Christian community consists of a hierarchy in which every Christian has a place corresponding to the degree of spiritual perfection he has attained, and the business of the *didaskalos* [teacher] is to give each class of soul the food it needs. The different aspects of himself that Jesus manifests in the Gospel (to the woman with the issue of blood he shows himself a Healer, to the sinful woman a Redeemer, to Mary of Magdala and John the beloved disciple a Master) symbolize the different ways in which he should be presented to different classes of people. And we are to notice that the woman with the issue of blood touches the fringe of his garment, the sinful woman his feet, the Magdalen his head and John his heart.[31]

A third factor which creates differentiation within religious groups is the natural division according to *age, sex,* and *descent.* Though for different reasons, the young as well as the old will be somewhat set apart and play different roles individually and collectively in the life of a religious community.[32] The preparatory stage in which the full privileges of membership are yet withheld ends with the initiation into full participation. Different groups within the ranks of youth may be formed according to age—infants, younger and older adolescents. Though in a body the aged may function as a "senate," a "presbytery," or as "elders," it will be as individuals that the seer, the prophet, the teacher, or the master will play an important role in the natural or specifically religious group.

Men and women are often separated in the *cultus* or in certain functions while they may mix freely in other activities of a religious character. In ancient Rome, women were excluded from the service of the *Ara Maxima* and men from the temple of the *Bona Dea*.[33] Cult-associations existed for both men and women of different age levels and some were comprised of both sexes. While in some religious communities only men may be religious functionaries, in others this role is reserved for women, and in still others both sexes are eligible for such service.

Differentiation according to descent may mean that racial qualifications are practiced according to which the members of certain "races" are excluded from full or partial participation in religious rites. There are many examples of this in Africa, Asia, Europe, and the Americas. It may also mean that certain privileges with regard to the religious life and its activities are limited to members of one or several special racial groups. It is at this point that universal and tribal (particular) faiths are most definitely at variance. Differentiation according to descent also includes distinctions made on the basis of historical events, such as conquest, war, and so forth. We have differentiation according to descent where a group of people is barred from partial or full participation in worship and other functions of a religious nature by virtue of belonging to a particular political, cultural, or ethnic unit, be it actual or fictitious.

Fourth, there may be differentiation according to *status*. This principle may be looked upon as a combination of a number of factors creating diversity. The "democratic" notion of the equality of all believers is a late product in the history of religions, and, strictly speaking, is rarely ever carried through in practice. Where no differences suggest themselves on the basis of the three previously mentioned criteria, distinctions of a nonreligious character will make themselves felt. There are differences in property, in functions within society, and in rank. As Liston Pope has written: "Religion, despite the close association of its institutions with the class structure, is neither simply a product nor a cause, a sanction or an enemy, of social stratification. It may be either or both, as it has been in various societies at various times." [34] Differentiation within a religious community according to these factors is, of course, more frequently than not "unofficial"; it exists *de facto* rather than *de jure*. More often than not the wealthy are accorded special privileges; the boss, chief, or the political leader wields unwarranted influence, the noble man or woman, or otherwise highly situated personage, is given special preference although a religious sanction of such distinction does not exist. Yet there are mythological and theological explanations in some religious communities which justify differences of status, especially in certain primitive and Indo-European societies, and in India and Japan. The difference between legitimate and illegitimate distinctions of this kind is of great importance for the development and history of cult-fellowship. History has shown both mild and violent protests against the status quo; some of these protests have led to reformations and secessions.

The actual structure of the religious group with which we have thus far been concerned may be reflected in its constitution.

This is a legal term, and it should be reserved for designating an organization prescribed and guaranteed by religious law. This is to say that in small religious communities and in those which are of a pneumatic character, there are usually few differences and there is little that can be called law. On the other hand, the constitutions regulating the life of the Christian church in its various forms,[35] as well as Judaism and Islam, Hinduism and Zoroastrianism, Buddhism and Confucianism, were or are highly complex. The principles of canon law in all these ecclesiastical bodies are invariably drawn from basic theological formulations or religious insights, and there is considerable margin for the interpretation of these principles. In an earlier work I have developed the distinction between egalitarian and hierarchical organizations and suggested the terms "minimum" and "maximum" types.[36] Only within a constitution can the differentiations according to function, charisma, natural factors, and status become legalized and sanctioned.

What existed *de facto* becomes so *de jure*. There are examples of religious groups inside and outside Christianity which adopted strict constitutions immediately upon coming into existence, or shortly thereafter. However, the constitution of the major Catholic, Protestant, and sectarian Christian Churches, of the Jewish, Islamic, and Parsee bodies, of the Buddhist and of the Jaina Samgha, and of Confucianism is in each case the result of complex historical developments. The constitution regulates the duties and rights of the religious functionary (clergy) and of the laity, and it defines the order of the clergy. Further, it regulates the forms of worship and of service. It defines the holy law, develops middle principles of its application, and may include casuistry.

In his earlier study, the author has enumerated and analyzed some of the types of constitutions of religious groups. Natural communities and especially religious communities may be ordered by such constitutions. Kinship or local cults, secret or mystery societies, brotherhoods, ecclesiastical bodies, monastic orders, or independent and sectarian groups have all developed constitutions. They include regulations concerning the relationship between the community and the numen, the nature of the government of the body, the norms by which it is to exist, the method of representation used, matters of discipline (admission and expulsion), material contributions, and so on. As there may be some latitude for regional and other differences, so there will also be provisions for permanent and temporary conditions. Broadly speaking, a more democratic or a more authoritarian order is determined by the regulation of the relation of the whole institution to its government or leadership, of its parts to the whole (the individual congregation) and of the individual to the higher sociological and ecclesiastical units. The various functions and orders in the culture are defined according to the constitution of the group.

As fundamental as the problem of the communication of religious experience is that of religious authority. Allowing for a few exceptions among skeptics, religious individualists, and anarchists, we are all inclined to agree that there is and must be authority in religious matters,[37] for it seems preposterous to claim that everything should start *de novo* as if there had never been any communication between God and man. God has revealed himself to man, and the history of religion is the story of man's understanding and appropriation of this self-disclosure. "By these contacts with the unseen, the individual may become the 'organ' or 'mouthpiece' of the divine." [38] In an earlier work which continues the previous studies of Weber, Scheler, Otto, Znaniecki, and others, the author has outlined the typology of bearers of religious authority.[39] This typology, which includes founder, reformer, prophet, seer, magician, diviner, saint, priest, and *religiosus,* indicates the degrees of authority which personal of official charisma confers upon the *homo religiosus*. But not all claims to authority can be honored. All religions have been faced with the task of distinguishing between true and false prophets, between genuine and spurious saints. What are the criteria by which such distinctions can be made, and with whom does the competence rest to make them? It has been all too true that the authority of one speaking in the name of religion has been taken to be self-authenticating. The vicious circle which is established between the claim and the demonstration of its validity on such grounds has been the curse of many a religious tradition in many a religious community. In fact, none has escaped it. And yet, in the case of every individual claim, there is the opportunity of weighing it in the light of the total revelation of the divine nature and character. If we were right in stating in our first chapter that truth can only be one and hence, knowledge of the truth must ultimately be also unified, then consistent coherence with what has been revealed in the course of man's history cannot count for naught. "Each immediate religious experience must be set in relation with our total range of experience and thought; untested experience is not trustworthy." [40] It can only be the depth of religious insight and truth which guarantees the veracity and legitimacy of the claim of a *homo religiosus,* of a group of leaders speaking in the name of religion, or of a religious institution.

The question of how we may test authorities is also discussed in Wenger's interesting analysis of the problem of truth in religion. "The authority that men recognize in religion," he states, "is one who, in his character and manner of life, gives the impression of having insight into truths that ordinary men cannot fathom." [41] He also stresses the necessity of seeing larger contexts: "The expert in religious truth must be one who has, implicitly or explicitly, a capacity to see the whole of life and to have a message adequate for it." [42]

The question of motivation takes on great importance when assessing the validity of any claim to religious authority. Are the motives pure or mixed? If they are mixed, where does personal ambition or desire for power, wealth, or well-being begin and end? The study of personality has made great strides since the time of Freud, Jung, Pareto, and others who investigated the problems of the so-called subconscious mind. We have become convinced that the relationship between conscious reasoning and the drives which propel it need close scrutiny in all cases where much depends upon the character of this relationship.

It has been said that the meaning of the sacred dance is "the affirmation of the cohesion of the group in its communion with nature, with the ancestors, with the sources of life." [43] It will always be difficult to analyze and describe the spirit which prevails in a group united by a common religious experience, a common faith, and a common worship. An intensely religious group will always be a highly integrated group. The solidarity which characterizes the members both binds them together and sets them off from outsiders. There is a wide gamut of tokens and signs by which the members of a given cult-group can be identified. They range from outward marks or emblems (painted or tattooed signs or patterns, lacerations, or pieces of garments or vestments) to attitudes revealing a characteristic spirit. While in some religious groups little value is placed upon the identification of members—a varying degree of participation being not only tolerated but officially recognized—other groups think in strict terms of membership. In this case, admission other than by inherited right is made dependent upon the fulfillment of definite obligations of varying character. Criteria for membership in good standing are established, and membership is voted or decided upon by a competent body or by persons. Discipline is enforced, and provisions for the exclusion of the unworthy are made. Thus it is possible to determine who may or may not be considered as a good Christian, Jew, Moslem, Parsee, Buddhist, Jain, or Confucian. In each case there are individual actions, courses of action, or attitudes which are considered definitely out of harmony with, or actually contrary to, the spirit of the particular cult-group by the standard of basic religious principles or according to traditions or customs within the community of faith. The range of violations is very wide and extends from the infraction of a rule concerning dress, food, or participation in activities to the violation of basic moral ordinances by outright criminal acts.

There have been discussions within Jewish, Moslem, Hindu, Buddhist, and Christian theologies as to what constitutes a true believer and to what degree the existent community may be said to represent the ideal community. The latter may or may not be identified with an instance of the past—such as mythical beginnings, the primary circle of a founder and his disciples, or some brotherhood in history. The fellowship may bear eschatological features, such as messianism in Judaism, Christianity, Islam, Hinduism, and Buddhism. In many religious communities certain mythical or historical figures are regarded as prototypes of the true believer; frequently the founder or outstanding prophets and leaders play this paradigmatic role. The emulation of their virtues and attitudes becomes a guide to perfection. This ideal may be broken down still further and the exemplary man, woman, elder, or youth recognized in persons of the most distant or recent past. They become "saints." Their names may serve as the designation for a group of followers.

While students of religious groups have given much attention both to the leading figures in religious life and to the ideal image which fires the imagination of the members of a religious community, less has been said about the "poor" follower. Hence, the processes of decline in religious societies needs more attention. Which convictions and practices are apt to be abandoned first, and which will be the last to go? Are the most characteristic convictions most likely to survive opposition, hostility, and persecution, or not? (By no means is it necessarily the central or essential feature of a religion which becomes its shibboleth.) [44]

It remains for us to consider now the religious group in its relation to the world at large. If we have thus far concentrated on the cult-community as a microcosm and studied it in relative isolation, this was not intended to deny the existence or importance of its relationship with other social groupings. There is a very wide range between the maximal identity of religion with other activities which prevail in primitive societies, and the tension between religion and other aspects of life and culture which exist on more advanced levels of cultural and religious development. Following Weber, we have elsewhere suggested three basically different attitudes toward the world: a naively positive, a negative, and a critically positive attitude.[45] The first is illustrated by the outlook of the Veda or by the Homeric epics, the second by the philosophy of Gnosticism or Buddhism, the third by the evaluation of the world in the monotheistic religions. Whatever the prevailing mood, the religious association takes precedence over all other forms of fellowship. Religious loyalty, in theory at least, outranks any other loyalty everywhere except in the modern Western world.[46]

There is a growing understanding in the West that the emancipation from religion of one sphere of activity after another has had some extremely serious and pernicious consequences. If we hold this view, we do not mean to defend the policies and attitudes of religious institutions or of their spokesmen in the past or present, but we do maintain the principle that religious values are either man's supreme values or they are no values at all. Religions differ as to whether the values of economics, sex, art, science, or politics offer the most serious competition to specifically religious values. Whereas some cult-communities place no limitations on trade or commerce, others demand severe restrictions. While some, far from being hostile to sexual gratification, are fond of symbolism and imagery taken from this area, the act of procreation and all that pertains to it are under heavy censure in others. In most religious groups the arts are expected to contribute their share to the cultic expression of religious experience, but some communities frown upon and exclude all aesthetically gratifying forms of worship. Under the aegis of religious tradition the pursuit of knowledge is assiduously cultivated in most societies, but in some instances it has led to a sharp antagonism between religion and science. As far as political activity is concerned, a variety of typologically different attitudes toward the state as the highest form of societal organization can be traced. It has to be understood, then, that association for any of these or for other purposes is differently evaluated on the basis of different religious experiences, and that the relationship between cult groups and other associations will differ correspondingly.

All is very simple in the case of the intimate religious community where practically all activities can be shared; in natural as well as in specifically religious groups of this size a close integration of activities and associations exists under the inspiration of religion. Where differentiation and specialization have progressed, it is more difficult to prevent partial or total emancipation of economic, artistic, or erotic interests and with it a conflict of loyalties. It is in the case of specifically religious groups that such conflicts are particularly frequent as their very emergence may represent a protest against certain political, economic, or moral conditions. Here religious sovereignty might actually clash with secular sovereignty, as in the case of feudal Western Christianity and of feudal Japanese and Tibetan Buddhism. There may also be friction or struggle between several religions competing within the same political realm. In developing certain basic religious institutions and principles, applying them to typical situations and even concrete cases, middle principles were formulated—as in the great systems of religious laws in Judaism, Islam, Hinduism, Confucianism, and the Catholic branches of Christianity. This was intended in many cases to arrest the process of the application of basic religious principles to a concrete situation at a given stage. The result was a conflict between traditional religion and the prevailing feeling and attitude of man.

It is interesting to apply a comparative study to the meaning and function which the notion of the religious community actually has for its members, especially in the case of the great mass cults. In Judaism, practically all orthodox, conservative, and liberal Jews have a definite and inclusive consciousness of being *one* in spite of rather deep-reaching differences and the existence of national variants such as pro- and anti-Zionism. Every individual and every congregation of Jews has an immediate sense of belonging to this great unit. Similarly, in Hinduism the consciousness of belonging to the community held together by the careful observance of the traditional rites and institutions is shared by hundreds of millions of followers, such significant differences in doctrine, cult, and organization as the divisions of different Sampradayas in Vaishnava—Shaiva, Shakta, and minor groups notwithstanding. It would be difficult to think that in any case the solidarity felt among Hindus as a religious community could be broken by any other principle of grouping, even the political. Less regionally bound than Hinduism, Islam has—in the past at least—represented a brotherhood with a solidarity which has superseded all other principles of association. Only in recent times has this solidarity been challenged by the claims of national loyalty. Very great geographical, ethnic, and cultural variations separate Moslems from each other, in addition to some important religious divisions (Sunna, Shia and her subdivisions, the four Madhabs, traditionalism, and Sufism). Yet they all join in the consciousness of belonging to the great brotherhood.

A somewhat peculiar situation prevails with regard to Buddhism. No overall organization exists; only in certain forms is there any higher unit beyond the individual congregation. There is the important division into "vehicles," with all that this means for the threefold expression in doctrine, cult, and organization. There are geographical, ethnic, and cultural variations. Yet a feeling for the unity of the Samgha does exist, and more than in the case of those religions previously discussed does the individual Buddhist as an individual follower "represent" the ideal which integrates the Samgha.

As with each of the other world religions, so also in Christianity the historical developments and the genius of the people who profess it are reflected in the type and degree of consciousness of solidarity. Early in its history, divisions have occurred on the basis of national, political, cultural, and religious differences. The key term *ecclesia* was used for the local congregation as well as for the total community of the followers of Christ—his "body," the church. In the early centuries various Oriental churches emerged, and in the eleventh century the great division of the Eastern and Western churches occurred. From the days of the Reformation a plurality of bodies existed with rival claims to representation of the true Christian communion. Beside the ecclesiastical bodies there were denominations, independent groups, sects, and so forth, which were typologically different in the integration of their fellowship. The feeling of solidarity did not extend to the whole of the Christian brotherhood; each of the major units into which the brotherhood was divided absorbed the main part of the loyalty of its members. It has been characteristic of the so-called ecumenical movement in Protestantism to have gained ground only during the last fifty years; for centuries the attempts in this direction were suspect and remained fruitless. It is instructive to compare the widest view of religious community, as well as the narrowest view, in different religions. In both Catholic and Protestant Christianity we have the congregation and the parish. Recently we have been given illuminating Catholic studies of parochial sociology in France and in the United States.[47] The author of *The Southern Parish*, Fichter, has rightly said that "a systematic understanding of the role of Catholicism in modern society requires a study not only of its values and meanings but more especially of the 'vehicles' employed to activate them and of the agents who believe in those values and employ those vehicles."[48] The parish is "the church in miniature,"[49] and the primary question is: Is the population of a parochial area homogeneous, religiously speaking? The answer is no. This study involved actual parishioners, non-Catholics, and lapsed Catholics.[50] The following are the standards by which the degree of activity can be approximately determined: the number of religious vocations coming from the parish, attendance at mass, at the sacraments, at weekday devotions, and at parochial activities, parish schools, numbers of converts, numbers of juvenile delinquents, mixed marriages, and the size of families.[51] Answering all these questions we begin to understand the wide margin which exists with regard to the degree of activity and hence to the nature of membership in a parish.

NOTES AND BIBLIOGRAPHY

LIST OF ABBREVIATIONS

AA	American Anthropologist, Organ of the American Anthropological Association. Washington, D.C., Judd & Detweiler, 1888–.
AAA Mem	American Anthropological Association Memoirs. Lancaster, Pa., 1905–.
AJS	American Journal of Sociology. Chicago, University of Chicago Press, 1895–1941.
AR	Archiv für Religionswissenschaft. Leipzig and Freiburg, 1898–.
EI	The Encyclopedia of Islam. Edited by M. T. Houtsma. Leiden, E. J. Brill; London, Luzac & Co., 1913–.
ERE	Encyclopedia of Religion and Ethics. Edited by James Hastings. Edinburgh, T. and T. Clark, 1908–27.
IRM	International Review of Missions. Edinburgh and London, Committee of the World Mission Conference, 1910–.
JBR	Journal of Bible and Religion. Edited by Ismar J. Peritz. National Association of Biblical Instructors, 1933–.
JRAI	Journal of the Royal Anthropological Institute.
RGG	Die Religion in Geschichte und Gegenwart. 2d ed. Edited by Hermann Gunkel and Leopold Zscharnack. Tübingen, J. C. B. Mohr (Paul Siebeck), 1927–32.
SBPAW	Sitzungsberichte der Preussischen Akademie der Wissenschaften. Berlin.
TLZ	Theologische Literaturzeitung. Edited by Emil Schürer *et al*. Leipzig, Hinrichs, 1876–.
ZMR	Zeitschrift für Missionskunde und Religionswissenschaft. Berlin Ostasien Mission (Steglitz), 1885–.
ZTK	Zeitschrift für Theologie und Kirche. Edited by D. J. Gottschick *et al*. Freiburg and Tübingen, J. C. B. Mohr, 1891–.

NOTES

NOTES TO INTRODUCTION

1. Petitpierre, *The Romance of the Mendelssohns*, pp. 236–37, n. 2.
2. *Ibid.*, pp. 97–98.   3. Hensel, *Die Familie Mendelssohn*.
4. See Wach, *Das Problem des Todes in der Philosophie unserer Zeit*.
5. Wach, *Der Erlösungsgedanke und seine Deutung*.
6. Heiler, "Joachim Wach" (Memorial Address), *The Divinity School News*, the University of Chicago, Vol. XXII (November, 1955).
7. Kitagawa, "Joachim Wach et la sociologie de la religion," in *Archives de Sociologie des Religions*, Vol. I (Janvier–Juin, 1956).
8. Wach, *Religionswissenschaft*, pp. 2–3, n. 4.
"Ist die Religionswissenschaft überhaupt eine 'Geisteswissenschaft?' die positive Beantwortung dieser Frage ist eine der Voraussetzungen, die dieser ganzen Arbeit zugrunde liegen. Wir sind allerdings der Überzeugung, dass zu den grossen Ausdruckszusammenhängen oder Systemen, in denen der Geist zu seinem Bewusstsein kommt, auch die Religionen gehören, in denen sich die religiöse Subjektivität objektiviert. Auch diese Objektivationen besitzen eine Struktur, die es für den Erkennenden zu verstehen gilt."
9. Hodges, *Wilhelm Dilthey: An Introduction*, p. 42.
10. Wach, *Types of Religious Experience*, p. 61.
11. *Ibid.*, p. 64.   12. *Ibid.*, p. 62.
13. Hodges, *Wilhelm Dilthey*, p. 68.

14. Taken from Wach's unpublished lecture notes on "Religion and Ethics."
15. *Ibid.* 16. Wach, *Typen religiöser Anthropologie*, p. 8.
17. *Ibid.*, pp. 11–12. 18. *Ibid.*, p. 15.
19. Wach, *Religious Experience*, p. 67.
20. Wach, *Religiöser Anthropologie*, pp. 15–16. 21. *Ibid.*, p. 17.
22. *Ibid.*, p. 20. 23. Wach, *Religious Experience*, p. 74.
24. *Ibid.*, p. 70. 25. Wach, *Religiöser Anthropologie*, p. 24.
26. Wach, *Religious Experience*, p. 78. 27. *Ibid.*, p. 64.
28. Wach, *Religiöser Anthropologie*, pp. 31–32.
29. *Ibid.*, p. 33. 30. *Ibid.*, pp. 34–35.
31. Wach, *Religious Experience*, p. 65.
32. Leeuw, *Religion in Essence and Manifestation*, pp. 243–44.
33. Kitagawa, "Joachim Wach et la sociologie de la religion," *Archives de sociologie des religions*, I (Janvier–Juin, 1956), 29.
34. Taken from Wach's unpublished lecture notes on "The Theories of Religious Communication."
35. *Ibid.* 36. *Ibid.*
37. Wach's unpublished notes on "Religion and Ethics."
38. Wach, "Religionssoziologie," in *Handwörterbuch der Soziologie*, Vierkandt, ed.

I am indebted to Professor James Luther Adams who made his unpublished summary translation of this article available to me.

39. Taken from Wach's unpublished manuscript, "Religion in America: The Sociological Approach to Religion and Its Limits."
40. See Shils, "The Present Situation in American Sociology," in *Pilot Papers*, II (June, 1947), 23–24.
41. Wach, *Sociology of Religion*, p. 108. 42. *Ibid.*, p. 16.
43. *Ibid.*, p. 108. 44. *Ibid.*, p. 8.
45. Wach, "Sociology of Religion," in *Twentieth Century Sociology*, Gurvitch, ed., p. 418.
46. Wach, *Sociology of Religion*, p. 2.
47. Pemberton, "Universalism and Particularity" (A review article of Wach's *Religionssoziologie*, 1951, and *Types of Religious Experience*, 1951), JBR, Vol. XX (April, 1952).
48. Wach, *Sociology of Religion*, p. 7.
49. Quoted in *ibid.*, p. 383.

NOTES TO INTRODUCTION

50. Quoted from William James's *The Varieties of Religious Experience* on the fly sheet of *Sociology of Religion*.

51. Wach, "The Christian Professor" (published by World Student Christian Federation, University Commission, December 10, 1947).

52. Wach, *Religious Experience*, p. 169.   53. *Ibid.*, pp. 169–70.

54. See Kraemer, ed., *On the Meaning of History*, p. 3.

55. Quoted in Wach, *Religious Experience*, pp. 185–86.

56. Wach, "Comparative Study of Religion," in *The Philosophy of Sarvepalli Radhakrishnan,* Schilpp, ed., p. 452.

57. *Ibid.*

58. Wach, "Redeemer of Men," *The Divinity School News*, XV (November 1, 1948), 6.

59. *Ibid.*   60. Wach, *Religious Experience*, p. 14.

61. Wach, *Religionswissenschaft,* Chap. IV.

62. Wach, *Religious Experience*, p. 14.

63. See Kitagawa, "Theology and the Science of Religion," *Anglican Theological Review*, Vol. XXXIX (January, 1957).

64. Wach, *Religious Experience*, pp. 229–30.

65. *Ibid.*, p. 228.   66. *Ibid.*, p. 30.   67. *Ibid.*, p. 47.

68. *Ibid.,* p. vii.

69. See Tillich, *Systematic Theology*, I, 215 f., for Tillich's views on Otto's idea of the holy.

70. Wach, *Religious Experience,* Chap. III.

71. *Ibid.*, p. 229.   72. *Ibid.*

73. Quoted in Wach, "General Revelation and Religions of the World," JBR (April, 1954), p. 92.

74. Wach, "Comparative Study of Religion," *The Philosophy of Sarvepalli Radhakrishnan,* Schilpp, ed.

75. *Ibid.*, p. 449.   76. *Ibid.*, p. 447.   77. *Ibid.*, p. 450.

78. *Ibid.*, p. 453.   79. *Ibid.*, p. 449.   80. *Ibid.*, p. 450.

81. See Kitagawa, "Theology and the Science of Religion," *Anglican Theological Review,* Vol. XXIX (January, 1957).

82. Wach, "General Revelation and Religions of the World," JBR (April, 1954), p. 86.

83. *Ibid.*   84. *Ibid.*   85. *Ibid.*, p. 85.   86. *Ibid.*, p. 91.

87. *Ibid.*, p. 88.   88. Quoted in *ibid.*, p. 91.

89. *Ibid.*, pp. 88–91.   90. Wach, *Religious Experience*, p. 230.

91. *Ibid.*, pp. 230-31.   92. Quoted in *ibid.*, p. 231.

93. Wach, *Meister und Jünger*.

94. See Kitagawa, "A Glimpse of Professor Wach," Chicago Theological Seminary *Register,* Vol. XLV (November, 1955). See also his Memorial Address in the University of Chicago, *Divinity School News,* Vol. XXII (November, 1955).

NOTES TO CHAPTER I

1. Jordan, *Comparative Religion in Genesis and Growth.* See also the survey of twenty-five years later: Haydon, "History of Religions," in *Religious Thought in the Last Quarter Century,* Smith, ed., pp. 140 ff.

2. Hardy, "Zur Geschichte der vergleichenden Religionsforschung," AR, IV (1901), 45 ff., 97 ff., esp. 193 ff.; Pinard de la Boullaye, *L'Étude comparée des religions;* Mensching, *Geschichte der Religionswissenschaft;* Wach, "On Teaching History of Religions," in *Pro Regno pro Sanctuario,* pp. 525 ff.

3. See the discussion of nomenclature by Jordan, *Comparative Religion,* pp. 7 ff. For the emancipation of the general study of religion from theology, see Wach, *Religionswissenschaft.*

4. For a study of the development of comparative studies in the nineteenth century, see Rothacker, *Einleitung in die Geisteswissenschaften,* Chap. LV; also p. 136, n. 1; pp. 237 ff.; Jordan, *Comparative Religion.*

5. *Elements of the Science of Religion* (1896-99); see Tiele, "On the Study of Comparative Theology," in *World Parliament of Religions,* Barrows, ed., I, 583 ff. His first publication dates from 1853. On the "Leyden" School, see Jordan, *Comparative Religion,* pp. 179 ff.

6. For a criticism, see Otto on Wundt's theory of religion in *The Idea of the Holy,* p. 15, and W. E. Hocking on Hegel in *Living Religions and a World Faith,* pp. 102 ff. See also Widengren, *Religionens Ursprung.*

7. Marett, *Tylor.*

8. For a discussion of "objectivity" and "impartiality," see Hodges, *The Philosophy of Wilhelm Dilthey.*

9. Dussaud, *L'Oeuvre scientifique d'Ernest Renan.*

10. Dieterich, "H. Usener," AR, VIII (1905), 1 ff.

11. An important repository of findings for this era was the *Archiv für Religionswissenschaft*, from 1898, ed. by Dieterich and others. See also the *Journal of the American Oriental Society*, from 1843.

12. See "Religionsgeschichtliche Schule," RGG, Vol. IV; also Gruppe, *Geschichte der Klassischen Mythologie und Religionsgeschichte*, Sec. 88.

13. Eduard Lehmann, "Der Lebenslauf der Religionsgeschichte," *Actes du Ve congrès d'histoire des religions*, pp. 44 ff.

14. See Fleure, "J. G. Frazer," *Man*, Vol. LIV (1954).

15. See Lowie, *The History of Ethnological Theory*, Chap. IX; and "Biographical Memoir of Franz Boas," *Biographical Memoirs, National Academy of Sciences*, XXIV (1947), 303 ff.

16. For the development and the methods of anthropology in Europe and America, see Marett, *Tylor*; Lowie, *Ethnological Theory*; Evans-Pritchard, *Social Anthropology*, Chaps. II, III; Forde, "The Integration of Anthropological Studies," JRAI, Vol. LXXVII (1948); the discussions in Tax, ed., *An Appraisal of Anthropology Today*; Eggan, "Social Anthropology and the Method of Controlled Comparisons," AA, 56 (1954), esp. pp. 748 ff. For a criticism of some major concepts of leading historians of religions see Radin, *Die religiöse Erfahrung der Naturvölker*, Chap. 1.

17. Clarke, *Ten Great Religions*. On this author see Bolster, *J. F. Clarke*, pp. 296, 303. Barrows is especially remembered for his activity in connection with the World Parliament of Religions, 1893. See Barrows, *A Memoir*. Toy's *Introduction to the History of Religions* (1913) was reprinted as late as 1948 by Harvard University Press. See also, on the "American School," Jordan, *Comparative Religion*, pp. 197 ff., 462 ff.; and Hume, "The Study of the History of Religions" (reprinted from *Christian Education*).

18. For the methodological notions of Dilthey, who is to be regarded as one of its principal exponents, see esp. Vols. I, V, and VII of his *Gesammelte Schriften*, and Hodges, *Wilhelm Dilthey*.

19. A comprehensive study and appraisal of the work of Troeltsch does not exist as yet, either in English or in German. Meanwhile, see Mandelbaum, *The Problems of Historical Knowledge*, Chap. IV, pp. 155 ff.

20. See Schweitzer, "Die Bedeutung des Historismus für die

Theologie," *Studium Generale,* Thiel, ed., VII (No. 8, 1954), 501 ff., an important reassessment of the effect of historism on theology and of theology on historicity.

21. See Überweg, *Die deutsche Philosophie des 19. Jahrhunderts;* Farber, *Philosophic Thought in France and the United States;* Lyotard, *La Phénoménologie.*

22. In America especially, William James's name marks the transition. Besides his classic study of the *Varieties of Religious Experience,* see his correspondence: Perry, *The Thought and Character of William James as Revealed in Unpublished Correspondence.*

23. Otto, *Idea of the Holy.* See Heiler, "Die Bedeutung R. Ottos für die vergleichende Religionsgeschichte," in *Religionswissenschaft in Neuer Sicht,* pp. 13 ff.; R. F. Davidson, *Rudolf Otto's Interpretation of Religion;* Wach, *Types of Religious Experience,* Chap. X.

24. Hügel, *Essays and Addresses on the Philosophy of Religion,* I, 2; II, 5. See Nédoncelle, *Baron Friederich von Hügel.*

25. Webb, *Religious Experience.* There is no monograph on his work.

26. The development of our studies in this second period (and in the third) has been traced by Puech, "Bibliographie générale," in *Mana,* and for Scandinavia by Widengren, "Die religionswissenschaftliche Forschung in Skandinavien," *Zeitschrift für Religions- und Geistesgeschichte,* V (1953), 193 ff., 320 ff. Masson-Oursel, "La connaissance de l'Asie en France depuis 1900," *Revue Philosophique,* Nos. 7–9 (1953), pp. 342 ff.; Padovani, "La Storia delle religioni in Italia," *Semaine Internationale d'ethnologie religieuse,* IV (1925), 47 ff.

27. See the symposium by Miller *et al., Religion and Freedom of Thought,* contributions of Miller, Calhoun, Pusey, and Reinhold Niebuhr.

28. For a historical orientation, see Davies, *The Problem of Authority in the Continental Reformers.* For a balanced systematic treatment, see Temple, *Nature, Man and God,* Chap. XIII; Kruger, "Das Problem der Autorität," in *Offener Horizont,* pp. 44 ff. Antiauthoritarian is Zaehner, "Dogma," *Hibbert Journal,* III (1954), 9 ff.

29. H. W. Schneider, *Religion in Twentieth Century America,* p. 33.

30. Farnell, *The Attributes of God*, p. 10, wrote correctly that the intellectual student of the science of religion "may be merely devoted to truth and indifferent to the possibly far-reaching practical results of his work." He adds that it is clear that such results, direct or indirect, are inevitable.

31. Troeltsch, *Die Absolutheit des Christentums und die Religionsgeschichte*, p. 51.

32. *Types of Experience*, Chap. 1.

33. Richardson, *Christian Apologetics*, Chap. V.

34. The author has frequently addressed himself to this question. See "Zur Methodologie der Religionswissenschaft," ZMR (1923); "Zum Problem der externen Würdigung der Religion," ZMR (1923); *Religionswissenschaft;* "Sinn und Aufgabe der Religionswissenschaft," ZMR (1935); *Das Verstehen*, Vols. I–III. See also Bollnow, *Das Verstehen*.

35. "Comprendre et rendre compréhensible la modalité du sacré" is the task, according to Eliade, *Traité d'histoire des religions*, p. 19.

36. See Pinard de la Boullaye, *L'Etude comparée*, I, 30 ff.

37. Webb, *God and Personality*, p. 84.

38. This was the postulate of some of the authors treated in our history of nineteenth-century hermeneutics and is strongly stressed by Bultmann in "Das Problem der Hermeneutik," in *Glauben und Verstehen*, II, 211 ff. See Dinkler, "Existentialist Interpretation of the New Testament," *Journal of Religion*, XXXII (1952), 87 ff. See also Bollnow, *Das Verstehen*, pp. 37 ff.

39. Pinard de la Boullaye, *L'Etude comparée*, pp. 31 ff.

40. Wach, *Sociology of Religion*, Chap. VI.

41. Allport, *The Individual and His Religion;* Grensted, *Psychology of Religion*.

42. "The real weight of the 'evidence' which is accepted as sufficient ground for assurance can only be judged by a mind of the right kind and with the right kind of training." Taylor, "The Vindication of Religion," *Essays Catholic and Critical*, Selwyn, ed., p. 39.

43. The excellent article by Earle, "The 'Standard Observer' in the Sciences of Man," *Ethics*, LXIII (1953), 293 ff., stresses that "man" in distinction from the data of the sciences proper is not a "public

datum," that he is objective only for the "total nature of man." Accordingly the wise man, the lover, the poet, the saint is the true observer (296 f.).

44. Whitehead, *Process and Reality; Religion in the Making*. Hartshorne, "Whitehead's Idea of God," in *The Philosophy of A. N. Whitehead*, Schilpp, ed., pp. 513 ff.; also, "Religious Bearings of Whitehead's Philosophy," *Reality as Social Process*, Chap. XIV.

45. See Morgan, *Emergent Evolution;* and *The Interpretation of Nature*.

46. Morgan, *Emergent Evolution*.

47. *Ibid.*, pp. 129 f.   48. *Ibid.*, p. 279.

49. Samuel Alexander, *Space, Time and Deity*. See McCreary, "The Religious Philosophy of S. Alexander," *Journal of Religion*, XXVII (No. 2), 103 ff.

50. Temple, *Nature, Man and God*. See Iremonger, *Life of William Temple*. A comprehensive treatment of Temple's thought has not as yet appeared.

51. Ferré, *The Christian Understanding of God*, Chaps. I and II.

52. Richardson, *Christian Apologetics*.

53. Moses, *Religious Truth and the Relation between Religions*.

54. *Ibid.*, p. 20.   55. *Ibid.*, p. 19.   56. *Ibid.*

57. Temple, *Nature, Man and God*, p. 129.

58. Emmet, *Whitehead's Philosophy of Organism*, p. 52.

59. *Ibid.*, p. 53. For the history of this idea see Wach, *Das Verstehen*, I, 38, n. 2.

60. Richard de St. Victor, *De Gradibus Charitatis*, as quoted in J.-P. Migne, ed., *Patrologiae Cursus Completus*, Series Latina, Vol. 176, col. 1195.

61. In his article "Das Problem der Hermeneutik," in *Glauben und Verstehen*, II, 211 ff., Bultmann stresses, without wanting to make light of the actual and potential contributions of the grammatico-historical interpretation, the necessity of a living relationship (*Lebensverhältnis, Interesse*). We follow him here, whereas his theory of *Vorverständnis* is open to misunderstanding. Dilthey wisely limited the task of interpretation, properly so called, to expressions of life in fixed form. The loose use of the term "hermeneutic" and "interpretation" by Heidegger and his followers is misleading.

NOTES TO I: MEANING AND METHOD

62. Wach, "Understanding," in *Jubilee Book for Albert Schweitzer*, Roback, ed., pp. 131 ff. See also, Schultz, "Wesen und Grenze der Theologischen Hermeneutik," ZTK, XIX (1938), 283 ff.
63. Otto, *Idea of the Holy*, p. 63.
64. Otto, *Die Anschauung vom heiligen Geiste bei Luther*.
65. Bultmann, "Das Problem der Hermeneutik," in *Glauben und Verstehen*, pp. 216 ff.; Dinkler, "Existentialist Interpretation of the New Testament," *Journal of Religion*, Vol. XXXII (1952).
66. Dinkler, "Existentialist Interpretation of the New Testament," *Journal of Religion*, XXXII (1952), 94.
67. Wach, *Das Verstehen*, I, 89. Schultz, "Die Grundlagen der Hermeneutik Schleiermachers," ZTK, XXXIII (1953), 158 ff.; also, Bollnow, *Das Verstehen*, pp. 49 f.
68. Hartmann, *New Ways of Ontology*. See Friedrich Schneider, *Philosophie der Gegenwart*, pp. 28 ff.
69. Hartmann, *Ontology*, p. 43, and Chap. V.
70. *Ibid.*, p. 47.   71. *Ibid.*, Chap. IX.   72. *Ibid.*, p. 118.
73. *Ibid.*, p. 87.   74. *Ibid.*   75. *Ibid.*, p. 119.
76. *Ibid.*, p. 41.
77. Friedrich Schneider, *Philosophie der Gegenwart*, pp. 52 ff.
78. Hartmann, *New Ways*, Chap. XI.
79. *Ibid.*, p. 103 (cf. p. 44).   80. *Ibid.*
81. *Ibid.*, p. 116.   82. *Ibid.*, p. 122.
83. Northrop, *The Meeting of East and West*. The "undifferentiated" aesthetic continuum as elementary and primary is discussed on pp. 394 ff.
84. On intuition as the source of true knowledge (*panna*) in early Buddhism, see Keith, *Buddhist Philosophy*, pp. 90 f., 128 ff.
85. Datta, *The Six Ways of Knowledge*.
86. A pramana is an active and unique cause of knowledge. *Ibid.*, p. 27.
87. *Ibid.*, pp. 20 f.   88. *Ibid.*, Book VI. See p. 243.
89. *Ibid.*, pp. 328 ff., 339.
90. Brightman, *A Philosophy of Religion*, p. 16.
91. See Pinard de la Boullaye, *L'Etude comparée*, Vol. II, Chaps. III–VII; Pettazzoni, "Aperçu introductif," *Numen*, I (No. 1, 1954), 1 ff.

92. Mainage, *Les Religions de la préhistoire;* E. O. James, *The Beginnings of Religion;* Finegan, *The Archaeology of World Religions;* Lehman, "Die Religionsgeschichte des Palaeolithikum," AR, XXXV (1938), 288 ff.; Widengren, *Religionens Ursprung;* Bidney, "The Ethnology of Religion: The Problem of Human Evolution," AA 56 (1954), 1 ff.

93. Troeltsch, *Gesammelte Schriften,* III.

94. While Gibbon and Burckhardt (in *Force and Freedom*), who have been greatly interested in assessing the role of religion in history, are widely quoted, J. G. Droysen's contribution to both formal and material theory is much neglected. See Huber, ed., *Historik,* abbreviated translation by Andrews, *Outlines of the Principles of History.* Also, Wach, "Droysen's Lehre vom Verstehen," Chap. II in *Das Verstehen,* III.

95. The *Lehrbuch der historischen Methode* (especially its fifth and sixth editions) is and remains a standard work, not frequently enough consulted.

96. See Friedrich, *Entzifferung verschollener Schriften und Sprachen.*

97. See Dobschütz, *Vom Auslegen des Neuen Testament;* Schultz, "Wesen und Grenze der theologischen Hermeneutik," ZTK, XIX (1938), 283 ff.; Bultmann, "Das Problem der Hermeneutik," *Glauben und Verstehen;* Schweitzer, "Das Problem der Hermeneutik in der gegenwartigen Theologie," TLZ, V (No. 7, 1950), 467 f.; Jentsch, "Verstehen und Verständlichmachen," TLZ, 76 (1951), 641 ff.

98. Wach, *Das Verstehen,* Vol. III, on the growth of philological and archaeological hermeneutics.

99. See n. 3; Radcliffe-Brown, "Religion and Society," JRAI, LXXV (1945/46), 33, errs when he designates the "experimental method of social anthropology" as "the only one."

100. Widengren, "Stand und Aufgaben der iranischen Religionsgeschichte," *Numen,* I (1954), 17, emphasizes that "philology alone does not make a student a historian of religions, any more than a historian of law, medicine, or economics."

101. Here the work of Dilthey (esp. *Gesammelte Schriften,* I and V, 139 ff., 241 ff.) is again of decisive methodological importance. He himself refers often to the influence of Maine de Biran who, not

accidentally, has been much discussed in modern French religious thought. See Cresson, *Maine de Biran:* "Ce qui a assuré à Maine de Biran l'influence qu'il a eue . . . c'est la place immense qu'il a donnée dans sa philosophie, à cette observation intérieure qu'il appelle l'expérience du 'sens intime' " (p. 82).

102. P. E. Johnson, *Psychology of Religion,* pp. 19 ff., gives a brief historical survey.

103. See above, n. 7. Pinard de la Boullaye enumerates three methods: introspection, extrospection, and experimentation. *L'Etude comparée,* II, 286 ff., 289 ff., 303 ff.

104. See Wach, "Sociology of Religion," *Twentieth Century Sociology,* Gurvitch, ed., Chap. XIV.

105. Schoeck, *Soziologie,* pp. 255 f.

106. Fustel de Coulanges, *La Cité antique.*

107. Durkheim, *Les Formes élémentaires de la vie religieuse.* Cf. Parsons, *The Structure of Social Action,* Chaps. VIII–XII. Alpert, "Emile Durkheim and Sociologismic Psychology," AJS, XLV (1940), 65 ff.

108. Weber, "Wirtschaft und Gesellschaft," *Grundriss der Sozialökonomik,* III, Chap. IV; *Gesammelte Aufsätze zur Religionssoziologie.* See also Parsons, *Essays in Social Theory,* Chap. V. On Max Weber as a sociologist of religion, see Wach, *Einleitung in die Religionssoziologie,* Appendix on Max Weber.

109. Troeltsch, *Gesammelte Schriften,* Vols. I, IV.

110. Sombart, *Der moderne Kapitalismus.*

111. Scheler, *Die Wissenformen und die Gesellschaft.* See also *The Nature of Sympathy.*

112. See Friedrich Spiegelberg, *Living Religions of the World,* for a study of the origin and development of phenomenology.

113. Husserl, *Logische Untersuchungen; Ideen zu einer reinen Phänomenologie;* and *Méditations Cartésiennes.* Also, Farber, *The Foundation of Phenomenology;* Breda, "Aus dem Husserl Archiv zu Löwen," *Jahrbuch der Görresgesellschaft,* LXII (No. 2, 1953), 240 ff.

114. See *Jahrbuch für Philosophie und Phänomenologie.* A very good new brief orientation is Lyotard, *La phénoménologie,* Part I, "Husserl," Part II, "Phénoménologie et sciences humaines."

115. See *Vom Ewigen im Menschen*. For a criticism, see Troeltsch, *Gesammelte Schriften*, Vols. III, V; Hessen, *Max Scheler*.

116. Scheler, *Vom Ewigen*, p. 391.

117. *Revue d'histoire et philosophie religieuse*, XXI (1951), 405 ff. See again Pettazzoni, "Aperçu introductif," *Numen*, I (No. 1, 1954).

118. *Revue d'histoire et philosophie religieuse*, XXI (1951), 407. "Le principle eidétique a pour but de rechercher l'Eidos, c'est à dire ce qu'il y a d'essentiel dans les phénomènes religieux."

119. *Ibid.*, p. 408.

120. *Festschrift für Alfred Bertholet*, Baumgartner, ed.

121. *Ibid.*, p. 269.

122. Dilthey, *Gesammelte Werke*, VIII, 100: "Diese Typenunterscheidung soll ja nur dienen, tiefer in die Geschichte zu sehen, und zwar vom Leben aus."

123. See Wach, *Religionswissenschaft*, Chap. III, pp. 94 ff.; Parrish, *The Classification of Religions*; W. E. Hocking, *Living Religions*, p. 63; Northrop, *East and West*, Chaps. VIII, X; Mensching, *Vergleichende Religionswissenschaft*.

NOTES TO CHAPTER II

1. W. C. Smith, *Inaugural Lecture*, p. 49.

2. Malinowski, *Magic, Science and Religion*, pp. 20, 68.

3. Radcliffe-Brown, "Religion and Society," JRAI, LXXV (1945/46), 33 ff.

4. *Ibid.*, p. 43. He stresses religion as "an important or essential part of the social machinery," *ibid.*, p. 33. See below, Chap. V.

5. William James, *The Varieties of Religious Experience*. For criticism see Moore, *Theories of Religious Experience with Special Reference to James, Otto and Bergson*.

6. Richardson, *Christian Apologetics*, p. 115.

7. Kierkegaard, the founder of modern Existentialism, isolates individual religious (Christian) experience, and both German and French existentialists (Heidegger, Jaspers, Sartre, Marcel) have followed him with this emphasis. Lowrie, *Kierkegaard*, pp. 426 ff., 524 ff.; Eduard Lehmann, *Grundtvig*, p. 64. Fitzpatrick, in "Kierkegaard and the Church," JR, XXVII (No. 4, 1947) 255 ff., sees it differently.

8. Webb, *Religious Experience*, pp. 28 f.

9. Berthold, "The Meaning of Religious Experience," JR, XXXII (1952), 263 ff., 265. He rightly states that "The analysis of experience cannot itself settle the question of what is experienced."

10. See Mouroux, "Sur la notion de l'expérience religieuse," *Recherches de sciences religieuses*, XXXIV (1947), 5 ff.

11. Kay, *The Nature of Christian Worship*, pp. 54 ff., 58.

12. Buddhism too, following its founder, has often stressed that observation and experience rather than metaphysical deliberations are the starting point of its path. See, for example, Keith, *Buddhist Philosophy*, pp. 57 f.

13. See Allport, *The Individual and His Religion*, pp. 125 ff.

14. Scheler, *Vom Ewigen im Menschen;* Herring, *Phénoménologie et philosophie religieuse;* Grensted, *Psychology of Religion*.

15. Tillich, *Systematic Theology*, I, 157.

16. Wach, *Types of Religious Experience*, pp. 32 ff., 35.

17. Emmet, *The Nature of Metaphysical Thinking*, p. 17.

18. Hence we take exception to Hartshorne's statement: "To say nature is worthy of being loved and to say there is a God are perhaps not ultimately distinguishable assertions." *Reality as Social Process*, pp. 177 f. See also the definition of faith, p. 163.

19. "The psychologist can do no more than examine our *response* to the ultimate reality so far as that response can be seen and recorded." Grensted, *Psychology*, p. 16.

20. Bedoyère, *The Life of Baron von Hügel*, p. 296. See Hartshorne, *Reality as Social Process*, Chap. IV.

21. Hügel, *Selected Letters, 1896–1924*, p. 261.

22. Mouroux "Sur la notion de l'expérience religieuse," *Recherches de sciences religieuses*, XXIV (1947), p. 13, finds "L'expérience est l'acte par quoi la personne se saisit en relation avec . . . Dieu." For Marcel's theory of religious experience, see the unpublished dissertation of Cain, "Gabriel Marcel's Theory of Religious Experience."

23. *Ibid.*, p. 26: "L'expérience religieuse est dynamique par essence." *Ibid.*, p. 28: "Une perpétuelle recherche. . . ."

24. *Ibid.*, p. 27. "Dieu n'est jamais découvert au sens strict."

25. This is the core of my argument in "Radhakrishnan and the Comparative Study of Religion," in *The Philosophy of Sarvepalli Radhakrishnan*, Schilpp, ed., pp. 443 ff.

26. "The most concrete experiences are those to which I must re-

spond with the whole man." Cotton, *Christian Knowledge of God*, p. 92. See also Mouroux, "Sur la notion de l'expérience religieuse," *Recherches de science religieuses*, XXXIV (1947), p. 10; Mowinckel, *Religion and Kultus*, p. 125.

27. Mouroux, "Sur la notion de l'expérience religieuse," *Recherches de sciences religieuses*, XXXIV (1947), p. 10.

28. Webb, *Religious Experience*, p. 39.

29. Thornton, "The Christian Concept of God," in *Essays Catholic and Critical*, p. 124.

30. Ferré suggests interesting consequences of this "integration" for the concept of the Deity as body, in *The Christian Understanding of God*.

31. Swami Akhilananda, *Hindu Psychology and the West*, Chap. XIII; *Mental Health and Hindu Psychology*, Chap. I. See also Chaps. XIII, XIV.

32. Swami Akhilananda, *Hindu Psychology*, pp. 205 f.

33. Swami Akhilananda, *Mental Health*, pp. 11 f.

34. See Mackintosh, *Types of Modern Theology*, esp. Chaps. II, III, IV.

35. Marett, *The Threshold of Religion*, p. xxix.

36. Allport, *Individual*, pp. 16 f.

37. Harrison, *Ancient Art and Ritual*, p. 38.

38. See below, Chap. III, on religious anthropology.

39. For Christian anthropology, see Reinhold Niebuhr, *The Nature and Destiny of Man;* for Eastern: Hilliard, *Man in Eastern Religions*. Also see below, Chap. III.

40. Puech, *Le Manichéisme*, p. 72; "La gnose est en même temps théologie et cosmologie."

41. This is sensed though not quite carried through by Redfield, *The Primitive World and Its Transformations*, Chap. VI.

42. See the analysis of the aesthetic attitude in Hospers, *Meaning and Truth in the Arts*, pp. 4 ff.

43. Allport, *Individual*, Chap. IV.

44. Tillich, *Systematic Theology*, I, 212.

45. See the beautiful stories collected by Buber, *Die Erzählungen der Chassidim*.

46. See Nicholson, *The Mystics of Islam;* and the great study of

Massignon, *La Passion d'al Hosayn Ibn Mansour al Hallaj*. Also Margaret Smith, *Studies in Early Mysticism in the Near and Middle East*, Part II.

47. Hooper, *Hymns of the Alvars;* Rajogopalachariar, *The Vishnuite Reformers of India;* Kennedy, *The Chaitanya Movement; Indian Theism*.

48. G. U. Pope, *The Tiruvacagam or Sacred Utterances . . . of Manikka-Vacagar;* Katiresu, *A Handbook of Saiva Religion;* Schomerus, *Sivaitische Heiligenlegenden;* Arno Lehman, *Die sivaitische Frömmigkeit der tamulischen Erbauungsliteratur*.

49. Swami Nikhilananda, *Ramakrishna*, p. 48.

50. Zimmer, Jung, ed., *Der Weg zum Selbst*.

51. See the stimulating phenomenological analysis by Bugbee on "The Moment of Obligation in Experience," *Journal of Religion*, XXXIII (No. 1, 1953), 1 ff.

52. "World view can be seen as a characteristic attitude of obligation toward that which man finds in his universe." Redfield, *Primitive World*, p. 99.

53. William James, *Varieties*, p. 121.

54. Radhakrishnan, *Religion and Society*.

55. For a discussion of the faith and work relationship in Islam, see Wensinck, *The Muslim Creed*, Chaps. I, III, and VII; Goldziher, *Koranauslegung*, pp. 160 f.

56. Bedoyère, *Von Hügel*, 296.

57. See Dewick, *The Christian Attitude to Other Religions*, Chap. I.

58. See Braden, *War, Communism and World Religions*.

59. See Constantin, "The Gospel to Communists," IRM, XLI (April, 1952) 202 ff.

60. Bergson, *The Two Sources of Morality and Religion*, p. 102.

61. Firth, *Elements of Social Organization*, p. 216. See also Bidney, "The Ethnology of Religion and the Problem of Human Evolution," AA (No. 56, 1954), on religion as an authentic and enduring element of human experience.

62. Marett, *Sacraments of Simple Folks*, p. 3.

63. Evans-Pritchard, *Social Anthropology*, p. 128.

64. Redfield, *Primitive World*, p. 94.

65. Otto, *Idea of the Holy*, pp. 119 f.

NOTES TO II: NATURE OF EXPERIENCE

66. Webb, *Religious Experience*, p. 37.

67. "Perhaps the most striking fact about subjective religion is the contrast between its essential simplicity when, well-formed, it is playing its part in the economy of the personal life and its *extreme complexity* in the process of forming." Allport, *Individual*, p. 8.

68. *Offener Horizont*, p. 73.

69. Andrae, *Die Frage nach der religiösen Anlage*, pp. 72, 77 f.

70. Radin, *Primitive Religion*, Chap. I.

71. See below, Chap. V.

72. "Grace," says Von Hügel, "so little interferes with, or even simply adds itself on to, or runs parallel with the autonomy of the spiritual personality, that it actually *constitutes* that personality." *Selected Letters*, p. 91.

73. Marett, *Threshold of Religion*, p. xxv; and Faris, *The Nature of Human Nature*.

74. Marett, *Faith, Hope and Charity in Primitive Religion*, p. 5. Firth, *Social Organization*, p. 216.

75. Thornton, "The Christian Concept of God," in Selwyn, ed., *Essays Catholic and Critical*, p. 135.

76. Wenger, "The Problem of Truth in Religion," in Payne, ed., *Studies in History and Religion Presented to H. Wheeler Robinson;* pp. 159 ff., 164.

77. Hooke, *Babylonian and Assyrian Religion*, pp. 26 f.

78. On Shiva as Satguru, see Schomerus, *Der Caiva-Siddhanta*, pp. 290 ff. That Shiva himself appears and instructs is necessary because it is Shiva alone who indwells the souls from eternity, knows their true state and what they need, *ibid.*, p. 301. On the seven *diksha*, through gaze, contact, oral teaching, shastras (texts), yoga, see *ibid.*, pp. 315 ff.

79. For the identification of instruction and perfection in Confucianism in the *Chung-Yung* and *Ta-hsuch*, see Groot, *Universismus*, pp. 62 ff., 71 ff.; and E. R. Hughes, *The Great Learning and the Mean in Action*, pp. 105 ff., 145 ff.

80. Wach, *Meister und Jünger;* Benoit, "Direction spirituelle et Protestantisme," *Etudes d'histoire et de philosophie religieuse* (No. 37, 1940). See Rabbow, *Seelenführung*.

81. See Underwood, *Conversion: Christian and Non-Christian*. On

the time factor, see pp. 13 f.; on gradual and sudden conversion, Chap. XII.

82. For the "subitism" (suddenness doctrine) and the "gradualism" in Chinese Buddhist thinking (especially of the eighth century A.D.) and the parallels elsewhere, see Demieville, "Le Miroir spirituel," *Sinologica*, I (1947), 112 ff. For the gradual character of the instruction of Shiva (by hearing, meditation, understanding, *samadhi*) according to the *Siddhanta*, see Schomerus, *Der Caiva-Siddhanta*, p. 316.

83. "Le principe effective du soufism est la culture organisée de l'expérience religieuse." Gibb, *La structure de la pensée religieuse de l'Islam*, p. 45.

84. See below, Chap. IV.

85. Hügel, *Selected Letters*, p. 206. Gardet and Anawati, *Introduction à la théologie musulmane*, pp. 338 f., "la verité divine est une et simple; mais la nature de l'esprit humain est telle que nous ne pouvons saisir cette verité que sous son mode complexe. *Cognita sunt in cognoscente secundum modum cognoscentis.*"

86. We would rather side with Ferré than with Tillich in characterizing the Christian concept of the nature of Ultimate Reality as love rather than being. See Tillich, *Systematic Theology*, I, Chap. II.

87. See Hartshorne and Reese, *Philosophers Speak of God*, p. 167.

88. Müller, *Life and Religion*, p. 56.

89. Baillie, *Our Knowledge of God*, p. 174.

90. *Ibid.*, p. 16.   91. Hügel, *Eternal Life*, p. 368.

92. See Otto, *The Idea of the Holy*, Chap. I.

93. Thornton, "The Christian Concept of God," in *Essays Catholic and Critical*, Selwyn, ed., p. 126.

94. Glasenapp, *Madhvas Philosophie des Vishnuglaubens*, pp. 33-39.

95. Hügel, *Selected Letters*, p. 90.

96. Zimmer, in Campbell, ed., *Philosophies of India*, pp. 560 f.

97. Tillich, *Systematic Theology*, I, 271.

98. Hartshorne and Reese, *Philosophers*, Introduction. See below, Chap. III.

99. Wach, "General Revelation and Religions of the World," JBR, XXII (No. 2, 1954), 83 ff.

100. See Razek, "La Révélation dans l'Islam," *Transactions of the*

Fifth International Congress of History of Religions, 1929, p. 270 ff.

101. Underhill, *An Anthology of the Love of God*, p. 42.

102. Nédoncelle, *Baron Friedrich von Hügel*, p. 76.

103. Eliade, *Traité d'histoire des religions*, p. 38, relates the wide range of "hierophanies" in the world of primitive religion to the Christian notion of the freedom of God, "de prendre n'importe quelle."

104. Ferré, *Christian Understanding*, p. 158.

105. Temple, *Nature, Man and God*, pp. 306 f.

106. Otto, *Idea of the Holy*, pp. 147 ff.

107. "Revelation," ERE, X, 745 ff.

108. *Ibid.*, p. 746. On *wahj* (revelation) in Islam, see Andrae, *Die Person Muhammeds*, pp. 179 ff.

109. Wenger, "The Problem of Truth in Religion," in Payne, ed., *Studies in History and Religion Presented to H. Wheeler Robinson*, pp. 159 ff.

110. Hartshorne, *Reality*, p. 165.

111. Ferré, *Christian Understanding*, p. 167.

112. Wenger, "The Problem of Truth in Religion," in Payne, ed., *Studies in History and Religion Presented to H. Wheeler Robinson*, p. 167.

113. Scheler, *Vom Ewigen im Menschen*.

114. Wach, "Inkarnation," RGG, III, 267 f.

115. Mozley, "The Incarnation," in Selwyn, ed., *Essays Catholic and Critical*. Hartshorne and Reese, *Philosophers*, p. 37, interpret Incarnation as an "implicit expression of divine passivity and passion."

116. Schroeder, *Introduction to the Pancaratra*, pp. 35 ff., 152.

117. A brief summary on Pillai Lokacarya's Five Articles appears in Otto, *Vishnu Narayana*, p. 105.

118. Bhandarkar, *Collected Works*, IV, 74 ff. For the Buddhist trikaya doctrine see Wach, *Types of Experience*, Chap. VI.

119. As yet we are not concerned with *conceptualization* but rather with *apprehensions*. The former will be discussed in Chap. III.

120. For a Catholic statement echoing Otto, see Mouroux, "Sur la notion de L'expérience religieuse," *Recherches de sciences religieuses*, XXXIV (1947), 20 f.: "Un dieu 'clair' ne peut être qu'une idée, et donc un néant."

121. Marett, *Threshold of Religion*, pp. 183 ff.

122. Smith, ed., *African Ideas of God*, pp. 17, 21; Parrinder, *African Traditional Religion*, p. 21; Griaule, *Dieu d'eau*, Preface; Deschamps, *Les religions de l'Afrique noire*, pp. 5 ff.

123. Gaster, "The Religion of the Canaanites," in Ferm, ed., *Forgotten Religions*, pp. 120 f.

124. Söderblom, "Die Gottheit als Wille," *Das Werden des Gottesglaubens*, Chap. VIII.

125. Thornton, "The Christian Concept of God," in Selwyn, ed., *Essays Catholic and Critical*, p. 123.

126. Ferré, *Christian Understanding*, pp. 16 ff.

127. "It appears to us that the religious founders were trying to express not the absence of succession and of effect in deity but the transcendental or categorically supreme form of these." Hartshorne and Reese, *Philosophers*, p. 36. Not only succession and effect but other "attributes" may be interpreted this way.

128. Otto, *Idea of the Holy*, pp. 120 ff.

129. Tillich, *Systematic Theology*, I, p. 212.

130. Wilder, *Eschatology and Ethics in the Teachings of Jesus*, p. 137.

131. *Ibid.*, p. 141.

132. Gaster, "The Religion of the Canaanites," in Ferm, ed., *Forgotten Religions*, pp. 119 ff., distinguishes "el" (innate power) and "baal" (energy) as two types of concept.

133. See the discussion of Al Ghazzali's notion of divine power in Hartshorne and Reese, *Philosophers*, pp. 107 f. See the discussion of the *ilapiygat*, the great theses on the deity, "l'essentiel de la théologie musulmane," in Gardet and Anatawi, *Introduction*, p. 329.

134. Farnell, *Attributes of God*, p. 11; Chaps. VII–IX, on "power."

135. See Ohm, *Die Liebe zu Gott in den nichtchristlichen Religionen*.

136. See Hartshorne, *Reality*, esp. Chap. VII, p. 130.

137. Tillich, *Systematic Theology*, I, 238.

138. Temple, *Nature, Man and God*, pp. 324 ff.

139. *Ibid.*, p. 347. Cf. reference to Ferré's statement above.

140. See Wach, "General Revelations and Religions of the World," JBR, XXII (1954), 83 ff.

141. Richardson, *Christian Apologetics*, p. 129.

142. Farnell, *Attributes of God*, p. 19, agrees with Fowler's demonstration of the superiority of the old Roman religious temperament as compared with that of the Greek, "in respect to awe, reverence, etc." Pp. 186 f., especially 188.

143. Marett, *Threshold of Religion*, p. 20.

144. "In an article published in *Folklore* in the year 1900, he [Marett] analyzed, with psychological knowledge and skill, the experiences that underlay animism, and came to the conclusion that behind the logic was emotion, the *recoil from the uncanny and the mysterious,* 'that basic feeling of awe which drives a man, ere he can think or theorize upon it, into personal relations with the supernatural.'" Hartland, *Ritual and Belief, Studies in the History of Religion*, p. xii.

145. Marett, *Threshold of Religion*, pp. 186, 187. See Otto, *Idea of the Holy*, Chaps. IV–VI, esp. p. 55; Mouroux, "Sur la notion de l'expérience religieuse," *Recherches de sciences religieuses*, XXXIV (1947), pp. 9 f., discusses the Holy as an object of (1) adoration, (2) love (both qualified by the fact of sin).

146. Thornton, "The Christian Concept of God," in Selwyn, ed., *Essays Catholic and Critical*, p. 126.

147. Scholem, *Major Trends in Jewish Mysticism*, esp. Lecture VII.

148. Goldziher, *Die Richtungen der islamischen Koranauslegung*, pp. 211 ff.

149. Schroeder, *Introduction to the Pancaratra*, pp. 32 f. on the six gunas; Glasenapp, *Madhvas Philosophie des Vishnuglaubens*, p. 33.

150. Farnell, *Attributes of God*, pp. 177 ff. See *ibid.*, on the prevalence of the merciful aspect in Greek religion. See also Farnell, *Greece and Babylon*, p. 145.

151. For the dual notions of judgment and grace, majesty and beauty, see below, Chap. III.

152. That is, bhakti-devotion, Amida Buddhism, and Pietism. For the latter, see McNeill, *Modern Christian Movements*, Chap. II.

153. Some Christian religious thinkers, such as Meland and Ferré, refuse to recognize the legitimacy of this aspect and stress, along with the immanence, the tenderness of God. See Ferré, *Christian Understanding*, Chap. V. Also, Hartshorne's criticism of Islamic theology:

Philosophers, pp. 106 ff., esp. pp. 110, 111; and his comment on Whitehead, *ibid.*, pp. 273 ff.

154. "The attempt of some theologians to disparage the cognitive bearing of faith becomes a pretense that can scarcely be distinguished from nonsense," Cotton, *Christian Knowledge*, p. 103. See Baillie, *Our Knowledge of God*, Chap. III, pp. 143, 166 ff., 181, 207; and also Mouroux, "Sur la notion de l'expérience religieuse," *Recherches de sciences religieuses*, XXXIV (1947), pp. 18 f. See also Ferré, *Christian Understanding*, pp. 3 ff.

155. Moses, *Religious Truth and the Relation between Religions*, p. 17.

156. Datta, *Six Ways of Knowledge*.

157. Gardet and Anawati, *Introduction*, pp. 46 f., 304, 309, 330 ff., 347 ff., 372.

158. See the use of this term by Hartshorne, *Reality*, pp. 69 ff.

159. Mouroux, "Sur la notion de l'expérience religieuse," *Recherches de sciences religieuses*, XXXIV (1947), 14, 20. "L'expérience est toujours quelque chose d'éprouvé et de vécu." "L'expérience religieuse est la conscience de cette réponse à l'appel . . . la conscience de l'unification de l'être."

160. In *Philosophers Speak of God*, Hartshorne states that the idea of God, "the supremely excellent or all-worshipful being, first reaches vivid consciousness in an emotional and practical, not in an explicitly logical or analytic form," and that this preanalytic form is not practically simple. But "the dearth of logical technique is partly compensated for by a richness of insight into the fundamental experience from which alone a meaningful idea of God can be derived" (p. 1).

161. See the interesting analysis of Aldrich, "The High and the Holy," *Journal of Religion*, XXXIV (1954), 106 ff.

162. Otto, *Idea of the Holy*, p. 7: "We count this the very mark and criterion of a religion's high rank and superior value, that it should have no lack of *conceptions* about God." See pp. 60 f., 146. He emphasizes the difference between *knowing* and understanding conceptually on p. 139.

163. The roots of Indian philosophical and theological thought are shown to lie in magic by Schomerus, *Der Caiva-Siddhanta*, p. 18.

164. See Mauss, "Esquisse d'une théorie générale de la magie,"

Sociologie et Anthropologie, pp. 1 ff., defines as "magic" all rites which are not part of an organized cult, that is, "private, secret, mysterious. . . ." He rightly points out that magic is not divided into different forms, as religion is with its "autonomous" institutions, sacrifice, and priesthood, p. 81. For a survey, see Webster, *Magic: A Sociological Study;* also, Martino, *Mondo Magico*.

165. Weizsäcker, *The History of Nature,* Introduction, and p. 190.

166. See also Schubart, "Verschlingungstrieb und Magie," in Seifert, ed., *Religion und Eros*.

167. See the excellent article by Earle, "The 'Standard Observer' in the Sciences of Man," *Ethics,* LXIII (1953), 293 ff. The "anyone" is contrasted here with the wise man, the lover, the poet, as the "observer." "To understand the meaning of each requires more than the registration of sense data" (p. 296).

168. Mauss points out the similarities between the magician and the scientist. "Esquisse d'une théorie générale de la magie," *Sociologie et Anthropologie,* p. 69.

169. Marett, *Threshold of Religion,* Chap. VII.

170. *Ibid.,* p. 201.

171. Jaeger, *Theology of the Early Greek Philosophers,* p. 98.

172. See Söderblom, "Holiness," ERE, VI (1914), 731 ff.

173. Marett, *Threshold of Religion,* p. 193.

174. Caillois, *L'Homme et le sacré*.

175. See Söderblom, *Das Werden des Gottesglaubens,* Chap. III. For a criticism, see Radin, *Die religiöse Erfahrung der Naturvölker,* Chap. I; Marett, "The Concept of Mana," *Transactions of the Third International Congress of History of Religions,* pp. 46 ff.

176. Farnell, *Attributes of God,* pp. 186 f.

177. Eliade, *Traité,* pp. 15, 24 ff. The same in *Le Mythe de l'éternel retour*.

178. Again, Eliade, *Traité,* p. 16: "C'est toujours dans une certaine situation historique que le sacré se manifeste."

179. For an interesting example of the difference in the religious attitudes, notions, and practices within one area caused by physical conditions, See Oppenheim, "Assyro-Babylonian Religion," Ferm, ed., *Forgotten Religions,* pp. 67 f. (dichotomy of southern and northern Mesopotamia; security and uncertainty; reliable and unpredictable deity).

180. Underhill, *Worship*, Chap. II.
181. Filiozat, *Magie et médicine*.
182. See Jacobi, *The Psychology of C. G. Jung*.
183. Weizsäcker, *Autobiographie*.
184. Roberts, *Psychotherapy and a Christian View of Man*. Also, Allport, "Psychology, Psychiatry and Religion," *Andover-Newton Bulletin*, XLIV (1952).
185. Hiltner, "Psychotherapy and Christian Ethics"; *Self-Understanding*.
186. Hügel, *Eternal Life*, p. 332.
187. Pittenger, *Sacraments, Signs and Symbols;* Watts, *Behold the Spirit;* Schubart, "Verschlingungstrieb und Magie," in Seifert, ed., *Religion und Eros*.
188. Watts, *Behold the Spirit*. See also Johnson, ed., *Religious Symbolism*, esp. Chaps. III, IX, XI.
189. Webb, *The Historical Element in Religion*, p. 27.
190. Wach, "Comparative Study of Religion," in Schilpp, ed., *The Philosophy of Sarvepalli Radhakrishnan*, pp. 443 ff., 452.
191. Wenger, "The Problem of Truth or Religion," in Payne, ed., *Studies in History and Religion Presented to H. Wheler Robinson;* Moses, *Religious Truth and the Relation between Religions*.
192. Moses, *Religious Truth and the Relation between Religions*, Chap. X.

NOTES TO CHAPTER III

1. Green, *Personal Record: 1929–1939*, p. 80.
2. Webb, *Transactions of Third Congress of History of Religions*, II, 416.
3. Eliade, *Traité d'histoire des religions*, p. 17: "Les grandes expériences ne se resemblent pas seulement par leur contenu, mais souvent aussi par leur expression."
4. Tiele, *Einleitung in die Religionswissenschaft*, I, 259.
5. See the symposium on "Are Religious Dogmas Cognitive and Meaningful?" *Journal of Philosophy*, LI (March, 1954), 145, esp. the statements of Aldrich, pp. 145 f.
6. Gelb, *A Study of Writing*, p. 1.
7. Otto, *The Idea of the Holy*, Chap. IX.
8. W. E. Hocking, *Living Religions and a World Faith*, p. 39.

9. See Otto, *Idea of the Holy,* Chap. III.
10. W. E. Hocking, *Living Religions,* p. 40.
11. Following Proclus, Creuzer, in his *Symbolik und Mythologie der alten Völker,* distinguishes veiled and unveiled expression. The former (*endeixis*) uses symbols, myths, and images. Pp. 22 ff.
12. See Otto on "indirect means of expression," *Idea of the Holy,* pp. 64 ff., 67.
13. For Zen Buddhism, which stresses the non-verbal expression, see the publications of Suzuki, such as *Essays in Zen Buddhism,* Essay VI.
14. Hartshorne and Reese, *Philosophers Speak of God,* p. 1.
15. On the concrete and "syncretic" character of primitive thought, see Werner, *Comparative Psychology of Mental Development,* pp. 213 ff., 267 ff. There are some fine remarks on the meaning of religious expression in Aldrich, "The High and the Holy," *Journal of Religion,* XXXIV (1954), 106 ff., 109.
16. See the discussions in India on the *Sabda-Pramana,* Datta, *The Six Ways of Knowledge,* pp. 256 ff.
17. Harrison, *Ancient Art and Ritual,* p. 35.
18. Daniélou, "The Problem of Symbolism," *Thought,* XXV (1950), 423; Eliade, *Images et symboles;* Machle, "Symbols in Religion," JBR, XXI (1953), 163 ff.; Fremgen, *Offenbarung und Symbol;* E. W. Smith, "African Symbolism," JRAI, LXXXII (1952), 13 ff.; Johnson, ed., *Religious Symbolism.*
19. Urban, *Language and Reality,* p. 580.
20. Underhill, *Worship,* p. 29. E. W. Smith, "African Symbolism," JRAI, LXXXII (1952), 13, quotes Monod's excellent, brief definition of the symbol as "signe visible d'une réalité invisible."
21. Bevan, *Symbolism and Belief,* p. 29.
22. Langer, *Philosophy in a New Key.*
23. Ewer, *A Survey of Mystical Symbolism.*
24. Kay, *The Nature of Christian Worship,* pp. 73, 76.
25. Quick, *The Christian Sacrament,* Chap. I. See below, Chap. IV.
26. Pittenger, *Sacraments, Signs and Symbols,* p. 9. See Johnson, ed., *Religious Symbolism,* a series of fourteen essays.
27. Lubac, "Note sur le symbolisme comparé de l'art bouddhique et de l'art chrétien primitif," *Aspects du Bouddhism,* pp. 80 ff.;

Fleming, "Religious Symbols Crossing Cultural Boundaries," in Johnson, ed., *Religious Symbolism*, Chap. V.

28. Eliade, *Traité d'histoire des religions*, p. 22. See also Chaps. I, XIII.

29. Oppenheim, in "Assyro-Babylonian Religion," in Ferm, ed., *Forgotten Religions*, p. 72, distinguishes two types of symbols: (1) natural (plants); (2) man-made (weapons).

30. Hartshorne, *Reality as Social Process*.

31. Webb, *God and Personality*, p. 264.

32. Whitehead, *Religion in the Making*, p. 131.

33. On the psychological unity and indivisibility of emotion and reason, affection and cognition—and hence of the different fields of expression—see Allport, *The Individual and His Religion*, pp. 16 ff.

34. Hügel, *Essays and Addresses on the Philosophy of Religion*, p. 3. See "Man as an Amphibian," in Pittenger, *Sacraments, Signs and Symbols*, Chap. II.

35. See the end of this chapter.

36. Otto, *Idea of the Holy*, p. 67, speaks of the spell exercised by the "only half intelligible or wholly unintelligible language of devotion," instancing it with "ancient traditional expressions."

37. See Gruppe, *Die griechischen Culte und Mythen;* also *Geschichte der Klassischen Mythologie und Religiongeschichte*. For the earlier history of the concept of myth, see Hartlich and Sachs, *Der Ursprung des Mythosbegriffes in der modernen Bibelwissenschaft*, especially on Heyne's and on De Wette's roles. See also Steinthal, "Allgemeine Einleitung in die Mythologie," AR, III (1900), 249 ff.

38. For the controversy on the concept of myth of Bultmann and his followers, see Bartsch, ed., "Kerygma und Mythus," in *Theologische Forschung;* Dinkler, "Existentialist Interpretation of the New Testament," *Journal of Religion*, XXXII (No. 2, 1952), 90 ff.; and Wilder, "Biblical Hermeneutic and American Scholarship," in *Neutestamentliche Studien für Rudolf Bultmann*, pp. 24 ff.

39. Leeuw, "Die Bedeutung des Mythus," *Festschrift für Alfred Bertholet*, pp. 287 ff.

40. Steinthal, "Allgemeine Einleitung in die Mythologie," AR, III (1900), 249 ff., 297 ff. See Wach, *Das Verstehen*, III, Chap. III, devoted entirely to Steinthal.

41. See in addition to the series of volumes of the *Mythology of All Races,* Krappe, *Mythologie universelle.*

42. Urban, *Language and Reality,* p. 588.   43. *Ibid.,* p. 593.

44. Malinowski, *Magic, Science and Religion,* pp. 122, 86.

45. Langer, *Philosophy,* p. 143.

46. Griaule, "La Connaissance de l'homme noire," in *La Connaissance de l'homme au XXe siècle;* Dieterlen, *Essai sur la religion Bambara:* "les mythes une sophie," p. 1. See also E. W. Smith, "African Symbolism," JRAI, LXXXII (1952), 30: "African mythology expresses speculative thought in symbolical guise."

47. Malinowski, *Magic,* p. 78.   48. Langer, *Philosophy,* p. 143.

49. Jaeger, *The Theology of the Early Greek Philosophers,* pp. 173 f.

50. This view of Cassirer's has influenced many scholars in various fields. For an interpretation of the structure of thought in primitive man, see Werner, *Comparative Psychology,* Chap. X. This is "concrete," "affective," "syncretistic," and "diffuse" (in terms of "undivided totalities"). The sun as a personified being in myth: p. 300; on mythical space: pp. 169 ff.; and on time: pp. 182 ff.

51. Jacobi, *The Psychology of C. G. Jung.* See also an unpublished Ph.D. thesis of the University of Chicago by Thomas Altizer.

52. Eliade, *Le Mythe de l'éternel retour.*

53. Mowinckel, *Religion und Kultus;* Hooke, *Myth and Ritual;* Spence, *Myth and Ritual in Dance, Game and Rhyme;* Gaster, *Thespis.* Also, *Proceedings of the Seventh International Congress of the History of Religions.*

54. Urban, *Language,* p. 589.

55. Campbell, *The Hero with a Thousand Faces,* offers a comparative study of the adventure and the transformations of the hero in the myths of many races.

56. Toy, *Introduction to the History of Religions,* and Hooke, *Babylonian and Assyrian Religion,* pp. 63 ff., offer different typologies (myths of origin, of organization, and of evaluation).

57. "Die Mythologie ist, wenn sie tot ist, von einer schrecklichen Hartnäckigkeit." Ortega y Gasset in *Offener Horizont,* p. 76. See also Johnson, ed., *Religious Symbolism,* pp. 159 ff.

58. Redfield discusses the growth and systematization of reflection

and critical thought in primitive societies, in *The Primitive World and Its Transformations*, pp. 115 ff.

59. The beginning of doctrine may be seen in the brief philosophical summaries such as the *Sutras* of Badarayana in Brahmanism or the *Mulamadhyamika Karikas* of Nagarjuna in Mahayana Buddhism.

60. I do not think that Jaeger is right when he says in his *Theology*, p. 4: "Theology is a mental attitude which is characteristically Greek, and has something to do with the great importance which the Greek thinkers attribute to the *logos*, for the word *theologia* means the approach to God or the gods by means of the *logos*. To the Greeks God became a problem." Very similar things could be said of the Hindu thinkers to whom God also "became a problem." See also p. 62: "Sects, dogmas, and theology, indeed, are definite products of the Greek mind."

61. In Vaishnavism the transition from the Alvars to the Acaryas marks the development of doctrine proper, according to Otto, *Vishnu Narayana*, pp. 59 ff. Similarly, in Shaivism the rise of the trika teachers in Kashmir, and in the south, a work like the *Saiva-Siddhanta* (Schomerus, *Der Çaiva-Siddhanta*, and Paranjoti, *Saiva Siddhanta* [London: Luzac, 1938], or the *Siva-hānabodham: A Manual of Saiva Religious Doctrine*). This thirteenth-century treatise is interpreted by Shiva Jnana yogi in the eighteenth century, *ibid.*, pp. 30 ff.

62. "But a *theologian* is, by definition, a person who accepts as positive reality the *symbols* by which a religious experience of whatever kind has expressed itself," Gibb, *La Structure de la pensée religieuse de l'Islam*, p. 41.

63. W. E. Hocking, *Living Religions*, pp. 94 ff.

64. *Ibid.*, p. 168.

65. Alan Richardson, *Christian Apologetics*, p. 125.

66. Ferré, *The Christian Understanding of God*, p. 7.

67. Dilthey, "Das Wesen der Philosophie," in *Gesammelte Shriften*, V, 339–417; *Offener Horizont, Festschrift für Karl Jaspers*, p. 74.

68. Hartshorne, *Reality*, pp. 163, 164.

69. Jaeger, *Theology*, pp. 55, 56.

70. *Ibid.*, p. 56. In all thought, according to Ortega y Gasset, (*Offener Horizont*, p. 75), a depth dimension (often unconscious

basic traditions), a ground level, consisting of conscious principles, and an adversary thought which differs, are present.

71. Poussin, *Transactions of the Third International Congress of the History of Religions, 1908*, II, 32. See also his *Bouddhisme*, pp. 8 ff., 54 ff.

72. See also Beckh, *Der Buddhismus*, pp. 22 ff. Keith, *Buddhist Philosophy*, p. 34, stresses faith as "an indispensable preliminary," and "the root of correct knowledge."

73. Poussin, *Transactions of the Third International Congress of the History of Religions, 1908*, II, 35 f. Also, Organ, "Reason and Experience in Mahayana Buddhism," JBR, XX (1952), 77 ff.

74. For the Buddha's enlightenment as complete intuition, see Keith, *Buddhist Philosophy*, p. 39.

75. Poussin, *Transactions of the Third International Congress of the History of Religions, 1908*, II, 43; *Bouddhisme*, pp. 130 f.

76. Farnell, *The Attributes of God*, p. 6.

77. Gardet and Anawati, *Introduction à la théologie musulmane*. See above, notes to Chap. II, p. 159.

78. See Schacht, "Taklid," EI, IV, 563 ff.

79. Sweetman, in his *Islam and Christian Theology*, pp. 72 ff., has confronted the teachings of the two religions on seven major topics of doctrine. For the relation between rational (*agli*) and traditional (*sam i*) argument, see Gardet and Anatawi, *Introduction*, p. 351.

80. Gardet and Anatawi, *Introduction*, pp. 309, 347, 372.

81. Nyberg, "Al-Mu'tazila," EI, III, 787–93.

82. *Ibid.*, p. 86.

83. See the statement of Randall, "Symposium," *Journal of Philosophy*, II (No. 5, 1954), 159, to the effect that the religious function of religious doctrines is one to which any cognitive claim is irrelevant. This function, he says, is "not to furnish knowledge but to strengthen religious faith." They serve as "instruments of unification" (p. 162).

84. Puech, *Le Manichéisme*, p. 62: "[revelation] C'est une science absolue, totale et directe, une explication intégrale et évidente de toutes choses."

85. Harnack, *Die Entstehung der Christlichen Theologie und des Kirchlichen Dogmas*.

86. Zaehner, "Dogma," *Hibbert Journal*, III (No. 7, 1954), 9 ff.:

"Dogmas, then, are nothing less than the presuppositions on which a member of any given religion bases his life" (p. 18). This article is critical of all dogma.

87. Nielson, in *Oral Tradition,* discusses the role of oral tradition in the Near East and in the Old Testament and illustrates the method of the traditional historical school (Engnell). For India, see Renou and Filiozat, *L'Inde classique,* p. 515.

88. See Bertholet, "Die Macht der Schrift in Glauben und Aberglauben," *Abhandlung der Deutschen Akademie der Wissenschaften.*

89. Ballou, ed., *The Bible of the World;* Martin, *Seven Great Bibles;* Braden, *The Scriptures of Mankind;* Leipoldt and Morenz, *Heilige Schriften;* Bouquet, *Sacred Books of the World.*

90. Leipoldt and Morenz, *Heilige Schriften,* Chaps. VIII–XII, discuss secrecy surrounding sacred writings, their use in the home, their interpretation and magical use in the ancient Mediterranean world.

91. To the Vedanta-Sutra of Bedarayana alone, no less than thirty *bhasyas* have been found. Schomerus, *Caiva-Siddhanta,* p. 6.

92. Dobschütz, "Interpretation," ERE, VII, 390; Grant, *The Bible in the Church.* See also: Bertholet, "Über kultische Motivverschiebungen," SBPAW, XVIII (1938), 22; Grant *et al,* "History of the Interpretation of the Bible," *The Interpreter's Bible,* I, 106 ff., 115 ff., 127 ff.

93. Goldziher, *Die Richtungen der islamischen Koranauslegung;* p. 84 for the *fecunditas sensus.* Also, on exegesis and *kalam* see Gardet and Anatawi, *Introduction,* pp. 394 ff. (types of meaning of words in proper [*haqiqa*] and metaphorical [*majaz*] sense).

94. See Dilthey, "Die Entstehung der Hermeneutik," *Gesammelte Schriften,* V (1924), 317 ff.

95. Goldziher, *Vorlesungen über den Islam,* Chap. II.

96. On the shahada, see Wensinck, *The Muslim Creed,* Chap. II, tracing the antecedents in the traditions (*hadith*), esp. pp. 23 f., 27 f., 32 f., and stressing the *personal* form ("I believe . . ."), p. 102.

97. Temple, "Revelation," in Baillie, ed., *Revelation,* p. 91.

98. Schaff, *The Creeds of Christendom.*

99. Jaeger, *Theology,* p. 91.

100. Neumann, "Judaism," in Jurji, ed., *The Great Religions of the Modern World,* pp. 224 ff.

101. Modi, *The Religious Ceremonies and Customs of the Parsees*, pp. 182 ff.

102. Wensinck, *The Muslim Creed*. See Gardet and Anawati, *Introduction*, pp. 137 ff., 180.

103. MacDonald, *Development of Muslim Theology, Jurisprudence and Constitutional Theory*, Chap. III.

104. Elder (trans.), *A Commentary on the Creed of Islam*.

105. Hügel, *The Mystical Element in Religion*, p. 71.

106. *Ibid.*, p. 65.

107. For the sociological implications of the "protest," see Wach, *Sociology of Religion*, Chap. V.

108. Tillich, *Systematic Theology*, I, 60.

109. In his study, *Die Absolutheit des Christentums*, p. 79, Troeltsch enumerates four central topics: God, the world, the soul, and the higher life.

110. See Raven, *Natural Religion and Christian Theology*, II, Chap. I.

111. E. O. James, *The Concept of Deity*. See also Cotton, *Christian Knowledge of God*; Ferré, *Christian Understanding*; Bhattacharyya, *The Foundations of Living Faiths*.

112. Tillich, *Systematic Theology*, I, 220.   113. *Ibid.*, p. 239.

114. Hartshorne and Reese, *Philosophers*, Preface.

115. *Ibid.*, pp. 15 ff., on the five questions asked: is God eternal? is He temporal? is He conscious? does He know? and does He include the world?

116. Thornton, "The Christian Concept of God," in Selwyn, ed., *Essays Critical and Catholic*.

117. Webb, *God and Personality*, I, 139.

118. Tillich, *Systematic Theology*, I, 212.

119. Jaeger, *Theology*, p. 72.

120. "One of the most striking features of Mesopotamian religion is the enormous number of gods whose names have been preserved in the various religious texts." Hooke, *Babylonian and Assyrian Religion*, p. 23.

121. Usener, *Götternamen*; Cassirer, *Language and Myth*; Farnell, *The Attributes of God*, Chap. III.

122. Monier-Williams, *Hinduism*, p. 168.

123. Tillich, *Systematic Theology*, I, 222.

124. Lamotte, *Le Traité de la grande vertu de la Sagesse de Nagarjuna*, I, 142: "Le triple monde est peuplé par dieux."

125. Cassirer, *Language and Myth*, p. 73.

126. Söderblom, *Das Werden des Gottesglaubens*, Chap. IV; Marot, "Der primitive 'Hochgott,'" *Actes du Ve congrès international d'histoire des religions*, 1929, p. 87; Bidney, "The Ethnology of Religion and the Problem of Human Evolution," AA 56 (1954), 1 ff.

127. Widengren, *Hochgottglaube im alten Iran*. He ties together the notions of a high god, of his identification with celestial bodies or the sky and with destiny. See also Eliade, *Traité*, Chap. II.

128. See Duchesne-Guillemin, *Ormazd et Ahriman*.

129. Duchesne-Guillemin, "Zoroastre," in Dumézil, ed., *Les Dieux et les hommes*, II, 148 ff., 150.

130. Hodgson, *The Doctrine of the Trinity*, p. 102. See also Ferré, *Christian Understanding*, pp. 64 ff. See Söderblom, "The Place of the Christian Trinity and the Buddhist Tiratna among Holy Triads," *Transactions of the Third International Congress of the History of Religions, 1908*, II, 391 ff. See also Lamotte, *Traité de Sagesse*, I, 140.

131. Hodgson, *Doctrine of the Trinity*, p. 132.

132. Tillich, *Systematic Theology*, I, 228.

133. Temple, *Nature, Man and God*, pp. 259 ff., 305, 319, 321.

134. On the term, "to theion" in early Greek speculation, see Jaeger, *Theology*, p. 203, n. 44. Eliade (*Traité*, p. 32) opposes the interpretation of *mana* as a "universal" impersonal force.

135. Schebesta, "Das Problem des Urmonotheismus," in *Anthropos*, XLIX (1954), 689 ff.

136. Buber, *I and Thou*.

137. Webb, *God and Personality*, pp. 80 ff.

138. Temple, *Nature, Man and God*, p. 54.

139. *Ibid.*, p. 312: the excuse on Whitehead.

140. Tillich, *Systematic Theology*, I, 245. See also Ferré, *Christian Understanding*, Chaps. II, III.

141. Webb, *God and Personality*, pp. 249 ff.

142. Otto, *Vishnu Narayana*; Schomerus, *Caiva-Siddhānta*, pp. 62 ff.; On *ekagrata*: Otto, *Die Gnadenreligion Indiens und das Christentum*, pp. 30 ff.

143. Webb, *God and Personality*, p. 79.   144. *Ibid.*, p. 81.

145. Farnell, *Attributes*, pp. 116 f., stresses the nearness of the deity who worked and moved in nature.

146. Schomerus, *Caiva-Siddhānta*, pp. 67 ff., 74 ff. On the five Shaktis: Paranjoti, *Saiva Siddhānta*, pp. 89 ff.

147. See Poussin, "Bodhisattva," in ERE, II (1910), 738 ff.; Lamotte, *Traité de Sagesse*, I, 241 ff. Definition of the *bodhisattva:* Wach, *Types of Religious Experience*, pp. 114 ff.; Dayal, *The Bodhisattva Doctrine in Buddhist Sanskrit Literature*.

148. W. E. Hocking, *Living Religions*, p. 110.

149. Allport, *Individual*, pp. 1 ff.

150. Hartshorne, *Reality*, pp. 148 ff. See also Brightman, *The Problem of God;* and *A Philosophy of Religion*, pp. 301 ff.

151. Redfield, making use of the English equivalent of the German term *Weltanschauung*, suggests a thorough investigation of "world views," defined as "the way a people characteristically look outward upon the universe." *Primitive World*, Chap. IV, p. 85.

152. On the relation of God to the world, see the contributions of the school of Whitehead which tends to stress the notion that the deity needs a world. Hartshorne, *Reality*, pp. 148 ff., trying to establish the superiority of "God-with-the-world" to "God-alone," as the concrete is superior to the "abstract." Creation, in Whitehead's view, is not a "condescension" of deity but his "very life" (p. 204). See Hartshorne and Reese, *Philosophers*, Introduction. See also, Ferré, *Christian Understanding*, pp. 59 ff., for an analysis of the status of relations in Christian thought.

153. See the extremely complex and highly systematic cosmology of the Sudanese Dogon and Bambara which the expeditions of Griaule have helped to explore, in *Dieu d'eau*. Also, Dieterlen, *Essai sur la religion Bambara*.

154. See Milne, *Modern Cosmology and the Christian Idea of God*. Also, Burtt, *Types of Religious Philosophy*, Chap. XIV.

155. For the Shaiva Siddhantin, Shiva is the fire, the boiling water is the universe. Shiva exists in the fire invisibly. Schomerus, *Caiva-Siddhānta*, p. 83.

156. Linton, *Ethnology of Polynesia and Micronesia*, pp. 171 ff.

157. Saussure, "La cosmologie religieuse en Chine, dans l'Inde

NOTES TO III: EXPRESSION IN THOUGHT

et chez les prophètes hébreux," *Actes du Congrès International d'Histoire des Religions*, II (1923), 77.

158. Maspero, *Les Religions chinoises*, pp. 179 ff.

159. Kraemer, "Sumerian Religion," in Ferm, ed., *Forgotten Religions*, pp. 56 f.

160. Frazer, *Creation and Evolution in Primitive Cosmogonies*. Also, Farnell, *Greece and Babylon*, pp. 179 ff.

161. See the description of the cosmic awakening of the Shakti of Vishnu to a first, pure creation according to the Ahirbudhnyd samhita: Schroeder, "Pancaratra," pp. 29 ff., in *A Descriptive Catalogue of the Sanskrit Manuscripts in the Adyar Library*, I (Madras, The Oriental Publishing Co., Ltd., 1908).

162. Matthews, trans., *Shiva-jnana-bodham*, I, 7.

163. Keith, *Buddhist Philosophy*, p. 73. On the world systems composing the universe in Buddhism, pp. 92 ff.

164. Otto, *Vishnu Nārāyana*, pp. 102, 105 ff.

165. See *Sociology of Religion*, Chap. III.

166. See Eliade, "Shamanism," in Ferm, ed., *Forgotten Religions*, pp. 299 ff., on the structure of the cosmos, the *axis mundi*, etc.

167. Jaeger, *Theology*, p. 116.

168. Groot, *Universismus*, Chaps. I, II.

169. See also Werner, *Comparative Psychology*, p. 311.

170. "Les analogies de la création chez Çankara et chez Proclus," *Revue Philosophique* (1953), pp. 329 ff.

171. Otto, *Die Gnadenreligion*, pp. 29, 52, 53.

172. Leeuw, "Die Bedeutung des Mythus," in *Festschrift für Alfred Bertholet*, pp. 290 ff.

173. Richard Hocking, "Some Types of Historical Consciousness in Chinese and Indian Thoughts," *Papers of the Ecumenical Institute*, V (1949), 19 ff.

174. See Jedin, "Kirchengeschichte als Heilsgeschichte," *Saeculum*, V, 2 (1954), 119 f.

175. Even Jaspers speaks of "Christus die Achse der Geschichte," *Vom Ursprung und Ziel der Geschichte*, pp. 8 ff. See p. 212 on faith.

176. Daniélou, "Saint Irénée et les origines de la théologie de l'histoire," *Recherches de sciences religieuses*, XXXIV (1947), 227 ff.; Puech, "Temps, histoire et mythe dans le christianisme des premières

siècles," *Proceedings of the Seventh Congress for the History of Religions*, pp. 33 ff.

177. For the Christian notion of history, see Troeltsch, *Der Historismus und seine Überwindung;* Bernheim, *Lehrbuch der historischen Methode;* Toynbee, *A Study of History,* esp. Vol. VII; Nichols, "Religion in Toynbee's History," *Church History,* XXVII (1948), 99 ff.; Zahn, *Toynbee und der Problem der Geschichte,* pp. 36 ff.; Reinhold Niebuhr, *Faith and History;* Löwith, *Meaning in History;* Daniélou, *The Salvation of the Nations,* Chap. V; Butterfield, *Christianity and History;* Nichols, "Church History and Secular History," *Church History,* XIII (1944), 87 ff.

178. According to Otto, *Die Gnadenreligion,* p. 63, we owe to Christianity the "rationality" of history.

179. Eliade, *Le Mythe.*   180. *Ibid.,* pp. 163, 237.

181. *Ibid.,* pp. 136, 228.

182. *Ibid.,* Chap. IV. Eliade points out that only small "élites" are *conscious* of the situation, that is, feel the "terror of history."

183. The anti-intellectualism of Nietzsche, Bergson, Sorel, Pareto, Klages, Freud, and Jung, and even of Van der Leeuw—a romantic heritage—prepares the way.

184. Eliade, *Le Mythe,* pp. 229 ff.

185. See Randall, *The Making of the Modern Mind;* Brinton, *The Shaping of the Modern Mind.*

186. Whale, *Christian Doctrine,* p. 180.

187. See Wilder, *Eschatology and Ethics in the Teachings of Jesus,* esp. Chap. VI on the universality of speculation about what is to come.

188. *Ibid.,* p. 7.   189. *Ibid.,* p. 8.

190. Whale, *Christian Doctrine,* p. 183.

191. Otto, *Die Gnadenreligion,* pp. 49 ff.

192. Otto, *The Kingdom of God and the Son of Man.*

193. Otto, *Die Gnadenreligion,* p. 54.

194. Wach, *Typen der religiösen Anthropologie.* See *Types of Religious Experience,* Chap. IV.

195. Reinhold Niebuhr, *Nature and Destiny.*

196. Hilliard, *Man in Eastern Religions.* See also McKenzie, *Two Religions,* Chap. V; and Bleeker, ed., *Anthropologie Religieuse.*

NOTES TO III: EXPRESSION IN THOUGHT

197. Ratschow, *Magie und Religion*. See also Schubart, *Religion und Eros*.
198. Dieterlen, *Essai sur la religion bambara*, p. 56.
199. Leenhardt, *Do Kamo*.
200. Elkin, *The Australian Aborigines*, esp. Chap. VIII.
201. Werner, *Comparative Psychology*, Chap. XIII.
202. *Ibid.*, p. 424.
203. See several papers in *Actes du Ve congrès d'histoire des religions*, 1929.
204. Tempels, *Bantu filosofie*; Dieterlen, *Essai sur la religion bambara*; Parrinder, *West African Psychology*.
205. For Chinese notions see Groot, *Universismus*, Chap. II.
206. Bousset, "Die Himmelsreise der Seele," in AR, LV (1901), 45 ff., 97 ff.
207. Eliade, *Le chamanisme et les archaiques techniques de l'extase*. See the Taoist notions in Maspero, *Le Taoisme*, pp. 13 ff., 83 ff.
208. Benedict, "The Concept of the Guardian Spirit in North America," AAA Mem, XXIX (1923).
209. Söderblom, *Les Fravashis*. Duchesne-Guillemin, "L'homme dans la religion Iranienne," in Bleeker, ed., *Anthropologie religieuse*, pp. 93 ff.
210. Das, *A Study of the Vedanta*, Chap. VII.
211. Otto, *Vishnu-Narayana*, pp. 102 ff.
212. Schomerus, *Der Caiva-Siddhanta*, and *Meister Eckhart und Manikka-Vassager*, pp. 32 ff.; Matthews (trans.), *Siva-nana-bodham*; Paranjoti, *Saiva Siddhanta*.
213. Garbe, "Sankhya," ERE, XI, 189 ff.
214. Stevenson, *The Heart of Jainism*, pp. 161 ff.
215. Keith, *Buddhist Philosophy*, Chaps. IV, V, LX, X, XIII, XIV. See Frauwallner, "Die Anthropologie des Buddhismus," in Bleeker, ed., *Anthropologie religieuse*, pp. 120 ff.
216. Keith, *Buddhist Philosophy*, pp. 57, 74 ff. For Pudgalvadins, see pp. 81 ff., 84 ff., in Poussin, *Bouddhisme*, pp. 156 ff.
217. Lamotte, *Traité de Sagesse*, p. 43.
218. Niebuhr, *Nature and Destiny*. See Sevenster, "Die Anthropologie des Neuen Testaments," in Bleeker, ed., *Anthropologie religieuse*, pp. 166 ff.

219. Burtt, *Types of Religious Philosophy*, Chap. XVI. Still the most comprehensive treatment of the Christian doctrine of sin is Julius Müller, *The Christian Doctrine of Sin*. Also, C. Ryder Smith, *The Bible Doctrine of Sin*.

220. See Foss, *The Idea of Perfection in the Western World*.

221. H. B. Alexander, "Sin (American)," in ERE, XI, 528 ff.

222. Carsartelli, "Sin (Iranian)," ERE, XI, 564.

223. Davids, "Sin (Buddhist)," ERE, XI, 533.

224. On the concept of sin in Confucianism, see Soothill, *The Three Religions of China*, Chap. X.

225. On the concept of sin in Babylonia, see Hooke, *Babylonian and Assyrian Religion*, pp. 99 f. On sin in Israel, see Frankfort, *The Intellectual Adventure of Ancient Man*, pp. 268 ff.

226. See the theory of the three *mala* (*paca*): anava, Karma, and maya-mala of the saiva siddhantin in Schomerus, *Der Caiva-Siddhānta*, Part III. There are five "enemies" for the sikh: lust, anger, greed, attachment, pride. See Sikhism in Ferm, ed., *Religion in the Twentieth Century*, p. 198.

227. See the comparative study on "Das mystische Zentralerlebnis Hindernde," in Schomerus, *Meister Eckhart und Mānikka Vasager* pp. 32 ff., 41 ff.

228. This issue caused the great division in Buddhism (Hinayana and Mahayana). See Wach, *Types of Experience*, Chap. VI.

229. Farnell, *Attributes*, pp. 181 ff.

230. For the vivid discussions in Islam, see Goldziher, *Koranauslegung*, pp. 147 ff.

231. Handman, *The Christian Doctrine of Grace*.

232. In modern western philosophy of religion the notion has been expressed that what man does makes a difference to God, so that "we can feel that every moment of our lives contributes a unique quality to the divine experience . . . and the finer the quality the richer the life of God." Hartshorne, *Reality*, p. 151.

233. Hartshorne and Reese, *Philosophers*, p. 234.

234. Schomerus, *Der Caiva-Siddhānta*, Chap. VI.

235. Otto, *Vishnu-Nārāyana*, pp. 109 ff., esp. 122 ff.; and **Gnadenreligion**, p. 34.

236. For Madhva, see Glasenapp, *Madhvas*, pp. 80 ff.

237. Stevenson, *The Heart of Jainism*.
238. Jaeger, *Theology*, p. 88.
239. On the Vadagalai, see Rangachari, *The Sri Vaishnava Brahmans*, pp. 37 ff.
240. Glasenapp, *Madhvas*, pp. 76 ff., 80 ff.
241. Moulton, *The Treasure of the Magi*, p. 39.
242. Schomerus, *Meister Eckhart*, pp. 158 ff.; *Der Caiva-Siddhānta*, pp. 367 ff., 380 ff. Paranjoti, *Saiva Siddhanta*, Chap. VIII.
243. Otto, *Vishnu-Nārāyana*, p. 115.
244. Glasenapp, *Madhvas*, pp. 98 ff., 108 ff.
245. Goldziher, *Koranauslegung*, pp. 102 ff.; Subhan, "The Nature of Summum Bonum in Islam," *Islamic Culture*, XXI (1947), 353 ff.; Schimmel, "Zur Anthropologie des Islams," in Bleeker, ed., *Anthropologie religieuse*, pp. 140 ff.
246. See Hartshorne's exposition in *Reality*, pp. 151, 160.

NOTES TO CHAPTER IV

1. For the twin concepts of "act" and "intention," well known to continental phenomenology (Brentano, Husserl, Scheler, Hartmann), and their significance, see Allport, *The Individual and His Religion*, pp. 125 ff. For Judaism, Heschel, "Symbolism and Jewish Faith," in Johnson, ed., *Religious Symbolism*, pp. 52 ff., stresses the *centrality of the act*. ("The act of studying is more important than the possession of knowledge," pp. 73 f.)
2. Hügel, *Selected Letters*, p. 261.
3. Leeuw, *Religion in Essence and Manifestation*, p. 376.
4. Scheler, *Vom Ewigen in Menschen*. Rightly does Mouroux object to any concept of experience as pure passivity: ". . . disons que l'éprouvé est le fait des *actes* aussi bien que des *états*," *Recherches de sciences religieuses*, XXXIV (1947), p. 14. He defines religious experience as the act by which man feels himself to be in relationship with God (p. 18).
5. Burnouf, *La science des religions*, p. 33.
6. W. E. Hocking, *Living Religions and a World Faith*, p. 46.
7. Will, *Le culte*, I, 407 ff. Similarly, referring to Loisy and Robertson Smith, Radcliffe-Brown, "Religion and Society," JRAI, LXXV (1945/46), 34.
8. Mowinckel, *Religion und Kultus*.

9. Underhill, *Worship*, p. 6. See also Fremgen, *Offenbarung und Symbol*, esp. pp. 25 ff., 253 ff.

10. Will, *Le Culte*, p. 17. See Frobe-Kapteyn, ed., "Mensch und Ritus," in *Eranos Jahrbuch*, XIX (1950). Eliade, *Traité d'histoire des religions;* also *Proceedings of the Seventh Congress for the History of Religions*, 1951.

11. The avowed inadequacy of *all* worship is stressed by Taylor, "Vindication of Religion," in Selwyn, ed., *Essays Catholic and Critical*, pp. 76 f. For Judaism, see the agreement on this point of the two otherwise differing views of Heschel and Kaplan in Johnson, ed., *Religious Symbolism*, Chaps. IV, XII.

12. Underhill, *Worship*, p. 27.

13. Ferré, *The Christian Understanding of God*, pp. 34 f.

14. Will, *Le Culte*, p. 13.

15. Bhandarkar, *Collected Works*, IV, 57 f., 78, on modes of worship; Bhattacharyya, "Religious Practices of the Hindus," *Religion of the Hindus*, Chap. 5; Rangachari, *The Sri Vaishnava Brahmans*, Chap. XIII, esp. pp. 87 ff.

16. Modi, *The Religious Ceremonies and Customs of the Parsees*, pp. 83 ff.

17. For attempts to stress participation and comprehension of the rites within the Roman Church, see the interesting discussion of Koenker, *The Liturgical Renaissance in the Roman Catholic Church*, esp. Chap. IV.

18. Will, *Le Culte*, p. 19.

19. Underhill, *The Life of the Spirit and the Life of Today*, p. 36.

20. Kay, *The Nature of Christian Worship*, p. 16.

21. Underhill, *Worship*, p. 77.

22. Kay, *Christian Worship*, pp. 18, 19.

23. Will, *Le Culte*, II, 95.

24. For trends in public worship in contemporary America, see Schneider, *Religion in Twentieth Century America*, Chap. V.

25. Underhill, *Worship*, p. 23; Wach, *Types of Religious Experience*, p. 45.

26. See Firth, *Elements of Social Organization*, pp. 222 ff., for a modern anthropologist's appraisal of the nature and function of ritual.

27. Heinz Werner, *Comparative Psychology of Mental Development*, p. 402.

28. Eliade, *Traité*, p. 24.

29. Marett, *Sacraments of Simple Folks*.   30. *Ibid.*, p. 18.

31. For the reinterpretation of the motivation of cultic acts, see Bertholet, "Über Kultische Motivverschiebungen," SBPAW, XVIII (1938), 3 ff.

32. Buber, *Die Erzählungen der Chassidim*, p. 647.

33. For recent developments in Roman Catholicism in the other direction, see Koenker, *Liturgical Renaissance*. He makes reference to Moehler's conception of the Church as an "organism created by inner spirit" (p. 35), in contrast with Reinhold's description of the Church as the "well-oiled, precise juggernaut of perfect organization with a propaganda front, a party line and complete absorption of the individual" (p. 37).

34. Pfister, "Kultus," in Kroll, ed., *Pauly-Wissowa Real Encyklopaedie* IX, 2106 ff. See also Leeuw, *Religion in Essence*, and Eliade, *Traité*, esp. Chaps. X and XI.

35. Wissowa, *Religion und Kultus der Römer*, pp. 300 ff.

36. Kramer, "Sumerian Religion," and Oppenheim, "Assyro-Babylonian Religion," both in Ferm, ed., *Forgotten Religions*, pp. 51 f., 73 ff. Hooke, *Babylonian and Assyrian Religion*, p. 26, refers to Ekur, "The House of the Mountain," the famous temple in Nippur whose name became a general designation for a temple. See Chap. IV. On the *ziggurat*, see p. 50.

37. Eliade, *Traité*, Chap. X, and below, note 41.

38. Groot, *Universismus*, Chaps. XII, XIII. See Leeuw, *Religion in Essence*, Sec. 57.

39. Everett Hughes, *Cycles and Turning Points*.

40. Wissowa, *Religion und Kultus*, p. 366. On the Roman Calendar, see Fowler, *The Religious Experience of the Roman People*, Chap. V.

41. Eliade, *Le Mythe de l'éternel retour*.

42. In his study of the Liturgical Movement in the Roman Catholic Church, Koenker says: "For those living the liturgical life, the Church calendar has come to take precedence over the civil calendar; following the Church year is seen as integral to an appreciation of the great religious truths," *Liturgical Renaissance*, p. 58.

43. Leeuw, *Religion in Essence,* p. 56. Oesterley, "Early Hebrew Festival Rituals," in Hooke, ed., *Myth and Ritual,* Chap. VI. For a description of the New Year festival, see Hooke, *Babylonian Religion,* pp. 58 ff., and its ritual, Appendix, pp. 103 ff.

44. Harrison, *Ancient Art and Ritual* and *Prolegomena to the Study of Greek Religion.* See also Oppenheim, "Assyro-Babylonian Religion," and Gaster, "The Religion of the Canaanites," in Ferm, ed., *Forgotten Religions.*

45. Otto, *The Idea of the Holy,* pp. 71 f. On silence, darkness, and emptiness as means of expression of the numinous, see Mensching, *Das heilige Schweigen.* On meditation in Hinduism, see Schomerus, *Der Caiva-Siddhanta,* p. 371 (the Five Letters); and Heiler, *Die Stufen der buddhistischen Versenkung.*

46. Marett, *The Threshold of Religion,* p. 171.

47. Eric Werner, "The Origin of Psalmody," *Hebrew Union Almanach* (1954), p. 343 (dialogue, pantomine, antiphony).

48. Farnell, *The Attributes of God,* pp. 13 f. Hooke, *Babylonian Religion,* pp. 37 ff. (Tammuz liturgies).

49. On the highly standardized Navaho chants, see Wyman, "The Religion of the Navaho Indians," in Ferm, ed., *Forgotten Religions,* pp. 349 ff.

50. Nath, "A Survey of the Sri Chaitanya Movement," *The Cultural Heritage of India,* II, 131 ff.; Bargellini, *San Bernhardino di Siena.*

51. See Revon, "Les Anciens Rituels du Shinto considérés comme formules magiques," *Transactions of the Third International Congress of the History of Religion, 1908,* I, 165 ff.

52. On the role of music in the Confucian cultus, see Groot, *Universismus,* p. 154.

53. Underwood, "The Dramatic Representation of Regeneration," in *Conversion: Christian and Non-Christian.*

54. Cuisinier, *La Danse sacrée en Indochine et en Indonésie.* Also, Granet, *Danses et legendes de la Chine ancienne.*

55. Marrett, *Threshold of Religion,* pp. 175, 180. On this subject, see also Harrison, *Art and Ritual,* pp. 43 ff.

56. On the leaping dance of the Canaanites, see Gaster, "The Religion of the Canaanites," in Ferm, ed., *Forgotten Religions,* pp. 131 f.

57. Oesterley, *The Sacred Dance*. Also Sachs, *World History of the Dance*.

58. Eric Werner, "The Origin of Psalmody," *Hebrew Union Almanach* (1954), pp. 327 ff.

59. Leeuw, *Religion in Essence*, Sec. 65.

60. Will, *Le Culte*, I, 23.

61. On the gift as exchange, see Mauss, "Essai sur le don," *Sociologie et anthropologie* (1923/24), pp. 145 ff.

62. See Farnell, *Greece and Babylon*, pp. 230 ff. Farnell discusses the use of fire, wine, incense, and other gifts in sacrifice (Chap. XIII). On the ancient Near Eastern and Greek notions of sacrifice, see Yerkes, *Sacrifice in Greek and Roman Religions and Early Judaism;* Hooke, *Babylonian Religion*, pp. 45 f., 57 ff.; Pittenger, *The Christian Sacrifice*.

63. Underhill, *Worship*, p. 48.

64. Kay, *Christian Worship*, p. 19.

65. Leeuw, *Religion in Essence*, Sec 50. Landtman, "The Actual Beginnings of Offerings," *Actes du Ve Congrès d'Histoire des religions, 1929*, pp. 44 ff.

66. Leeuw, *Religion in Essence*, p. 330.

67. "Worship is the best dana or giving," Poussin, "Worship," ERE, XII, 758.

68. Tachibana, *The Ethics of Buddhism*, p. 228.

69. Kay, *Christian Worship*, p. 20.

70. Hooke, *Babylonian Religion*, pp. 57 f. There he discusses three types of use of a *puhu*, or substitute.

71. *Proceedings of the Seventh International Congress of the History of Religions, 1950*, pp. 142 ff.

72. Farnell, *Greece and Babylon*, pp. 268 ff., on woman in Mesopotamian temple ritual.

73. J. E. Harrison, *Greek Religion;* Leeuw, *Religion in Essence*, Sec. 50; Yerkes, *Sacrifice*. Oesterley, "Early Hebrew Festival Rituals," in Hooke, ed., *Myth and Ritual*.

74. Underhill, *Worship*, p. 51.   75. Heiler, *Das Gebet*.

76. Kay, *Christian Worship*, pp. 29 ff.

77. On Mesopotamia, see Hooke, *Babylonian Religion*, Chaps. VIII, IX. He discusses the three aspects of the diviner's work: (1) biru

(vision), (2) purussu (decision), (3) ittu (sign); and the methods of the barū.

78. Eliade, *Techniques du yoga*.

79. Fowler, *The Religious Experience of the Roman People*, Chap. XIII.

80. Deubner, "Lustrum," AR, XVI (1913), 134 ff.; Wissowa, *Religion und Kultus*, p. 327.

81. See J. E. Harrison, *Greek Religion*, Chaps. II, III; Scheftelowitz, "Die Sündentilgung durch Wasser," AR, XVII (1914), 353 ff.; Tachibana, *Ethics of Buddhism*, Chap. XI; Maass, "Segnen, Weihen, Taufen," AR, XI (1922), 241 ff.; Farnell, *Greece and Babylon*, Chap. IX and 283 ff. Also, Drower, *The Mandaeans of Iraq and Iran*, esp. Chap. VII.

82. Mensching, *Vergleichende Religionswissenschaft*, p. 112.

83. See also Eliade, *Traité*, Chap. V, on aquatic symbolism.

84. Modi, *The Religious Ceremonies and Customs of the Parsees*, Chaps. IV and V. On the sacred fire, see Chap. IX.

85. Farnell, *Attributes*, pp. 186 ff., 190 f.

86. Tachibana, *Ethics of Buddhism*, pp. 159 ff. "Whether moral or religious, purity and purification in Buddhism are solely concerned with spiritual matters" (p. 176).

87. Hooke (*Babylonian Religion*, p. 56) compares the Egyptian and the Babylonian *pit-pi*, and could have included the corresponding Hindu ceremony.

88. Quick, *The Christian Sacraments*, p. 108.

89. Marett, *Sacraments of Simple Folks*, Chap. I.

90. For the Hindu samskara, see Radhakrishnan, *Religion and Society*, pp. 135 ff. The most important of the forty are the name-giving (*namakaratta*), initiation (*upanayana*), marriage (*vivaha*), and funeral (*antyesti*) ceremonies.

91. Bulgakov, *The Orthodox Church*, p. 131.

92. Quick, *Christian Sacraments*, Chaps. V and VI.

93. *Ibid.*, p. 106.   94. *Ibid.*, p. 101.   95. *Ibid.*, pp. 217 ff.

96. See Nock, "Hellenistic and Christian Sacraments," *Proceedings of the Seventh Congress for the History of Religions*, pp. 53 ff., rightly states "there was no category of sacraments" (p. 60).

97. Kay, *Christian Worship*, pp. 24 ff.

98. See Mattuck, *Jewish Ethics*, pp. 131 f., on the study of the Law as form of religious devotion and the good life.

99. Hooke, *Babylonian Religion*, p. 56, says that common to nearly all Babylonian myths was the idea that "man was created for 'dullu,' i.e., the service of the gods."

100. Loewe, in ERE, XII, 806.

101. McKenzie, *Two Religions*, p. 57.

102. Wilder, *Eschatology and Ethics in the Teachings of Jesus*, p. 131.

103. *Ibid.*, p. 154. 104. Groot, *Universismus*, Chaps. I, II.

105. Oakeshott, *Experience and Its Modes*, p. 256.

106. *Ibid.*, p. 337.

107. Marett, *Faith, Hope and Charity in Primitive Religion*, p. 11.

108. Marett, *Threshold of Religion*, pp. 187 f.

109. Mattuck, *Jewish Ethics*, Chap. XVIII. "The good life, according to Judaism is also the religious life" (p. 142).

110. Sneath, *The Evolution of Ethics as Revealed in the Great Religions*.

111. Otto, *Die Gnadenreligion Indiens und das Christentum*, pp. 55 f., 62.

112. Mattuck, *Jewish Ethics*. "At its best, Jewish ethical conduct has in it the spirit of worship" (p. 49). "That ethical conduct brings men to God is the first corollary from the Jewish doctrine of the Law" (p. 26).

113. Dawson, *The Ethical Religion of Zoroaster*.

114. Donaldson, *Studies in Muslim Ethics*.

115. Tachibana, *Ethics of Buddhism*, p. 257. According to him, *dharma*, in the sense of righteousness, justice, "may be said to imply virtue or morality in general, and therefore not merely righteousness, but the whole of ethics" (pp. 259 f.). See there quotations from the Scriptures on those "established on *dharma* and endowed with *sila*."

116. Donaldson, *Muslim Ethics*, Chap. III; "Sharia," EI.

117. Mitra, *The Ethics of the Hindus*.

118. Preisker, *Das Ethos des Urchristentums*, p. 129.

119. For some general principles and enumerations of particular virtues in the Qur'an, see Donaldson, *Muslim Ethics*, Chap. II.

120. "In Judaism, the *imitatio Dei* was identified by Philo with

life according to the Law," Mattuck, *Jewish Ethics,* Chap. VI. "The imitation of God is a motive invoked for Ethics," says Wilder, *Eschatology,* pp. 131 ff. See there pp. 151 ff., 200 ff., on the example of Jesus. For the Muslim notions (al tahalluk bi ahlāk Allāh), see Goldziher, *Vorlesungen über den Islam,* Chap. I, Sec. 9, n. 1. See there also, the imitation of Mohammed and the companions. Andrae, *Die Person Muhammads,* pp. 190 ff. Also, Donaldson, *Muslim Ethics,* pp. 60 ff., 64. For Shiitic Islam, see Goldziher, *Vorlesungen,* Chap. IV, pp. 3, 5.

121. Groot, *Universismus,* p. 33; Imitation of Tao and perfection and "sainthood" are discussed in Chap. III.

122. Glasenapp, *Der Jainismus,* p. 359.

123. For (five) types of Christian piety, including that of the *Imitatio,* see Kuehn, *Toleranz and Offenbarung.*

124. See Winternitz, *Geschichte der indischen Literatur,* pp. 263 ff.; Poussin, *Bouddhisme,* Chap. IV; "Boddhisattva," ERE, II, 739 ff.

125. See Saunders, *The Ideals of East and West,* a survey on the ethics of different religions. On the Chinese concept of virtue, see Groot, *Universismus,* Chap. III.

126. On Buddhism, Hinayana is discussed by Tachibana, *Ethics of Buddhism;* Mahayana is discussed by Poussin, *Bouddhisme,* Chap. IV, and Lamotte, *Traité de Sagesse.*

127. Weinrich, *Die Liebe im Buddhismus und im Christentum.* For the cardinal virtues of the Mahayana: ERE, II, 749 ff.

128. Tachibana, *Ethics of Buddhism,* pp. 53 ff., 63. See the 227 precepts for the full member of the Samgha, p. 80. See also p. 95, 183, and the detailed discussion of virtues in Part II.

129. For the "ten perfections" not found in canonical literature, *ibid.,* p. 154, n. 4.

130. Lamotte, *Traité de Sagesse;* Poussin, "Bodhisattva," ERE; and Wach, *Types of Experience,* pp. 112 ff.

131. Soothill, *The Three Religions of China,* p. 203. See also Chap. X.

132. Maspero, *Le Taoisme,* pp. 38 f., 85 ff., esp. 227 ff.; Wilhelm, *Laotse und der Taoismus,* pp. 46 ff.

133. Donaldson, *Muslim Ethics,* pp. 14 ff., 24 ff., 159 ff., 79 ff.

134. Bulgakov, *Othodox Church,* p. 149.

135. See Mensching, *Gut und Böse ins Glauben der Völker.*

NOTES TO CHAPTER V

1. For a fuller treatment, see Wach, *Sociology of Religion*. An additional bibliography has been included since the fifth printing (1949).

2. Pemberton, "Sociology of Religion," JBR, VII (1949), 35 ff. Yinger, "Present Status of Sociology of Religion," *Journal of Religion*, XXXI (1951), 194 ff. (sociology of religion as "a branch of scientific sociology, non-evaluating, objective, abstract"). Also, on the problem of the individual and society, see Thelen, "The Biblical Instruction and Comparative Religion," JBR, XX (1952), 71 ff.

3. In a very stimulating essay, "Formen der menschlichen Gemeinschaft," *Glauben und Verstehen*, II, 262 ff., Bultmann discusses four forms of human fellowship: those based on nature, on history, on art and science interests, and on religion—each having its laws and its dangers. The religious community is founded on faith; it may be a community of the "called," and, finally, a community of love.

4. Radin, *Die religiöse Erfahrung der Naturvölker*, Chap. II.

5. Marett, *The Threshold of Religion*, p. 137; see also Andrae, *Die Frage nach der religiösen Anlage*.

6. Marett, *Threshold of Religion*, p. 123. Marett sees the very need for a covenant arise in a conflict between associative and dissociative tendencies, in *Sacraments of Simple Folks*, p. 161.

7. Buber, *Die Erzählungen der Chassidim*, p. 228.

8. Mowinckel, *Religion und Kultus*, p. 125.

9. Andrae, *Die Frage der religiösen Anlage*, pp. 26 f., 33 ff., 46 ff., 51 ff.

10. Ferré, *The Christian Understanding of God*, p. 39. See Hartshorne, *Reality as Social Process*, Chap. I.

11. Mouroux, "Sur la notion d'expérience religieuse," *Recherches de sciences religieuses*, XXXIV (1947), 10.

12. *Ibid.*, p. 19.

13. Koenker, *The Liturgical Renaissance in the Roman Catholic Church*, p. 132. "Protestantism at its best is not individualistic, but it is infrequently seen at its best" (p. 137).

14. Kay, in *The Nature of Christian Worship*, Chap. II, "Corporateness in Worship," insists that corporate prayer is brought about by a number of people meeting at the same time and place, each

offering his own private prayers (pp. 47 f.), but that the individual is not swallowed up (pp. 54 ff.).

15. W. E. Hocking, *Living Religions and a World Faith*, pp. 44 ff.

16. Malinowski, *Magic, Science and Religion*, pp. 43 f.: "The anthropologist has done enough, when he has sown the value of a certain phenomenon for social integrity and for the continuity of culture." Radcliffe-Brown, "Religion and Society," JRAI, LXXV, pp. 33 ff.; "An orderly social life depends upon the presence in the minds of the members of sentiments which control the behaviour of the individual in relation to others" (pp. 34 f.).

17. "Sociology of Religion," in Gurvitch, ed., *Twentieth Century Sociology*, p. 428.

18. *Ibid.*

19. A satisfactory comparative study of the conception of the nature of the sacred community in primitive society which would avoid the shortcomings of the theories of Lévy-Bruhl, Durkheim, and the functionalists does not exist as yet.

20. See the article by Schmidt, "The Church," in *Bible Key Words*.

21. See "Jewish Community," in Landman, ed., *Universal Jewish Encyclopedia*, VI, 99 ff., 121 ff., on *mishpaha, edah, kahal, kenishta,* and *keneseth*.

22. Massignon, "L'Umma et ses synonymes," *Revue des études islamiques*, 1941–46, pp. 150 ff.; Gibb, "Ummah," *Shorter Encyclopedia of Islam*, pp. 603 ff. The term is a loan-word, referring to "linguistic and religious bodies of people who are the objects of the divine plan of salvation." The development leads from the ummah of the Arabs to the ummah of the Muslims. See also Lichtenstaedter, "Fraternization (Muakhat) in Early Islam Society," *Islamic Culture*, XVI (1942), 47 ff.

23. For the Hinayana notions of Samgha, see Tachibana, *The Ethics of Buddhism*, pp. 217 ff., 228 f. "Samgha" is defined by Nagarjuna as the reunion of several Bhiksu in the same place: Lamotte, *Le Traité de la grande vertu de la Sagesse de Nagarjuna*, I, 202 f. According to Buddhagosha, the Samgha presupposes "une communauté de vues et de préceptes" (*ibid.*, n. 3).

24. See H. R. Niebuhr, "The Norm of the Church," *Journal of Religious Thought*, IV (1946/47).

25. Wach, *Meister und Jünger;* Leeuw, *Religion in Essence and Manifestation,* Sec. 28.

26. See the studies of the leading French sociologist of religion, Le Bras. Also, see Desroche, "Areas and Methods of a Sociology of Religion, The Work of G. Le Bras," *Journal of Religion,* XXXV (1955), 34 ff.

27. Wach, *Sociology of Religion,* pp. 30 ff.

28. *Ibid.,* p. 42.   29. See Wach, *Meister und Jünger,* pp. 29, 56.

30. Wach, "Twentieth Century Sociology," in Gurvitch, ed., *Twentieth Century Sociology,* p. 431.

31. Daniélou, *Origen,* p. 47.

32. On the religion of age-groups, see Allport, *The Individual and His Religion,* Chaps. II, III.

33. Wissowa, *Religion und Kultus der Römer,* p. 405, n. 2. See also Schubart, *Religion und Eros,* on prophetesses and priestesses, pp. 187 f.

34. Liston Pope, "Religion and the Class Structure," *Annals of the American Academy of Political and Social Science* (March, 1948), p. 91.

35. Wolf, "Zur Rechtsgestalt der Kirche," *Bekennende Kirche,* pp. 254 ff.

36. Wach, *Sociology of Religion,* Chap. V, Sec. 9.

37. But see Jaeger's statement, *Theology of the Early Greek Philosophers,* p. 177: "The concept of *auctoritas,* which is later to be of such decisive importance for the attitude of the Church in questions of faith, is entirely missing in Greek thought."

38. Wach, *Sociology of Religion,* p. 335.   39. *Ibid.,* Chap. VIII.

40. Brightman, *A Philosophy of Religion,* p. 191.

41. "The Problem of Truth in Religion," *Studies in History and Religion,* pp. 177 ff.

42. *Ibid.,* p. 178.

43. Cuisinier, *La Danse sacrée en Indochine et en Indonésie,* p. 15.

44. For the discussions on the believer (*mu min*), the sinner (*fasig*) and the infidel (*kafir*) in Islam, see Gardet and Anawati, *Introduction à la théologie musulmane,* pp. 49 ff., 330 ff.

45. Wach, *Sociology of Religion,* pp. 44 ff.

46. See H. W. Schneider, *Religion in Twentieth Century America.*

47. Suhard, *Growth or Decline;* Michonneau, *Revolution in a City Parish;* Bishop, *France Alive;* Ward, *France Pagan?*

48. Fichter, *The Southern Parish,* Vol. I.

49. *Ibid.,* p. 4.   50. *Ibid.,* p. 14.

51. See Fichter, "A Typology of Parishioners," *Social Relations in the Urban Parish,* Part I. He suggests six criteria of determining membership in a parish: three institutional (baptism, residence, racial origin), and three personal (intention, observance, and social participation). He outlines (p. 11) the following four types of parishioners: nuclear, moral, marginal, and dormant.

BIBLIOGRAPHY

Akhilananda, Swami. *See* Swami Akhilananda.
Aldrich, Virgil C. "The High and the Holy," *Journal of Religion,* XXXIV (1954).
Alexander, Hartley B. "Sin (American)," ERE, XI.
Alexander, Samuel. Space, Time and Deity. London, Macmillan, 1920; 1950.
Allport, Gordon. The Individual and His Religion. New York, Macmillan, 1950.
────── Psychology, Psychiatry and Religion. Newton, Mass., *Andover-Newton Bulletin,* XLIV (1952).
Alpert, Harry. "Emile Durkheim and Sociologismic Psychology," AJS, XLV (1940).
Andrae, Tor. Die Frage nach der religiösen Anlage. Uppsala, Lundquist, 1932.
────── Die Person Muhammeds in Lehre und Glauben seiner Gemeinde. Stockholm, Norstedt, 1918.
Baillie, John. Our Knowledge of God. New York, Charles Scribner's Sons, 1939.
────── ed. Revelation. New York, Macmillan, 1937.
Ballou, Robert O., ed. The Bible of the World. New York, Viking, 1939.
Bargellini, Pierro. San Bernardino di Siena. 2d ed. Brescia, Morcelliano, 1934.
Barrows, John Henri. A Memoir. Chicago, Fleming H. Revell, 1904.
Bartsch, Hans Werner, ed. Theologische Forschung. 2d ed. Hamburg, H. Reich, 1951.

Baumgartner, Walter, ed. Festschrift für Alfred Bertholet. Tübingen, Mohr, 1950.

Beckh, Hermann. Der Buddhismus. 2d ed. Berlin, W. de Gruyter, 1925.

Bedoyère, Michael de la. The Life of Baron von Hügel. London, Dent, 1927.

Behier, E. "Les analogies de la création chez Çankara et chez Proclus," *Revue Philosophique,* July 1953. Paris, Presses Universitaires de France, 1953.

Benedict, Ruth. "The Concept of the Guardian Spirit in North America," AAA Mem, XXIX (1923).

Benoit, Jean Daniel. "Direction spirituelle et Protestantisme," in Etudes d'histoire et de philosophie religieuse, No. 37. Strassbourg, Paris, Alcan, 1940.

Bergson, Henri. The Two Sources of Morality and Religion. New York, Doubleday, 1954.

Bernheim, Ernst. Lehrbuch der historischen Methode. 5th, 6th eds. Leipzig, Duncker & Humblot, 1908.

Berthold, Fred. "The Meaning of Religious Experience," *Journal of Religion,* XXXII (1952).

Bertholet, Alfred. "Die Macht der Schrift in Glauben und Aberglauben," Abhandlungen der Deutschen Akademie der Wissenschaften, Phil. Klasse, 1948. Berlin, Akademischen Verlag, 1949.

—— "Über Kultische Motivverschiebungen," SBPAW, XVIII (1938).

Bevan, Edwyn R. Symbolism and Belief. London, Allen and Unwin, 1938.

Bhandarkar, Ramkrishna Gopal. Collected Works. Poona, Research Institute, 1929.

Bhattacharyya, Haridas. The Foundations of Living Faiths. Calcutta, University Press, 1938.

Bhattacharyya, Shiva. "Religious Practices of the Hindus," in Religion of the Hindus. New York, The Ronald Press, 1953.

Bidney, David. "The Ethnology of Religion and the Problem of Human Evolution," AA, 56 (1954).

Bishop, Claire Huchet. France Alive. New York, D. X. McMullan, 1947.

Bleeker, Claas Jouco, ed. Anthropologie Religieuse, Studies in the History of Religions. Leiden, Brill, 1955.
—— Proceedings of the Seventh International Congress for the History of Religions, 1950. Amsterdam, North-Holland Publishing Co., 1951.
—— "La Structure de la Religion," *Revue d'histoire et Philosophie religieuse*, XXI (1951).
Bollnow, Otto Friedrich. Das Verstehen. Mainz, Kirchheim, 1949.
Bolster, Arthur S. James Freeman Clarke. Boston, Beacon Press, 1954.
Bouquet, Alan Coates. Sacred Books of the World (Anthology). London, Penguin Books, 1954.
Bousset, Wilhelm. "Die Himmelsreise der Seele," AR, LV (1901).
Braden, Charles Samuel. The Scriptures of Mankind. New York, Macmillan, 1953.
—— War, Communism and World Religions. New York, Harper, 1953.
Breda, H. L. van. "Aus dem Husserl Archiv zu Löwen," *Jahrbuch der Görresgesellschaft*, 62, No. 2 (1953).
Brightman, Edgar Sheffield. A Philosophy of Religion. New York, Prentice-Hall, 1946.
—— The Problem of God. New York, Abingdon, 1930.
Brinton, Clarence Crane. The Shaping of the Modern Mind. New York, New American Library, 1953.
Buber, Martin. Die Erzählungen der Chassidim. Zürich, Manesse, 1949.
—— I and Thou. Translated by R. G. Smith. Edinburgh, T. and T. Clark, 1937.
Bugbee, Henry G. "The Moment of Obligation in Experience," *Journal of Religion*, XXXIII, No. 1 (1953).
Bulgakov, Sergei Nikolaevich. The Orthodox Church. London, Centenary Press, 1935.
Bultmann, Rudolf. "Das Problem der Hermeneutik," in Glauben und Verstehen, Vol. II. Tübingen, Mohr, 1952.
Burckhardt, Jacob Christoph. Force and Freedom, Reflections on History. Edited by James Hastings Nichols. New York, Pantheon, 1943.
Burnouf, Eugène. La science des religions. 3d ed. Paris, Maisonneuve, 1876.

Burtt, Edwin Arthur. Types of Religious Philosophy. Rev. ed. New York, Harper, 1951.

Butterfield, Herbert. Christianity and History. New York, Scribner's, 1950.

Caillois, Roger. L'Homme et le sacré. Paris, Presses Universitaires, 1939.

Cain, Seymour. Gabriel Marcel's Theory of Religious Experience (Unpublished Ph.D. dissertation). University of Chicago, 1956.

Campbell, Joseph. The Hero with a Thousand Faces. Vol. XVII of Bollingen Series. New York, Pantheon, 1949.

Carsartelli, Louis Charles. "Sin (Iranian)," ERE, XI (1921), 562–66.

Cassirer, Ernst. Language and Myth. Translated by Susanne K. Langer. New York, Harper, 1946.

Clarke, James F. Ten Great Religions. Boston, J. R. Osgood, 1875; 1883 (repr. Houghton Mifflin, 1913).

Constantin, Leonard. "The Gospel to Communists," IRM, XLI (April 1952).

Cotton, James Harry. Christian Knowledge of God. New York, Macmillan, 1951.

Cresson, André. Maine de Biran; Sa Vie, son oeuvre. Paris, Presses Universitaires, 1950.

Creuzer, Georg Friedrich. Symbolik und Mythologie der alten Völker. 3d ed. Leipzig, C. W. Leske, 1837.

Cuisinier, Jeanne. La Danse sacrée en Indochine et en Indonésie. Paris, Presses Universitaires, 1951.

Daniélou, Jean. Origen. Translated by Walter Mitchell. New York, Sheed and Ward, 1955. Originally published as Origène, Paris, La Table Ronde, 1948.

—— "The Problem of Symbolism," *Thought,* XXV (1950).

—— "Sainte Irenée et les origines de la théologie de l'histoire," *Recherches de sciences religieuses,* XXXIV (1947).

—— The Salvation of the Nations. London, Sheed, 1949.

Das, Saraj Kumar. A Study of the Vedanta. 2d ed. Calcutta, University of Calcutta, 1937.

Datta, Dhirendra Mohan. The Six Ways of Knowledge, A Critical Study of the Vedanta Theory of Knowledge. London, Allen & Unwin, 1932.

Davids, T. W., and Mrs. C. A. F. Rhys Davids. "Sin (Buddhist)," ERE, XI (1921), 533–34.

Davidson, Robert F. Rudolf Otto's Interpretation of Religion. Princeton, Princeton University Press, 1947.

Davies, Rupert Eric. The Problem of Authority in the Continental Reformers. London, Epworth, 1946.

Dawson, Miles Menander. The Ethical Religion of Zoroaster. New York, Macmillan, 1931.

Dayal, Har. The Bodhisattva Doctrine in Buddhist Sanskrit Literature. London, K. Paul, Trubner, 1932.

Demieville, Paul. "Le Miroir spirituel," *Sinologica*, I (1947).

Demos, Raphael, and C. J. Ducasse. "Symposium: Are Religious Dogmas Cognitive and Meaningful?" *The Journal of Philosophy*, LI (1954), 145–72.

Deschamps, Hubert Jules. Les Religions de l'Afrique noire. Paris, Presses Universitaires, 1954.

Desroche, Henri. "Areas and Methods of a Sociology of Religion, The Work of G. Le Bras," *Journal of Religion*, XXXV (1955), 34–47.

Deubner, L. "Lustrum," AR, XVI (1913).

Dewick, Edward Chisholm. The Christian Attitude to Other Religions (Hulsean Lectures). Cambridge, University Press, 1953.

Dieterich, Albrecht, ed. "Archiv für Religionswissenschaft," AR, 1898.

——— "H. Usener," AR, VIII (1905).

Dieterlen, Germaine. Essai sur la religion bambara. Paris, Presses Universitaires, 1951.

Dilthey, Wilhelm. Gesammelte Schriften. 11 vols. Leipzig and Berlin, Teubner, 1921–36. Vols. I (1922), V (1924), VII (1927), and VIII (1931).

Dinkler, Erich. "Existentialist Interpretation of the New Testament," *Journal of Religion*, XXXII (1952).

Dobschütz, Ernst von. "Interpretation," ERE, VII.

——— Vom Auslegen des Neuen Testament. Göttingen, Vandenhoeck, 1927.

Donaldson, Dwight Martin. "Sharīa," EI.

——— Studies in Muslim Ethics. London, S.P.C.K., 1953.

Drower, Ethel Stefana. The Mandaeans of Iraq and Iran. Oxford, Clarendon, 1937.
Droysen, Johann Gustav. Historik. Reedited by Rudolf Hübner. München, Oldenbourg, 1937. Abbreviated translation by E. B. Andrews, Outlines of the Principles of History. Boston, Ginn, 1893.
Duchesne-Guillemin, Jacques. "L'Homme dans la religion iranienne," in C. J. Bleeker, ed., Anthropologie religieuse. Leiden, Brill, 1955.
——— Ormazd et Ahriman, L'Aventure dualiste dans l'antiquité. Paris, Presses Universitaires, 1953.
——— "Zoroastre," in Georges Dumézil, ed., Les Dieux et les hommes. Paris, Maisonneuve, 1948.
Durkheim, Emile. Les formes élémentaires de la vie religieuse. Paris, Alcan, 1912. Translated by J. W. Swain, The Elementary Forms of the Religious Life. New York, Macmillan, 1915.
Dussaud, René. L'Oeuvre scientifique d'Ernest Renan. Paris, Geuthner, 1951.
Earle, William. "The 'Standard Observer' in the Sciences of Man," Ethics, LXIII (1953).
Eggan, Fred. "Social Anthropology and the Method of Controlled Comparisons," AA, 56 (1954).
Eissfeldt, Otto. "Religionsgeschichtliche Schule," RGG, IV.
Elder, Earl Edgar, trans. A Commentary on the Creed of Islam. New York, Columbia University Press, 1950.
Eliade, Mircea. Le Chamanisme et les techniques archaiques de l'extase. Paris, Payot, 1951.
——— Images et symboles. 2d ed. Paris, Gallimard, 1952.
——— Le Mythe de l'éternel retour, Archétypes et répétition. Paris, Gallimard, 1949.
——— "Shamanism," in Vergilius Ferm, ed., Forgotten Religions. New York, Philosophical Library, 1950.
——— Techniques du yoga. Paris, Gallimard, 1948.
——— Traité d'histoire des religions. Paris, Payot, 1949.
Elkin, Adolphus Peter. The Australian Aborigines. 2d ed. Sydney and London, Angus and Robertson, 1943.
Emmet, Dorothy. The Nature of Metaphysical Thinking. London, Macmillan, 1945.

—— Whitehead's Philosophy of Organism. London, Macmillan, 1932.

Evans-Pritchard, Edward Evan. Social Anthropology. Glencoe, Ill., Free Press, 1952.

Ewer, Mary Anita. A Survey of Mystical Symbolism. New York, Macmillan, 1933.

Farber, Marvin. The Foundation of Phenomenology. Cambridge, Harvard University Press, 1943.

—— Philosophic Thought in France and the United States. Buffalo, University of Buffalo Publications, 1950.

Faris, Ellsworth. The Nature of Human Nature. New York, McGraw-Hill, 1937.

Farnell, Lewis Richard. The Attributes of God (Gifford Lectures, 1924–25). Oxford, Clarendon, 1925.

—— Greece and Babylon. Edinburgh, T. and T. Clark, 1911.

Ferm, Vergilius T. A. Religion in the Twentieth Century. New York, Philosophical Library, 1948.

Ferré, Nels Frederik Solomon. The Christian Understanding of God. New York, Harper, 1951.

Fichter, Joseph Henry. The Southern Parish. Chicago, University of Chicago Press, 1951. Vol. I.

—— "A Typology of Parishioners," in Social Relations in the Urban Parish. Chicago, University of Chicago Press, 1954.

Filiozat, Jean. Magie et médicine. Paris, Presses Universitaires, 1943.

Finegan, Jack. The Archaeology of World Religions. Princeton, Princeton University Press, 1952.

Firth, Raymond William. Elements of Social Organization. New York, Philosophical Library, 1951.

Fitzpatrick, Mallary. "Kierkegaard and the Church," *Journal of Religion*, XXVII, No. 4 (1947).

Fleming, Daniel Johnson. "Religious Symbols Crossing Cultural Boundaries," in F. E. Johnson, ed., Religious Symbolism. New York, Harper, 1953.

Fleure, Herbert John. "J. G. Frazer," *Man*, LIV (1954).

Forde, C. D. "The Integration of Anthropological Studies," JRAI, LXXVII (1948).

Foss, Martin. The Idea of Perfection in the Western World. Princeton, Princeton University Press, 1946.

Fowler, William Warde. The Religious Experience of the Roman People. London, Macmillan, 1922.

Frankfort, H., H. A. Frankfort, and others. Intellectual Adventure of Ancient Man. Chicago, University of Chicago Press, 1946.

Frauwallner, Erich. "Die Anthropologie des Buddhismus," in C. J. Bleeker, ed., Anthropologie religieuse. Leiden, Brill, 1955.

Frazer, Sir James George. Creation and Evolution in Primitive Cosmogonies. London, Macmillan, 1935.

Fremgen, Leo. Offenbarung und Symbol, Das Symbolische als religiöse Gestaltung im Christentum. Gütersloh, Bertelsmann, 1954.

Friedrich, Johannes. Entzifferung verschollener Schriften und Sprachen. Berlin, Springer, 1954.

Frobe-Kapteyn, Olga, ed. "Mensch und Ritus," *Eranos Jahrbuch,* XIX (1950). Zürich, Rhein-Verlag, 1950.

Fustel de Coulanges, Numa Denis. La Cité antique. 13th ed. Paris, Machette, 1890. Translated by W. Small, The Ancient City. Boston, Lee, 1877.

Garbe, Richard. "Sankhya," in ERE, XI.

Gardet, Louis, and M. M. Anawati. Introduction à la théologie musulmane. Paris, Vrin, 1948.

Gaster, Theodor H. "The Religion of the Canaanites," in Vergilius Ferm, ed., Forgotten Religions. New York, Philosophical Library, 1950.

—— Thespis; Ritual, Myth and Dances in the Ancient Near East. New York, Schumann, 1950.

Gelb, Ignace J. A Study of Writing, The Foundations of Grammatology. Chicago, University of Chicago Press, 1952.

Gibb, Sir Hamilton Alexander Rosskeen. La structure de la pensée religieuse de l'Islam. Translated from English. Paris, Larose, 1950.

—— "Ummah," Shorter Encyclopedia of Islam. Leiden, Brill, 1953.

Glasenapp, Helmuth von. Der Jainismus, Eine indische Erlösungsreligion. Berlin, A. Häger, 1925.

—— Madhvas Philosophie des Vishnuglaubens. Bonn, Leipzig, K. Schroeder, 1923.

Goldziher, Ignaz. Koranauslegung. Leiden, Brill, 1920.

—— Die Richtungen der islamischen Koranauslegung. Reprint. Leiden, Brill, 1952.

—— Vorlesungen über den Islam. Heidelberg, Winter, 1910.

Granet, Marcel. Danses et legendes de la Chine ancienne. Paris, Alcan, 1926.

Grant, Robert M. The Bible in the Church, A Short History of Interpretation. New York, Macmillan, 1948.

—— et al. "History of the Interpretation of the Bible," in Vol. I of The Interpreter's Bible. New York, Abingdon-Cokesbury, 1952.

Green, Julian. Personal Record, 1929–1939. New York, Harper, 1939.

Grensted, Laurence William. Psychology of Religion. New York, Oxford University Press, 1952.

Griaule, Marcel. "La Connaissance de l'homme noire," in La Connaissance de l'homme au XXe siècle. Rencontres Internationaux de Genève, 1951.

—— Dieu d'eau. Paris, Ed. du chêne, 1948.

Groot, Jan Jakob Maria de. Universismus. Berlin, G. Reiman, 1918.

Gruppe, Otto von. Geschichte der Klassischen Mythologie und Religionsgeschichte. Leipzig, Teubner, 1921.

—— Die griechischen Culte und Mythen in ihren Beziehungen zu den Orientalischen Religionen. Leipzig, Teubner, 1887.

Hardman, Oscar. The Christian Doctrine of Grace. New York, Macmillan, 1947.

Hardy, H. "Zur Geschichte der vergleichenden Religionsforschung," AR, IV (1901).

Harnack, Adolf von. Die Entstehung der Christlichen Theologie und des Kirchlichen Dogmas. Gotha, L. Klotz, 1927.

Harring, J. Phénoménologie et philosophie religieuse. Paris, Alcan, 1926.

Harrison, Jane Ellen. Ancient Art and Ritual. New York, Holt, 1913.

—— Prolegomena to the Study of Greek Religion. Cambridge, Harvard University Press, 1922.

Hartland, Edwin Sidney. Ritual and Belief, Studies in the History of Religion. London, Williams & Norgate, 1914.

Hartlich, Christian, and Walter Sachs. Der Ursprung des Mythosbegriffes in der modernen Bibelwissenschaft. Tübingen, Mohr, 1952.

Hartmann, Nicolai. New Ways of Ontology. Chicago, Regnery, 1953.
Hartshorne, Charles. "Religious Bearings of Whitehead's Philosophy," in Reality as Social Process. Boston, Beacon; Glencoe, Ill., Free Press, 1953.
——— "Whitehead's Idea of God," in Paul Schilpp, ed., The Philosophy of A. N. Whitehead. Evanston, Northwestern University Press, 1941.
——— and W. L. Reese. Philosophers Speak of God. Chicago, University of Chicago Press, 1953.
Haydon, Albert Eustace. "History of Religions," in G. B. Smith, ed., Religious Thought in the Last Quarter Century. Chicago, University of Chicago Press, 1927.
Heiler, Friedrich. "Die Bedeutung Rudolf Ottos für die vergleichende Religionsgeschichte," in Religionswissenschaft in Neuer Sicht. Marburg, N. G. Elwert, 1951.
——— Das Gebet. München, Reinhardt, 1921. Translated by S. M. McComb, Prayer, A Study in the History and Psychology of Religion. London and New York, Oxford University Press, 1922.
——— "Joachim Wach" (Memorial Address), *The Divinity School News*, The University of Chicago, XXII, No. 4 (November, 1955).
——— Die Stufen der buddhistischen Versenkung. 2d ed. München, Reinhardt, 1922.
Hensel, S. Die Familie Mendelssohn. 6th ed., 8 vols. Berlin, B. Behr's, 1888.
Herring, J. Phénoménologie et philosophie religieuse. Paris, Alcan, 1926.
Hessen, Johannes. Max Scheler. Essen, Chamier, 1948.
Hilliard, Frederick H. Man in Eastern Religions. London, Epworth, 1946.
Hiltner, Seward. Psychotherapy and Christian Ethics. Unpublished Ph.D. dissertation. University of Chicago, 1952.
——— Self-Understanding. New York, Scribner's, 1951.
Hocking, Richard. "Some Types of Historical Consciousness in Chinese and Indian Thoughts," in *Papers of the Ecumenical Institute,* V (1949).
Hocking, William Ernest. Living Religions and a World Faith. New York, Macmillan, 1940.

Hodges, Herbert Arthur. The Philosophy of Wilhelm Dilthey. London, Routledge, 1952.
—— Wilhelm Dilthey, An Introduction. London, Routledge, 1944.
Hodgson, Leonard. The Doctrine of the Trinity (Croall Lectures). New York, Scribner's, 1944.
Hooke, Samuel H. Babylonian and Assyrian Religion. London, Hutchinson, 1953.
—— Myth and Ritual, Essays. London, Oxford University Press, 1933.
Hooper, J. S. M. Hymns of the Alvārs. Calcutta, Association Press, 1929.
Hospers, John. Meaning and Truth in the Arts. Chapel Hill, University of North Carolina Press, 1946.
Hügel, Baron Friedrich von. Essays and Addresses on the Philosophy of Religion. London, Dent, 1921, 1949.
—— Eternal Life. Edinburgh, T. and T. Clark, 1913.
—— Selected Letters, 1896–1924. London, Dent, 1927.
Hughes, E. R. The Great Learning and the Mean in Action. New York, Dutton, 1943.
Hughes, Everett. Cycles and Turning Points. National Council, Episcopal Church, 1952.
Hume, Robert E. "The Study of the History of Religions," an address at the Conference of the National Association of Biblical Instructors, 1922. Reprinted from *Christian Education*.
Husserl, Edmund. Ideen zu einer reinen Phänomenologie. Halle, Niemeyer, 1922.
—— Jahrbuch für Philosophie und Phänomenologische Forschung. Halle, Niemeyer, 1913.
—— Logische Untersuchungen. Halle, Niemeyer, 1900.
—— Méditations cartésiennes. Paris, Colin, 1931.
Iremonger, Frederic Athelwood. Life of William Temple. London, Oxford University Press, 1948.
Jacobi, Jolande. The Psychology of C. G. Jung. Revised ed., New Haven, Yale University Press, 1951.
Jaeger, Werner. Theology of the Early Greek Philosophers. Translated by E. S. Robinson. Oxford, Clarendon, 1947.

James, Edwin Oliver. The Beginnings of Religion. London, Hutchinson's University Library, 1948.
—— The Concept of Deity. London, Hutchinson's University Library, 1950.
James, William. The Varieties of Religious Experience. London and New York, Longmans, Green, 1929.
Jaspers, Karl. Vom Ursprung und Ziel der Geschichte. Zürich, Artemis, 1949.
Jedin, Hubert. "Kirchengeschichte als Heilsgeschichte," *Saeculum,* V, No. 2 (1954).
Jentsch, Werner. "Verstehen und Verständlichmachen," TLZ, 76 (1951).
Johnson, Frederick Ernst, ed. Religious Symbolism. New York, Harper, 1955.
Johnson, Paul Ernst. Psychology of Religion. New York, Abingdon, 1945.
Jordan, Louis Henry. Comparative Religion: Its Genesis and Growth. Edinburgh, T. and T. Clark, 1905.
Katiresu, S. A Handbook of Saiva Religion. Revised and reprinted. Madras, Natesan, 1950.
Kay, James Alan. The Nature of Christian Worship. London, Epworth, 1953.
Keith, Arthur B. Buddhist Philosophy in India and Ceylon. Oxford, Clarendon, 1923.
Kennedy, Melville T. The Chaitanya Movement. Calcutta, Association Press, 1925.
Kitagawa, Joseph M. "A Glimpse of Professor Wach," *The Chicago Theological Seminary Register,* XLV, No. 4 (1955).
—— "Joachim Wach" (Memorial Address), *The Divinity School News,* XXII, No. 4 (1955). University of Chicago.
—— "Joachim Wach et la sociologie de la religion," *Archives de sociologie des religions,* I, No. 1 (1956).
—— "Theology and the Science of Religion," *Anglican Theological Review,* XXXIX, No. 1 (1957).
Koenker, Ernest Benjamin. The Liturgical Renaissance in the Roman Catholic Church. Chicago, University of Chicago Press, 1954.
Kraemer, Hendrik, ed. On the Meaning of History. Geneva, The Ecumenical Institute, 1950.

Kramer, Samuel Noah. "Sumerian Religion," in Vergilius Ferm, ed., Forgotten Religions. New York, Philosophical Library, 1950.
Krappe, Alexander Haggerty. Mythologie universelle. Paris, Payot, 1930.
Krüger, Gustav. "Das Problem der Autorität," in Offener Horizont, Festschrift für Karl Jaspers. München, Piper, 1953.
Kuehn, Johannes. Toleranz und Offenbarung. Leipzig, F. Meiner, 1923.
Lamotte, Étienne. Le Traité de la grande vertu de la sagesse de Nagarjuna. Louvain, Muséon, 1944.
Landman, Isaac, ed. The Universal Jewish Encyclopedia. New York, The Universal Jewish Encyclopedia, Inc., 1942.
Landtman, G. "The Actual Beginnings of Offerings as Illustrated by a Primitive People," in Actes du Ve congrès international d'histoire des religions, 1929. Lund, Gleerup, 1929.
Langer, Susanne K. Philosophy in a New Key. New York, Penguin Books, 1942.
Leenhardt, Maurice. Do Kamo, La personne et le mythe dans le monde mélanésien. Paris, Gallimard, 1947.
Leeuw, Gerardus van der. "Die Bedeutung des Mythus," in Festschrift für Alfred Bertholet. Tübingen, Siebeck, 1926-32.
——— Religion in Essence and Manifestation. Translated by J. E. Turner. London, Allen & Unwin, 1938.
Lehman, R. "Die Religionsgeschichte des Palaeolithikum," AR, XXXV (1938).
Lehmann, Arno. Die sivaitische Frömmigkeit der tamulischen Erbauungsliteratur. Berlin, Heimatdienst, 1947.
Lehmann, Eduard. Grundtvig. Translated by A. Oster. Tübingen, Mohr, 1932.
——— "Der Lebenslauf der Religionsgeschichte," in Actes du Ve congrès international d'histoire des religions. Lund, Gleerup, 1929.
Leipoldt, Johannes, and Siegfried Morenz. Heilige Schriften. Leipzig, Harrassowitz, 1953.
Lichtenstaedter, Ilse. "Fraternization (Mua'khāt) in Early Islam Society," *Islamic Culture,* XVI (1942).
Linton, Ralph. Ethnology of Polynesia and Micronesia. Chicago, Field Museum of Natural History, 1926.

Lowie, Robert H. "Biographical Memoir of Franz Boas, 1858–1942," in *Biographical Memoirs of the National Academy of Sciences,* XXIV (1947), 303–22.

―――― The History of Ethnological Theory. New York, Farrar and Rinehart, 1937.

Löwith, Karl. Meaning in History. Chicago, University of Chicago Press, 1949.

Lowrie, Walter. Kierkegaard. New York, Oxford Press, 1938.

Lubac, Henri de. Aspects du bouddhisme. Paris, Ed. du seuil, 1951.

Lyotard, Jean F. La Phénoménologie. Paris, Presses Universitaires, 1954.

Maass, Ernst. "Segnen, Weihen, Taufen," AR, XI (1922).

McCreary, J. K. "The Religious Philosophy of S. Alexander," *Journal of Religion,* XXVII, No. 2.

MacDonald, B. Duncan. Development of Muslim Theology, Jurisprudence and Constitutional Theory. New York, Scribner's, 1903.

Machle, Edward J. "Symbols in Religion," JBR, XXI (1953), 163–69.

McKenzie, John. Two Religions: A Comparative Study of Some Distinctive Ideas and Ideals in Hinduism and Christianity. London, Lutterworth, 1950.

Mackintosh, Hugh Ross. Types of Modern Theology. London, Nisbet, 1954.

McNeill, John T. Modern Christian Movements. Philadelphia, Westminster, 1954.

Macnichol, Nichol. Indian Theism. London, Oxford University Press, 1915.

Mainage, Thomas L. Les religions de la préhistoire. Paris, Desclée, De Brouwer, & Co., 1921.

Malinowski, Bronislaw. Magic, Science and Religion. Glencoe, Ill., Free Press, 1948.

Mandelbaum, Maurice H. The Problem of Historical Knowledge. New York, Liveright, 1938.

Marett, Robert Ranulph. "The Concept of Mana," in Transactions of the Third International Congress for the History of Religions. Oxford, Clarendon, 1908.

―――― Faith, Hope and Charity in Primitive Religion. New York, Macmillan, 1932.

―――― Sacraments of Simple Folks. Oxford, Clarendon, 1933.

―――― The Threshold of Religion. London, Methuen, 1914.

―――― Tylor. New York, J. Wiley, 1936.

Marot, K. "Der primitive 'Hochgott,' " in Actes du Ve congrès international d'histoire des religions. Lund, Gleerup, 1929.

Martin, Alfred William. Seven Great Bibles. New York, F. A. Stokes, 1930.

Martino, E. de. Il Mondo Magico. G. Einaudi, 1948.

Maspero, Henri. Les Religions chinoises. Paris, Civilisations du Sud, 1950.

―――― Le Taoisme. Paris, Civilisations du Sud, 1950.

Massignon, Louis. La Passion d'al Hosayn Ibn Mansour al Hallāj. Paris, Geuthner, 1922.

―――― "L'Umma et ses synonymes. Notion de la communauté en Islam," in Revue des études islamiques, 1941–46. Paris, Geuthner, 1947.

Masson-Oursel, Paul. "La Connaissance de l'Asie en France depuis 1900," *Revue Philosophique,* Nos. 7 to 9 (1953).

Matthews, Gordon, tr. Siva-hānabodham, A Manuel of Saiva Religious Doctrine. Oxford, University Press, 1948.

Mattuck, Israel Isidor. Jewish Ethics. London, Hutchinson's, 1953.

Mauss, Marcel. "Esquisse d'une théorie générale de la magie," in Sociologie et Anthropologie. Paris, Presses Universitaires, 1950.

―――― "Essai sur le don," in Sociologie et Anthropologie. Paris, Presses Universitaires, 1950.

Mensching, Gustav. Das heilige Schweigen. Giessen, Topelmann, 1926.

―――― Geschichte der Religionswissenschaft. Bonn, Universität Verlag, 1948.

―――― Gut und Böse ins Glauben der Völker. 2d ed. Stuttgart, Klotz, 1950.

―――― Vergleichende Religionswissenschaft. 2d ed. Heidelberg, Quelle und Meyer, 1949.

Michonneau, Georges. Revolution in a City Parish. Westminster, Md., Newman Press, 1950.

Miller, Perry, *et al.* Religion and Freedom of Thought. New York, Doubleday, 1954.

Milne, Edward Arthur. Modern Cosmology and the Christian Idea of God (Cadbury Lectures, University of Birmingham). Oxford, Clarendon, 1952.

Mitra, Sisirkumar. The Ethics of the Hindus. Calcutta, University Press, 1925.
Modi, Jivanji Jamshedji. The Religious Ceremonies and Customs of the Parsees. 2d ed. Bombay, Karani, 1937.
Monier-Williams, Sir Monier. Hinduism. London, S.P.C.K., 1877.
Moore, John Morrison. Theories of Religious Experience with Special Reference to James, Otto and Bergson. New York, Round Table Press, 1938.
Morgan, Conway Lloyd. Emergent Evolution (Gifford Lectures, 1922). London, Williams and Norgate, 1923.
—— The Interpretation of Nature. New York, Putnam, 1906.
Moses, David G. Religious Truth and the Relation between Religions. Madras, The Christian Literature Society, 1950.
Moulton, James Hope. The Treasure of the Magi. London, Oxford, 1917.
Mouroux, J. "Sur la notion de l'expérience religieuse," *Recherches de sciences religieuses*, XXXIV (1947).
Mowinckel, Sigmund. Religion und Kultus. Translated by A. Schomer. Göttingen, Vandenhoeck, 1953.
Mozley, J. K. "The Incarnation," in E. G. Selwyn, ed., Essays Catholic and Critical. New York, Macmillan, 1926.
Müller, Granfel A., ed. Life and Religion, An Aftermath from the Writings of F. Max Müller by His Wife. New York, Doubleday, 1905.
Müller, Julius. The Christian Doctrine of Sin. Translated by W. Urwich. Edinburgh, T. and T. Clark, 1868.
Nath, Govinda. "A Survey of the Sri Chaitanya Movement," in The Cultural Heritage of India (Sri Ramakrishna Centenary Memorial). Calcutta; New York, 1937.
Nédoncelle, Maurice. Baron Friedrich von Hügel. Translated by M. Vernon. London, Longmans, Green, 1937.
Neumann, Abraham A. "Judaism," in Edward J. Jurji, ed., The Great Religions of the Modern World. Princeton, Princeton University Press, 1946.
Nichols, James H. "Church History and Secular History," *Church History*, XIII (1944).
—— "Religion in Toynbee's History," *Church History*, XXVII (1948).

Nicholson, Reynold Alleyne. The Mystics of Islam. London, G. Bell and Sons, Ltd., 1914.

Niebuhr, Helmut Richard. "The Norm of the Church," *Journal of Religious Thought*, IV (1946/47).

Niebuhr, Reinhold. Faith and History. New York, Scribner's, 1949.

—— The Nature and Destiny of Man. New York, Scribner's, 1942.

Nielson, Eduard. Oral Tradition, A Modern Problem in Old Testament Introductions. Chicago, Allenson, 1954.

Nikhilananda, Swami. *See* Swami Nikhilananda.

Nock, Arthur Darby. "Hellenistic and Christian Sacraments," in Proceedings of the Seventh International Congress for the History of Religions. Amsterdam, North-Holland Publishing Co., 1951.

Northrop, Filmer Stuart C. The Meeting of East and West. New York, Macmillan, 1946.

Nyberg, Henrik Samuel. "Al-Mu'tazila," in EI, III, 787–93. London, 1936.

Oakeshott, Michael Joseph. Experience and Its Modes. Cambridge, University Press, 1933.

Oesterley, William Oscar Emil. "Early Hebrew Festival Rituals," in S. H. Hooke, ed., Myth and Ritual. London, Oxford, 1933.

—— The Sacred Dance. Cambridge, University Press, 1923.

Ohm, Thomas. Die Liebe zu Gott in den nichtchristlichen Religionen. Krailling, Wewel, 1950.

Oppenheim, Leo. "Assyro-Babylonian Religion," in Vergilius Ferm, ed., Forgotten Religions. New York, Philosophical Library, 1950.

Organ, Troy Wilson. "Reason and Experience in Mahāyāna Buddhism," JBR, XX (1952), 77–83.

Ortega y Gasset, José. Contribution to Offener Horizont: Festschrift für Karl Jaspers. Munich, Piper, 1953.

Otto, Rudolf. Die Anschauung vom heiligen Geiste bei Luther. Göttingen, Vandenhoeck, 1898.

—— Die Gnadenreligion Indiens und das Christentum. Gotha, L. Klotz, 1930. Translated as Christianity and the Indian Religion of Grace. Madras, Christian Literature Society for India, 1929.

—— The Idea of the Holy. Translated by J. W. Harvey. London, Oxford, 1946. 10th impr.

—— The Kingdom of God and the Son of Man. Translated by F. V. Filson and B. L. Woolf. London, Lutterworth, 1938.

Otto, Rudolf (*Continued*)
—— Vishnu Nārāyana. Jena, Diederichs, 1917.
Padovani, Umberto Antonio. "La Storia delle religioni in Italia," *Semaine internationale d'ethnologie religieuse,* IV (1925). Paris, Geuthner, 1926.
Paranjoti, V. Saiva Siddhānta. London, Luzac, 1938.
Parrinder, E. Geoffrey. African Traditional Religion. London, Hutchinson's, 1954.
—— West African Psychology, A Comparative Study of Psychological and Religious Thought. London, Lutterworth, 1951.
Parrish, Fred Louis. The Classification of Religions. Scottdale, Penna., Herald Press, 1941.
Parsons, Talcott. Essays in Social Theory. Glencoe, Ill., Free Press, 1949.
—— The Structure of Social Action. New York, McGraw-Hill, 1937. 2d ed., Glencoe, Ill., Free Press, 1949.
Pemberton, Prentiss L. "Sociology of Religion," JBR, XVII (1949).
—— "Universalism and Particularity," JBR, XX, No. 2 (1952).
Perry, Ralph B. The Thought and Character of William James as Revealed in Unpublished Correspondence and Notes. Boston, Little, Brown, 1935.
Petitpierre, Jacques. The Romance of the Mendelssohns. Translated by G. Micholet-Cote. London, Dennis Dobson, 1947.
Pettazzoni, Raffaele. "Aperçu introductif," *Numen, International Review for the History of Religions,* I, No. 1 (1954).
Pfister, Friedrich. "Kultus," in Wilhelm Kroll, ed., Pauly-Wissowa Real-Encyclopaedie der Classischen Altertumswissenschaft, Vol. IX. Stuttgart, Metzler, 1921.
Pinard de la Boullaye, Henri. L'Étude comparée des religions, Essai critique. Paris, Beauchesne, 1922; 1925.
Pittenger, W. Norman. The Christian Sacrifice, A Study of the Eucharist in the Life of the Christian Church. New York, Oxford University Press, 1951.
—— Sacraments, Signs and Symbols. Chicago, Wilcox & Follett, 1949.
Pope, G. U., ed. and tr. The Tiruvacagam. Oxford, Clarendon, 1900.
Pope, Liston. "Religion and Class Structure," *Annals of the American Academy of Political and Social Science* (March, 1948).

Poussin, Louis de la Vallée. "Bodhisattva," in ERE, II (1910), 739–53.
—— Bouddhisme, Opinions sur l'histoire de la dogmatique. 4th ed. Paris, Beauchesne, 1925.
—— "Worship (Buddhist)" in ERE, XII (1922), 758–59.
Preisker, Herbert. Das Ethos des Urchristentums. 2d ed. Gütersloh, Bertelsmann, 1949.
Puech, Henri Charles. "Bibliographie générale," in Mana: Introduction à l'histoire des religions. Paris, Presses Universitaires, 1949.
—— Le Manichéisme. Paris, Civilisations du Sud, 1949.
—— "Temps, histoire et mythe dans le christianisme des premières siècles," in Proceedings of the Seventh International Congress for the History of Religions. Amsterdam, North-Holland Publishing Co., 1951.
Quick, Oliver Chase. The Christian Sacraments. London, Nisbet, 1927.
Rabbow, Paul. Seelenführung, Methodik der Exerzitien in der Antike. München, Kösel-Verlag, 1954.
Radcliffe-Brown, A. R. "Religion and Society," JRAI, LXXV (1945/46).
Radhakrishnan, Sir Sarvepalli. Religion and Society. London, Allen and Unwin, 1947.
Radin, Paul. Primitive Religion, Its Nature and Origin. New York, Viking, 1937.
—— Die religiöse Erfahrung der Naturvölker. Zürich, Rhein Verlag, 1951.
Rajogopalachariar, T. The Vishnuite Reformers of India. Madras, Natesan.
Randall, John Herman, Jr. The Making of the Modern Mind. Revised edition, Boston, Houghton Mifflin, 1940.
—— "Symposium," *Journal of Philosophy*, LI, No. 5 (1954).
Ratschow, Carl Heinz. Magie und Religion. Gütersloh, Bertelsmann, 1947.
Raven, Charles Earle. Natural Religion and Christian Theology (Gifford Lectures, 1951). Cambridge, Cambridge University Press, 1953.
Razek, M. Abdel. "La révélation dans l'Islam," in Transactions of the Fifth International Congress of History of Religions, 1929.
Redfield, Robert. The Primitive World and Its Transformations. Ithaca, Cornell University Press, 1953.
Renou, Louis, and Jean Filiozat. L'Inde classique. Paris, Payot, 1947.

Richard de St. Victor. De Gradibus Charitatis. Vol. 196 of Jacques Paul Migne, ed., Patrologia Cursus Completus, Series Latina. Paris, 1880.

Richardson, Alan. Christian Apologetics. New York, Harper, 1947.

Roberts, David E. Psychotherapy and a Christian View of Man. New York, Scribner's, 1950.

Rothacker, Erich. Einleitung in die Geisteswissenschaften. Tübingen, Mohr (Paul Siebeck), 1920.

Sachs, C. World History of the Dance. Translated by B. Schönberg. New York, Norton, 1937.

Saunders, K. The Ideals of East and West. New York, Macmillan, 1934.

Saussure, L. de. "La cosmologie religieuse en Chine, dans l'Iran et chez les prophètes hébreux," in Actes du congrès international d'histoire des religions, 1923. Paris, Champion, 1925.

Schacht, Joseph. "Taklīd," EI, IV, 629. London, 1934.

Schaff, Philip. The Creeds of Christendom (Bibliotheca Symbolica Ecclesiae Universalis). 6th ed., New York, Harper, 1931.

Schebesta, P. "Das Problem des Urmonotheismus, Kritik einer Kritik," Anthropos, XLIX (1954), 689–97.

Scheftelowitz, I. "Die Sündentilgung durch Wasser," AR, XVII (1914).

Scheler, Max Ferdinand. The Nature of Sympathy. Translated by P. Heath. Introduction by W. Stark. New Haven, Yale University Press, 1954.

——— Vom Ewigen im Menschen. Leipzig, Reinhold, 1923; 4th ed., Berne, Francke, 1954.

——— Die Wissenformen und die Gesellschaft. Leipzig, Neuer Geist, 1946.

Schilpp, Paul Arthur, ed. The Philosophy of Sarvepalli Radhakrishnan. New York, Tudor, 1952.

Schimmel, Annemarie. "Zur Anthropologie des Islams," in C. J. Bleeker, ed., Anthropologie religieuse. Leiden, E. J. Brill, 1955.

Schmidt, Karl Ludwig. "The Church," in Bible Key Words, from G. Kittel's Theologisches Wörterbuch zum Neue Testament. New York, Harper, 1951.

Schneider, Friedrich. Philosophie der Gegenwart. Basel, Reinhardt, 1953.

Schneider, Herbert Wallace. Religion in Twentieth Century America. Cambridge, Harvard University Press, 1952.
Schoeck, Helmut. Soziologie, Geschichte ihrer Probleme. Freiburg and München, K. Alber, 1952.
Scholem, Gershom Gerhard. Major Trends in Jewish Mysticism. New York, Schocken, 1941.
Schomerus, Hilko. Der Caiva-Siddhanta, Eine Mystik Indiens. Leipzig, Hinrichs, 1912.
—— Meister Eckhart und Mānikka-Vāsager. Gütersloh, Bertelsmann, 1936.
—— Sivaitische Heiligenlegenden. Jena, Diederichs, 1925.
Schroeder, F. O. Introduction to the Pāncarātra. Madras, Adyar, 1916.
Schubart, Walter. "Verschlingungstrieb und Magie," in F. Seifert, ed., Religion und Eros. 3d ed. München, Beck, 1952.
Schultz, Werner. "Die Grundlagen der Hermeneutik Schleiermachers," ZTK, XXXIII (1953).
—— "Wesen und Grenze der theologischen Hermeneutik," ZTK, XIX (1938), 283 ff.
Schweitzer, Wolfgang. "Die Bedeutung des Historismus für die Theologie," in M. Thiel, ed., Studium Generale, VII, No. 8 (1954).
—— "Das Problem der Hermeneutik in der gegenwärtigen Theologie," TLZ, V, No. 7 (1950).
Sevenster, Jan Nicolas. "Die Anthropologie des Neuen Testaments," in C. J. Bleeker, ed., Anthropologie religieuse. Leiden, Brill, 1955.
Shils, Edward A. "The Present Situation in American Sociology," in Pilot Papers, II, No. 2 (1947), London.
Smith, C. Ryder. The Bible Doctrine of Sin. London, Epworth, 1953.
Smith, Edwin William, ed. African Ideas of God. London, Edinburgh House Press, 1950.
—— "African Symbolism," JRAI, LXXXII (1952).
Smith, Margaret. Studies in Early Mysticism in the Near and Middle East. London, Sheldon Press, 1931.
Smith, Wilfred Cantwell. Inaugural Lecture. Montreal, McGill University, 1950.
Sneath, Elias Hershey, ed. The Evolution of Ethics as Revealed in the Great Religions. New Haven, Yale University Press, 1927.
Söderblom, Nathan. Les Fravashis, Étude sur les traces dans le

mazdéisme d'une ancienne conception sur la survivance des morts. Paris, Guimet, 1899.

——— "Die Gottheit als Wille," in Das Werden des Gottesglaubens. Leipzig, Hinrichs, 1926.

——— "Holiness (General and Primitive)," ERE, VI (1914), 731–41.

——— "The Place of the Christian Trinity and the Buddhist Tiratna among Holy Triads," in Transactions of the Third International Congress for the History of Religions. Oxford, Clarendon, 1908.

Sombart, Werner. Der moderne Kapitalismus. München and Leipzig, Duncker & Humblot, 1928.

Soothill, William Edward. The Three Religions of China. Oxford, Oxford University Press, 1929.

Spence, Lewis. Myth and Ritual in Dance, Game and Rhyme. London, Watts, 1947.

Spiegelberg, Friedrich. Living Religions of the World. New York, Prentice-Hall, 1956.

Steinthal, Heymann. "Allgemeine Einleitung in die Mythologie," AR, III (1900).

Stevenson, Mrs. Sinclair. The Heart of Jainism. London, Oxford, 1915.

Studies in History and Religion, Presented to H. Wheeler Robinson. London, Lutterworth, 1942.

Subhan, A. The Nature of Summum Bonum in Islam," *Islamic Culture,* XXI (1947).

Suhard, E. Cardinal. Growth or Decline. Translated by J. A. Corbett. South Bend, Ind., Fides, 1948.

Suzuki, Daisetz Teitaro. Essays in Zen Buddhism. London, Rider, 1926.

Swami Akhilananda. Hindu Psychology and the West. New York, Harper, 1946.

——— Mental Health and Hindu Psychology. New York, Harper, 1951.

Swami Nikhilananda. Ramakrishna, Prophet of New India. New York, Harper, 1942.

Sweetman, J. Windrow. Islam and Christian Theology. London, Lutterworth, 1945.

Tachibana, Shundo. The Ethics of Buddhism. London, Oxford, 1926.

Taylor, Alfred Edward. "Vindication of Religion," in E. G. Selwyn, ed., Essays Catholic and Critical. New York, Macmillan, 1926.

Tax, Sol, ed. An Appraisal of Anthropology Today. Chicago, University of Chicago Press, 1953.
Tempels, P. Bantu filosofie. Antwerp, de Sikkel, 1946.
Temple, William. Nature, Man and God (Gifford Lectures, 1932–34). New York, Macmillan, 1949.
Thelen, Mary Frances. "The Biblical Instruction and Comparative Religion," JBR, XX (1952), 71–76.
Thornton, Lionel Spencer. "The Christian Concept of God," in E. G. Selwyn, ed., Essays Catholic and Critical. New York, Macmillan, 1926.
Tiele, Cornelis Petrus. Einleitung in die Religionswissenschaft. Gothe, F. A. Perthes, 1899–1901.
——— Elements of the Science of Religion. New York, Scribner's, 1896–99.
——— "On the Study of Comparative Theology," in J. H. Barrows, ed., World Parliament of Religions. Chicago, Parl. Publishing Co., 1893.
Tillich, Paul. Systematic Theology, Vol. I. Chicago, University of Chicago Press, 1951.
Toy, Crawford Howell. Introduction to the History of Religions. Cambridge, Harvard University Press, 1948.
Toynbee, Arnold. A Study of History. 3 vols., 1st ed., London, Oxford, 1934.
Troeltsch, Ernst. Die Absolutheit des Christentums und die Religionsgeschichte. Tübingen, Mohr, 1902.
——— Gesammelte Schriften. 4 vols. Edited by Hans Baron. Tübingen, J. C. B. Mohr (Paul Siebeck), 1921–25.
——— Der Historismus und seine Uberwindung. Berlin, Heise, 1924.
Überweg, Friedrich. Grundriss der Geschichte der Philosophie. 5 vols. 12th ed. Edited by Karl Praechter. Berlin, Mittler, 1926–28. Vol. IV: Die deutsche Philosophie des 19. Jahrhunderts. Edited by T. K. Oesterreich.
Underhill, Evelyn. An Anthology of the Love of God. New York, McKay, 1953.
——— The Life of the Spirit and the Life of Today. New York, Dutton, 1922.
——— Worship. New York, Harper, 1937.
Underwood, Alfred Clair. Conversion: Christian and Non-Christian,

A Comparative and Psychological Study. New York, Macmillan, 1925.

Urban, Wilbur Marshall. Language and Reality: The Philosophy of Language and the Principles of Symbolism. London, Allen and Unwin, 1939.

Usener, Hermann. Götternamen. Bonn, F. Cohen, 1896.

Wach, Joachim. "The Christian Professor." Mimeo, distributed by the World Student Christian Federation, University Commission, December 10, 1947.

——— "Comparative Study of Religion," in Paul Schilpp, ed., The Philosophy of Sarvepalli Radhakrishnan. New York, Tudor, 1952.

——— "The Comparative Study of Religions." Unpublished Barrows Lectures, 1952.

——— Einleitung in die Religionssoziologie. Tübingen, Mohr, 1930.

——— Der Erlösungsgedanke und seine Deutung. Leipzig, Hinrichs, 1922.

——— "General Revelation and Religions of the World," JBR, XXII, No. 2 (1954).

——— "Inkarnation," RGG, III. 2d ed., 1929.

——— Meister und Jünger. Tübingen, Mohr, 1925.

——— "On Teaching History of Religions," in Pro Regno pro Sanctuario. Nijkerk, Callenbach, 1950.

——— Das Problem des Todes in der Philosophie unserer Zeit. Tübingen, J. C. B. Mohr, 1934.

——— "Redeemer of Men," *The Divinity School News*, XV, No. 4 (1948), University of Chicago.

——— "Religion and Differentiation within Society," in Sociology of Religion. Chicago, University of Chicago Press, 1944.

——— "Religion and Ethics." Unpublished lecture notes, University of Chicago.

——— "Religion in America: The Sociological Approach to Religion and Its Limits." Unpublished lecture notes, University of Chicago.

——— "Religionssoziologie," in Alfred Vierkandt, ed., Handwörterbuch der Soziologie. Stuttgart, Ferdinand Enke, 1931.

——— Religionswissenschaft, Prolegomena zu ihrer Grundlegung. Leipzig, Hinrichs, 1924.

―――― "The Theories of Religious Communication." Unpublished lecture notes, University of Chicago.
―――― Typen religiöser Anthropologie. Tübingen, Mohr, 1932.
―――― Types of Religious Experience. Chicago, University of Chicago Press, 1951.
―――― "Das Selbstverständnis des modernen Menschen," *Universitas*, X (1955), Stuttgart.
―――― "Sinn und Aufgabe der Religionswissenschaft," ZMR, 1935.
―――― "Sociology of Religion," in G. Gurvitch, ed., Twentieth Century Sociology. New York, Philosophical Library, 1945.
―――― Sociology of Religion. Chicago, University of Chicago Press, 1944.
―――― "Understanding," in A. A. Roback, ed., Jubilee Book for Albert Schweitzer. Cambridge, Sci-Art, 1945.
―――― Das Verstehen. 3 vols. Tübingen, Siebeck, 1926–32.
―――― "Zur Methodologie der Religionswissenschaft," ZMR, 1923.
―――― "Zum Problem der externen Würdigung der Religion," ZMR, 1923.
Ward, Maisie. France Pagan? New York, Sheed and Ward, 1949.
Watts, Alan Wilson. Behold the Spirit. New York, Pantheon, 1947.
Webb, Clement C. J. God and Personality (Gifford Lectures, 1918–19). New York, Macmillan, 1918.
―――― The Historical Element in Religion (L. Frey Lectures, 1934). London, Allen and Unwin, 1935.
―――― Religious Experience (Lecture, Oriel, 1944). London, Oxford, 1945.
Weber, Max. Gesammelte Aufsätze zur Religionssoziologie. 3 vols. Tübingen, Mohr, 1920–21.
―――― "Wirtschaft und Gesellschaft," in Grundriss der Sozialökonomik. Tübingen, Mohr, 1921.
Webster, H. Magic, A Sociological Study. Stanford, Stanford University Press, 1948.
Weinrich, F. Die Liebe im Buddhismus und im Christentum. Berlin, Töpelmann, 1935.
Weizsäcker, C. F. von. The History of Nature. Chicago, University of Chicago Press, 1949.

Wensinck, Arent Jan. The Muslim Creed. Cambridge, University Press, 1932.

Werner, Eric. "The Origin of Psalmody," in *Hebrew Union Almanach*, 1954.

Werner, Heinz. Comparative Psychology of Mental Development. Revised edition, Chicago, Follett, 1948.

Whale, John Seldon. Christian Doctrine. New York, Macmillan, 1941.

Whitehead, Alfred North. Process and Reality. New York, Macmillan, 1929.

—— Religion in the Making (Lowell Lectures, 1926). New York, Macmillan, 1926.

Widengren, George. Hochgottglaube in Alten Iran. Uppsala, Lundquist, 1938.

—— Religionens Ursprung. Stockholm, Diakonia Styrelsen's bokförlag, 1946.

—— "Die religionswissenschaftliche Forschung in Skandinavien," *Zeitschrift für Religions und Geistesgeschichte*, V (1953), 193 ff., 320 ff.

—— "Stand und Aufgaben der iranischen Religionsgeschichte," *Numen*, I (1954).

Wilder, Amos. "Biblical Hermeneutics and American Scholarship," in Neutestamentliche Studien für Rudolf Bultmann. Berlin, A. Töpelmann, 1954.

—— Eschatology and Ethics in the Teachings of Jesus. New York, Harper, 1939. Revised edition, 1950.

Wilhelm, Richard. Laotse und der Taoismus. Stuttgart, Frommann, 1925.

Will, Robert. Le Culte, Étude d'histoire et de philosophie religieuse. Paris, Alcan, 1925.

Winternitz, Moriz. Geschichte der indischen Literatur. Leipzig, Amelang, 1920.

Wissowa, Georg. Religion und Kultus der Römer. 2d ed., München, C. H. Beck, 1912.

Wolf, Erik. "Zur Rechtsgestalt der Kirche," in Bekennende Kirche. München, Kaiser, 1932.

Wyman, Leland Clifton. "The Religion of the Navaho Indians," in Vergilius Ferm, ed., Forgotten Religions. New York, Philosophical Library, 1950.

Yerkes, Royden Keith. Sacrifice in Greek and Roman Religions and Early Judaism. New York, Scribner's, 1952.

Yinger, John Milton. "Present Status of Sociology of Religion," *Journal of Religion,* XXXI (1951).

Zaehner, Robert Charles. "Dogma," *Hibbert Journal,* III, No. 7 (1954).

Zahn, E. F. J. Toynbee und das Problem der Geschichte. Köln, Westdeutscher Verlag, 1954.

Zimmer, Heinrich. Philosophies of India. Edited by J. Campbell. New York, Pantheon, 1951.

—— Der Weg zum Selbst (Shri Ramana). Edited by C. G. Jung. Zürich, Rascher, 1944.

INDEX

Abdu, Shaikh Muhammad, 71
Acharyas, 35
Adoration, 97, 98, 100, 101
African religions, aspects of Ultimate Reality, 47, 48; subjective factor in religious experience, 50; concept of God, 79, 80, 83; concept of man, 90; dance, 106; divination, 111; differentiations in cultic functions, 132
Aghoris, 95
Agl, 51
Aisvarya, 50
Akhilananda, Swami, 33
Alienum, 46
Allport, Gordon, 34, 84
American Council of Learned Societies, Committee on the History of Religions of the, xvi
American Indians, religion of: concept of God, 79, 80; guardian-spirit, 90; no classes of offenses, 93; worship, 101; dance, 106; differentiation of cultic functions, 130
Amidism, ways of attaining salvation, 95
Anawati, M. M., 70
Anlage, 39
Antar-atman, 91
Anthropology, functionalist school, 27; doctrine of man in Eastern and Western views, 34; as doctrine of man, 89-96; relationship between theology, ethics, and, 115; *see also* Man
Anyad, 46
Aparoksajnana, 96
Apprehension of religious experience, 45-46, 52

Arca, 46, 85, 103
Arul, 83
Asceticism, 94, 115-16
Ashvagosha, 41
Assyrian religion, 48, 50
Atman, 91
Atta, 91
Australian religions, religious communication, xxx; concept of God, 80; concept of man, 89; pre- and postexistence of souls, 95; dance, 106
Authority, religious, 135-37
Avataras, 46
Avidya, 91
Awareness, 51
Awe, 49
Axis mundi, 104
Aztec religion, 48, 50

Babylonian (Mesopotamian) religion, concept of history, 86; place of worship and symbolism, 104; calendar, 105; sacrifice, 108; divination, 111; differentiation in cultic functions, 130
Baillie, John, 51
Bala, 50
Baraka, 54
Berdyaev, Nicholas, 65
Be-sharia, 95
Bevan, Edwyn, 62
Bhakti, 34, 64, 94, 95, 96
Bhashyas, 73
Biologism, 37
Bleeker, Claas J., 25
Bodhisattva, 84
Body and soul, 55
Brahman, notion of, 82

Buddhism, concept of man, xxvii, xxviii, 91-92; religious community, xxx; religious experience, 33, 46; Ultimate Reality, 37; divine instruction, 40; faith and reason, 70; dogma, 71; confessions of faith, 73; *bodhisattva*, notion of the, 84; cosmology, 85, 86; Buddha, 92; grace, 94; destiny of soul, 96; divisions, 103; sacrifice, 107; ritual, 114; ethics, 116, 117-18; constitution, 134; messianism, 138; religious solidarity, 142; *see also* Amidism; Hinayana Buddhism; Mahayana Buddhism; *Samgha;* Tantrayana Buddhism; Zen Buddhism
Bulgakov, Sergei N., 113, 118

Cabala, 50, 82
Calendar, 105
Canaanite religion, 47, 48, 105
Canon law, 134
Caritra, 94
Carlyle, Thomas, xxxiv
Carya, 94
Cassirer, Ernst, 67
Caste system, xxx
Casuistry, systems of, 116-17
Categories, 19
Celtic religion, 111
Charisma, 130-31
Charity, 114, 117-18
Chinese religion, tendency toward monolatry, 80; cosmology, 85
Christianity, doctrine of man, xxvi, 89, 90, 92; Wach's attempt to relate *Religionswissenschaft* to, xliv; theology and revelation, xlv; understanding of doctrine of Holy Spirit, 18; truth, 21; intensity of religious experience, 35; aspects of Ultimate Reality, 47, 48; dogma, 71; confessions of faith, 73, 74; monotheism, 80; doctrine of Trinity, 80-81; eschatology, 88, grace, 94; life after death, 96; worship, 100; divisions, 103; sacrifice, 107; prayer, 110; sacraments, 113; ethics, 114, 116, 117-18; fellowship, 122; differentiation in cultic functions, 130; hierarchy, 131; law and constitution, 134, 141; messianism, 138; clashes between religious and secular loyalties, 140-41; religious solidarity, 142; *see also* Eastern Orthodox Church; Protestantism; Roman Catholicism
Classical writings, 72
Clergy, 134
Communication, religious, *see* Religious communication
Communism, 37
Community, religious, *see* Religious community
Conceptualization, 52
Confessions of faith, 73-75
Confucianism, concept of man, xxviii; transcendental faith, 37; divine instruction, 40; salvation through works, 95; ritual, 104; divination, 111; ethics, 118; differentiation in cultic functions, 130; law and constitution, 134, 141
Contemplation, 94
Conversion, 40
Corporate religions, 28
Cosmology, 77, 84-89
Cosmos, 86
Creeds, 73-74
Crime, 93
Culture-hero, 67
Cultus, 107, 121-22

Dana-katha, 107
Dance, 106, 137
De la Vallée-Poussin, Louis, 70
Determinism, 57
Devaram, 35
Devotion, 98, 100, 114, 127
Dharma, 96, 116, 117
Dharmakaya, 83
Dharma nairatyma, 92
Dhyana, 94
Dies dominica, 104
Dies religiosi, 105
Dies vitiosi, 105
Dilthey, Wilhelm, 69
Disciplina auguralis, 111
Divination, 111
Divine instruction, 40

INDEX

Djallal, 50
Djamal, 50
Doctrine, expression of religious experience in, 68-71; protests against, 75-76
Dogma, 71-72, 76

Eastern Orthodox Church, 118
Ecclesia, 124
Eckhart, Meister, 120
Edwards, Jonathan, 36
Egyptian religion, divine instruction, 40; tendency toward monolatry, 80; concept of history, 87; reincarnation theory, 91; life after death, 95; differentiation in cultic functions, 130
Eidetic vision, 25
Eikon, 103
Eliade, Mircea, 87-88, 104
Emanation (emergence), theory of, 84
Emergent evolution, 16-17, 19
Empathy, 8
Endeictic form of expression, 60
Eschatology, 88-89
Ethics, 114-18
Ethnic religions, 102
Etruscan religion, divination, 111
Evans-Pritchard, Edward Evan, 38
Evolutionary theory, 4, 16, 85
Ewer, Mary Anita, 62
Existentialism, 28
Experience, religious, *see* Religious experience

Faith, action and, 36; reason and, 70; confessions of, 73-75; statement of, concerning nature of Ultimate Reality, 76-77; emphasis of universal religions on, 102; propagation in universal religions, 119
Faqir's, 95
Farnell, Lewis R., 70
Fascinosum, 49, 50
Fear, 49
Fellowship, expression of religious experience in, 121
Feriae, 105
Ferré, Nels F. S., 45
Festivals, 127

Fichter, Joseph H., 143
Fiqh, 117
Force vitale, 47

Gardet, Louis, 70
Gemeinschaft, concept of, xxix-xxxiv
Gesellschaft, xxxi-xxxii
Gifford Lectures (Temple), 17
Glasenapp, Helmuth von, 117
Gnosticism, religion identified with knowledge, 51; cosmology, 86; journeys of the soul, 90; ways to attain salvation, 94
Grace, xlv, 94
Greek religion, concept of man, xxvi; contribution to three revealed religions, xxvii; religious communication, xxx; aspects of Ultimate Reality, 48; knowledge, 53; mythical expression, 66-67; reason, 69; pluralism of, 79; tendency toward monolatry, 80; Olympian gods, 83; Heraclitus' cosmology, 85-86; concept of history, 87; divination, 111
Griaule, Marcel, 66
Group worship, 110
Guilt, 93
Gunas, 50

Hamingya, 54
Hartmann, Nicolai, 19-20
Hartshorne, Charles, 41, 45, 69, 78
Health, 55
Heigl-Wach, Susi, xx
Heiler, Friedrich, xxi, 110
Hellenistic-Oriental religions, 113
Hermeneutics, xxiii, 18, 22, 73
Hierarchy, in religious communities, 131
Hinayana Buddhism, religious expression, 64; nature of God, 83; ethics, 118
Hinduism, interpretation of, xlii, xliii; true method of knowing, 20; religious experience, 33, 46; pathways shaping religious life, 34; divine instruction, 40; apprehension of Ultimate Reality, 43, 46, 48; forms of religious expression, 64; concept of

Hinduism *(continued)*
  God, 79, 82-83; Ramanuja, 82; concept of man, 91; grace, 94; interrelation of spiritual and material, 99; divisions, 103; sacrifice, 108-9; divination, 111; ritual, 114; ethics, 114, 116, 117; differentiation in cultic functions, 130; law and constitution, 134, 141; messianism, 138; religious solidarity, 141
Historicism, 5
History, historical approach to study of religions, 21-23; historical context in religious experience, 55-56; interpretation of, 86-87; eschatology, 88-89
History of religions, xxxviii, xli, 57
Hocking, William E., 68, 84
Holocaust, 109
Holy, experience of the, xl, xlv, 18, 24, 46
Holy Week, 105
Homo religiosus, religious experience, 31, 60-61; apprehension of Ultimate Reality, 46, 47; religious fellowship, 123; religious authority, 136
Horae, 104
Hsun-tse, 118
Hügel, Baron Friedrich von, 41, 42, 43
Husserl, Edmund, 24
Hvarenah, notion of, 82
Hymn, 106

Ibm, 51
Ibn Chaldun, 70
Idjma, 70
Idolatry, 64
Illud tempus, 67, 105
Imitatio, 117
Impersonalism, in concept of God, 80-83
Intellectualism, 64
Intent, as measure of genuineness of faith, 102
Iranian religion, interrelation of spiritual and material, 99-100
"Irenic effort," of Wach, xl-xliv
Islam, concept of man, xxvi; Wach on, xxxvii; intensity of religious experience, 35; opposition to any idea of embodiment, 46; aspects of Ultimate Reality, 48; knowledge, 51; faith, 70-71; dogma, 71; interpretation of sacred books, 73; confessions of faith, 73, 74; monotheism, 80; concept of God, 82, 84; cosmology, 86; journeys and destination of the soul, 90, 96; grace, 94; ways of attaining salvation, 95; divisions in, 103; ethics, 116, 117, 118; law and constitution, 134, 141; messianism, 138; religious solidarity, 141-42
Isq, 95
Isvara, manifestation of, 46

Jaeger, Werner, 66, 69, 74, 95
Jainism, religious community, xxx; Ultimate Reality, 37; cosmology, 85, 86; Triratna, 94; freedom of the soul, 95-96; ethics, 117
James, William, 28, 36
Japanese religion (Buddhism), clashes between religious and secular loyalties, 141
Japanese religion (folk), divination, 111
Jespers, Alfred, 25
Jnana, 34, 50, 64, 70, 94
Jubilee year, 105
Judaism, concept of man, xxvi; intensity of religious experience, 35; opposition to any idea of embodiment, 46; aspects of Ultimate Reality, 48; confession of faith, 73, 74; nature of God, 80, 82; cosmology, 86; Hasidim, 102; divisions, 103; ritual, 104; sacrifice, 109-10; divination, 111; sacramental acts, 113; ethics, 116, 117, 118; differentiation in cultic functions, 130; law and constitution, 134, 141; messianism, 138; religious solidarity, 141

Kahal, 124
Kalam, 70-71
Karma(n), 34, 64, 92, 96
Karuna, 118
Kawannah, 102

INDEX

Kirtan, 106
Knowledge, scientism and, 12, 14; Western and Eastern ways of knowing, 20-21; religious experience and, 51; term, 52; salvation attained through, 94
Kore, 85
Kriya, 94

Laity, 134
Langer, Susanne, 62, 66, 67
Language, 61, 126, 128-29; *see also* Symbolism
Leeuw, Gerardus van der, xxix, 107
Lila, 86
Logos, xxvii, xxix, 18, 25
Lustration, 111-12

Magic, 52-53, 112
Mahabba, 95
Mahayana Buddhism, doctrine of man, xxviii, 92; Wach's interpretation of, xl; manifestations of the deity, 46; majestic aspect of Ultimate Reality, 48; religious expression, 64; faith and reason, 70; nature of God, 79, 83; ways of attaining salvation, 94-95; cardinal virtues, 118; differentiation in cultic functions, 130
Maithuna, 109
Majestas dei, 48
Majestas tremenda, 47
Malamatija, 95
Malinowski, Bronislaw, 27, 66
Man, concept of, xxiv-xxix, 89-96; religious experience constitutive in nature of, 39-40; relationship to Ultimate Reality, 42; concept of deity and, 77; cosmology and, 89-90; *see also* Anthropology
Mandaeism, 86
Manichaeanism, 71, 86
Maori, cosmology of, 84-85
Marett, Robert R., on religious experience, 33-34, 39; concept of *homo religiosus*, 38; on magic, 53; on expression in fellowship, 122
Marga, 34

Marifa, 94
Marxism, 37, 56
Maya, 86
Mayan religion, 48, 105
Mazdaism, concept of God, 80
Melanesian religion, subjective factors in religious experience, 50; concept of God, 79; concept of man, 89
Metaphysics, 47, 48
Mexican religion, place of worship, 104; divination, 111; differentiation in cultic functions, 130
Middath ha-din, 50
Middath ha-rachamim, 50
Missionswissenschaft, xvi
Moksa, 96
Monier-Williams, Sir Monier, 79
Morgan, Lloyd, 16
Moses, D. G., 17, 51, 57
Mouroux, J., 32, 122
Müller, Max, xlvi, 3, 41-42
Muragaba, 94
Musnads, 73
Mysterium, 46
Mysterium fascinosum, xlv
Mysterium tremendum, xlv
Mystery religions, 95
Myth, mythical symbolism, 62; as theoretical expression of religious experience, 65-68; protests against mythical expression, 75
Mythos, xxvii, xxix

Nachfühlung, 8
Naojote, 74
Nazar, 51
Neoplatonism, xxvi, 86
Niebuhr, Reinhold, 50
Nirvana, 96
Nishta, 96
Niya, 102
Non-Christian religions, xlii, xlv-xlvi
"Numinous," Otto's concept of the, 24, 34

Olah, 109
Ontological stratification, theory of, 19
Opus operatum, 102
Ortega y Gasset, José, 39, 69

Otto, Rudolph, experience of the Holy, xl, 18, 24, 46; religious experience, xlvi, 49; critical studies of religion, 6; discovery of the "numinous," 24, 34; aspects of Ultimate Reality, 47

Para, 46
Parish, 143
Parsee, 112, 134
Pasa, 91, 96
Pasu, 91
Pater spiritualis, 40
Pati, 91
Perception, 20
Persecution, religious, *see* Religious persecution
Persian religion, 48; *see also* Mazdaism; Zoroastrianism
Personalism, in concept of God, 80-83
Personality, 90, 92
Phenomenology of religion, 24, 25
Philosophy, relationship between *Religionswissenschaft* and, xxxviii; science of religion needed by, 34; emancipation from theology, 69
Pilgrimages, 127-28
Pittenger, W. Norman, 62
Plato, xxvi, 18
Plurality of religions, xxxvi-xxxvii
Po, 85
Polydemonism, 79
Polynesian religions, tendency toward monolatry, 80; cosmology, 84; worship, 101; dance, 106; divination, 111; differentiation in cultic functions, 130
Polytheism, 79
Populism (racism), 38
Positivism, 33
Prajna, 118
Prakriti, 91
Prama, 20
Pramana, 20, 51
Pranas, 91
Prapatti, 94, 95
Prapti, 92
Pratika, 103
Prayer, 107, 110-11

Primitive religions, membership in tribal religions, 10; sacred vs. profane, 54; forms of expression of religious experience, 60-61; concept of God, 79; concept of man and cosmology, 89, 90; worship, 101-2, 105-6; dance and ritual, 106; divination, 111; religious community, 124, 125; *see also separate headings under geographical areas*
Profane vs. sacred, 53-54
Prophets, 103
Protestantism, religious experience involving integral person, 33; sacred writings, 73; ways of attaining salvation, 95; divisions, 103; ethics, 118; constitution, 134; ecumenical movement, 143
Pseudo religion, 37
Psychoanalysis, 23
Psychology of religion, 23, 33
Pudgala, 92
Pudgala nairatyma, 92
Pudgaluvadin, 92
Purification, 111-12
Purusha, 91

Quick, Oliver C., 62, 112, 113
Quran, 71

Racism (populism), 38
Radcliffe-Brown, A. R., 27
Radhakrishnan, Sarvepalli, xlii, xliii, 36
Ramadan, 105
Ramakrishna, Sri, 43, 46
Ramanuja, 82, 91
Reason, 68-69, 70-71
Redfield, Robert, 38
Reincarnation, 91
Relativism, 57
Religionsgeschichtliche Schule, 5
Religionswissenschaft, 3-6; Wach's interpretation, xiv-xv; European and American scholarship, xvi; methodological framework, xxiii-xxiv, xli; relationship between philosophy and,

xxxviii; Wach's attempt to relate Christian theology to, xliv
Religious communication, xxx, 135
Religious community, development of, xxix-xxx, 122-23; rapport with Ultimate Reality, xxxi; membership in tribal religions, 10; ability to understand religion of other groups, 10; two dimensions, 123-24; variations in, 125; size of group, 126-27; structure, 129; factors causing differentiation within, 129-33; *charisma*, 130; constitution, 133-35; membership, 137-38; clashes between religious and secular loyalties, 140-41
Religious experience, study of, as a division of *Religionswissenschaft*, xxiii; study of expressions, xxx, xxxix-xl; term, 13, 28; knowledge of aspects of, as approach to study of religions, 23; nature of, 27-58; as response to Ultimate Reality, 30-31, 32; criteria of, 31-37; through integral person, 32-33, 48; intensity, 35-36; issues in action, 36-37; universality, 38-39; apprehension of, and problem of truth, 45-46; subjective factor, 49-50; cognitive factor, 50-52; context, 54-57; expression in thought, 59-96; symbolism in expression of, 61; relationship between forms of expression and, 63-64; variations in different cultural, social, and religious settings, 63-64; means of intellectual expression, 65-72, 75; theoretical expression, 72-73; urge to express and limitations to which expression is subjected, 75-76; content of varied forms of intellectual expression, 76-96; expression in action, 97-120; expression in fellowship, 121-42
Religious persecution, 119
Religious tolerance, xxxv, xliii, 8
Religious truth, phenomenological approach to question of, xli; Moses's analysis of, 17, 57-58; highest goal of man, 21; claims to exclusive possession of, 29-30; in relation to man's apprehensions of religious experience, 45-46; religious authority and, 136-37
Religious understanding, 11, 18
Revelation, general vs. particular, xliv; two aspects of, xlv; human receptivity needed for, 40; media of, 43-45; marks of true revelation, 48-49
Richard of St. Victor, 18
Richardson, Alan, 17, 28, 69
Ritual, xxx-xxxi, 98, 105-7, 130
Roman Catholicism, religious experience involving integral person, 33; pluralistic aspect of divine reality, 79; divisions, 103; ethics, 117, 118; differentiation in cultic functions, 130; law and constitution, 134, 141; religious solidarity, 143
Roman religion, concept of history, 87; salvation through works, 95; place of worship and symbolism, 103, 104; time of worship, 105; divination, 111; differentiation in cultic functions, 130, 132
Rupa, 92

Sabbath, 104
Sabda, 20
Sacraments, 112-13; *see also* Symbolism
Sacred vs. profane, 53-54
Sacred writings, importance and interpretation, 72-74
Sacrifice, 107-10
Sakkid-ananda, 42
Sakti, 50
Salvation, 94
Samgha, 142
Samkhara, 92
Samkhya philosophy, 91
Samtana, 92
Samyagdarsana, 94
Sanctissimum, 103
Sanctuary, 103-4
Sanctum, 103
Sanna, 92

Scheler, Max, xl, 24, 64, 98
Science of religions, *see Religionswissenschaft*
Scientific method, 14-15
Sensus numinis, 38-40
Service, 98, 100, 114-16, 117, 127
Sesha, 86
Sex, religion and, 109; in differentiation of cultic functions, 131, 132; attitude of religious groups toward, 140
Shaivism, intensity of religious experience, 35; theology, 83, 91; ways of attaining salvation, 94, 95; religious community, 141
Shakta, 141
Shakti, 83
Shamanism, 90
Sharia, 117
Shema, 73
Shia, 142
Shintai, 103
Shintoism, 95, 130
Sin, 37, 49, 92-93
Skandavandin, 92
Skandha, 92, 96
Smith, Wilfred Cantwell, 27
Smrti, 73
Sociology of religion, as a division of *Religionswissenschaft,* xxiii, xxxi; tasks of, xxxi-xxxiii; emergence of, 23
Socrates, xxvi
Soul, 90-91, 95
Spiritualism, 64
Statism, 38
Sufism, divine instruction, 40; divine attributes, 50; impersonal notion of God, 82; religious community, 142
Sumerian religion, 85
Sunna, 70, 117
Sunnites, 142
Symbolism, as means of communication of religious group, xxx-xxxi; in religious experience and religious expression, 30, 61-63, 100; place of worship, 104; sacrifice and, 108-9; sacraments, 112-13; symbolic expression as bond of union of members of religious community, 127
Syncretism, 95
Synergism, 95

Tabu, 49
Tachibana, Shundo, 118
Tai, cosmology of, 85
Taklid, 51, 71
Tamim, 116
Tanha, 92
Tantrayana Buddhism, 84
Tantrism, 109
Taoism, concept of man, xxviii; conversion, 40; cosmology, 85; ethics, 114
Tawakkul, 94
Tawhid, 96
Taylor, Jeremy, 119
Tejas, 50
Teleios, 116
Telos, 86
Temenos, 103
Temple, William, *Nature, Man and God,* 17, 44; marks of true revelation, 48; nature of Ultimate Reality, 82
Theology, relationship between philosophy, history of religions, and, xxxviii; place of history of religions in, xlvi; task of, 9; apprehension of Ultimate Reality, 43; emancipation of philosophy from, 69; various concepts of deity, 77-84; relationship between anthropology, ethics, and, 115
Thornton, Lionel S., 78
Tibetan religion, 50, 141
Tiele, Cornelis P., 4
Tillich, Paul, 48, 76, 82
Time, attitudes toward, in various religions, 87; *see also* History
Tjurunga, 103
Tocqueville, Alexis de, xxxvi
Tolerance, *see* Religious tolerance
Toy, C. H., 67
Tremendum, 49, 50
Trinity, doctrine of, 80-81
Triratna, 94

INDEX

Trishna, 92
Troeltsch, Ernst, 8, 22
Truth, religious, *see* Religious truth
Typology of religion, 25-26

Ultimate Reality, religious community in rapport with, xxxi; in non-Christian religions, xlv; religious experience as a response to, 30-31, 32, 49; aspects of apprehension of, 42-45, 46-48; awareness of, 51-52; monism and pluralism, 79-80; personalism and impersonalism, 80-83; *Urmonotheismus,* 81; distance and nearness, 83-84; cosmological theories and, 84-85; adoration, 100; character of, and service, 115-16; *see also* Theology
Ummah, 124
Underhill, Evelyn, 62, 99, 100, 101
Understanding, religious, *see* Religious understanding
Universal religions, 102, 119
Uphadis, 91
Urban, W. M., 61, 65, 67
Urmonotheismus, 81

Vaishnavism, apprehensions of religious experience, 46; six attributes of God, 50; ways of attaining salvation, 94, 95
Vedana, 92
Vedic (Brahmanic) religion, concept of man, xxviii; caste system and religious community, xxx; aspects of Ultimate Reality, 48; six *pramanas,* 51; acosmistic world view, 86; ways of attaining salvation, 94-95; life after death, 95; purification, 112
Vhuha, 46
Vibhava, 46
Vice, 93
Vijnana, 70, 92
Virtue, 54, 117-18
Virya, 50
Vishnuism, intensity of religious experience, 35; question of apprehension of Vishnu, 42-43; nature of God, 83
Visio-beatifica, 96

Wach, Joachim, life and family background, xvii-xxii, xxxv; chief publications, xxii; academic career, xxii-xxiv; concept of man, xxiv-xxix; concept of *Gemeinschaft,* xxix-xxxiv; concept of religion, xxxiv-xl; irenic effort, xl-xliv; criticism of Radhakrishnan, xlii-xliii
Webb, Clement C. J., understanding of religions, 12; aspects of religious experience, 28, 32, 39, 55, 63; relation of God and man, 78; personalism in concept of God, 82
Weber, Max, 130
Weizsäcker, C. F. von, 52-53
Wenger, E. L., 44-45, 136
Wensinck, Arent Jan, 74
Werner, Eric, 90, 102
Whitehead, Alfred North, 15-16, 82
Wilder, Amos, 47
Will, Robert, 98, 99
Worship, 97-142; in non-Christian religions, xlvi; places of, 103-4; time of, 104-5; modes of, 105-7; prayer and sacrifice, 107-11; group worship, 110; preparatory acts, 111-12; partaking of sacraments as culmination of, 112-13; differentiation in cultic functions within religious group, 130
Wu-wei, 118

Yoga, 33, 94
Yogacara, 92

Zand, 73
Zebach, 109
Zen Buddhism, 40
Zoroastrianism, attributes of Ultimate Reality, 48; dogma, 71; confessions of faith, 73, 74; cosmology, 86; guardian-spirit, 90; blessedness, 95; purification, 112; ethics, 116, 117; law and constitution, 134

RELIGION

the comparative study of religions
joachim wach

Edited with an Introduction by Joseph M. Kitagawa

In this book, the outstanding religious historian Joachim Wach offers a profound investigation into the nature of religious experience. The result of a lifetime of scholarship and reflection, the book represents Professor Wach's efforts to develop and articulate a general framework in which scholars of different disciplines interested in religions, as well as adherents of diverse religious faiths, could understand each other. To construct this framework, he analyzes religious expression in thought (myth, doctrine, and dogma), practice (devotion and service), and fellowship (the religious community).

THE COMPARATIVE STUDY OF RELIGIONS reflects Professor Wach's deep belief that the distance separating East from West, and Christian from Jew and Moslem, could be lessened through a scientific study of religion or Religionwissenshaft. Professor Wach taught the history of religions throughout his academic career of thirty years at the University of Leipzig, Brown University, and the University of Chicago. At the time of his death in 1952, he was preparing this manuscript. His sister, Frau Susi Heigl-Wach, and Professor Joseph M. Kitagawa, with whom Professor Wach was closely associated at the Federated Theological Faculty of the University of Chicago, decided to retain the style and content of the book as much as possible. Professor Kitagawa presents, in the Introduction, a brief account of the life and thought of Joachim Wach.

". . . a wealth of insight into the nature, beliefs and function of religious man around the world. The book . . . will demand application on the part of those who are bold enough to read and study it. Those who do will remember it as one of the most rewarding books of their lives." P. H. Ashby, THE NEW YORK TIMES

Columbia University Press
New York and London

Printed in U.S.A.   ISBN 0-231-08528-1